This may be Jeremy's b̶........ w̶ḥat is more important than defending God's character? Jeremy shows in a scholarly but readable way that the traditional understanding of Hell does not actually exist. The Great News is that you don't have to defend or imagine God tortures people for beliefs while living for a short time on earth.

–Mike Edwards
What-God-May-Really-Be-Like.com

In *What is Hell?* Myers offers a very in depth, well-researched, and convincing reassurance that the modern orthodox teaching of the heinous doctrine of hell is undeniably false. There is no way, as Myers demonstrates with overwhelming evidence, that God's character could possibly be compatible with rejecting or torturing any of His/Her children for any length of time.

–Julie Ferwerda
Author of *Raising Hell: Christianity's Most Controversial Doctrine Put Under Fire*

I grew up in a strongly Hyper-Calvinist Church. They taught that my value as a human being was equal to brokenness and being no more than a mist. To add to this notion was the picture of eternal damnation awaiting those whom God did not choose to be saved. Damnation was a place called hell which was filled with fire and eternal misery without any escape. This is what I believed for decades until I read Jeremy Myers' latest book, *What is Hell?* His careful and balanced research into what the Bible was really teaching about hell is excellent. It debunks the 15th century view of the violent hell which came out of the confused thinking of church leaders of that time. This book is a must read for all people concerned about what happens to us in the afterlife. Jeremy demonstrates that a fiery hell doesn't exist after death, but instead exists in this life pulling people into misery, violence, grief, sorrow, and poverty. He shows that Christ has the keys to the gates of hell in this life, and has opened these gates so we can enter in and help those who are trapped within. Read his book it will bring you peace in your soul about eternity, especially if you accept Jesus for eternal life.

–Grahame Smith, Crisis Counselor
SoulCareCounselling.com

Forget what you think you know about hell! In straightforward language, Jeremy systematically rebuts the view of hell on which many Christians have been brought up. He demonstrates that the traditional understanding is based on coopting verses from Scripture to support extra-Biblical ideas. You will find this book both instructive and eye-opening with a surprising vision of what hell could really be like.

This book is certainly not another run-of-the-mill read. Though not pedantic, it is scholarly and quite thought provoking and challenging. It urges us to rethink don't-rock-the-boat theology. Jeremy exposes old wives tales about hell that most of us have been unwittingly fed and haplessly swallowed. Going through this book prayerfully will reveal the tremendous effort he has exerted, in love, to display God's ultimate goodness and grace.

CHRISTIAN QUESTIONS
VOLUME 4

WHAT IS HELL?

THE TRUTH ABOUT HELL AND HOW TO AVOID IT

J. D. MYERS

RedeemingPress.com

WHAT IS HELL?
The Truth About Hell and How to Avoid It
© 2019 by J. D. Myers

Published by Redeeming Press
Dallas, OR 97338
RedeemingPress.com

978-1-939992-66-6 (Paperback)
978-1-939992-67-3 (Mobi)
978-1-939992-68-0 (ePub)

Learn more about J. D. Myers by visiting RedeemingGod.com

Cover Design by Taylor Myers
TaylorGraceGraphics.com

JOIN JEREMY MYERS AND LEARN MORE

Take Bible and theology courses by joining Jeremy at
RedeemingGod.com/join/

Receive updates about free books, discounted books,
and new books by joining Jeremy at
RedeemingGod.com/reader-group/

WANT TO LEARN MORE?

Take the online course about hell.

If you have questions about hell,
get them answered in the online course about hell.

Learn more at RedeemingGod.com/Courses/

The course is normally $297, but you can
take it for free by joining the Discipleship Group at
RedeemingGod.com/join/

Other Books in the *Christian Questions* Series

Other Books by Jeremy Myers

Books in the *Close Your Church for Good* Series

All books are available at your favorite bookstore.
Learn about each title at the end of this book.

For the brave men and women
who daily follow Jesus
to the gates of hell.

.

TABLE OF CONTENTS

INTRODUCTION TO THE "CHRISTIAN QUESTIONS" BOOK SERIES

This "Christian Questions" book series provides down-to-earth answers to everyday questions. The series is based on questions that people have asked me over the years through my website, podcast, and online discipleship group at RedeemingGod.com. Since thousands of people visit the site every single day, I get scores of questions emailed in to me each month from readers around the world. Many of the questions tend to be around various "hot topic" issues like homosexuality, violence, and politics. Other questions, however, focus more on how to understand a particular Bible passage or theological issue. For example, I receive hundreds of questions a year about the unpardonable sin in Matthew 12.

I love receiving these questions, and I do my best to answer them. But after I answer the same question five or ten times, I realize that it might be better if I had a ready-made and easily-accessible resource I could invite people to read. This also provides the reader with a better explanation than I can give in a short email. For people who want the *full* experience, there are also online courses available for many of these questions at RedeemingGod.com/courses.

So the goal of this "Christian Questions" book series is to answer the questions that people send in to me. Below is the current list of books in the "Christian Questions" series. Most of these are not yet published, but I include the list to show you where the series is headed.

What is Prayer?

What are the Spiritual Gifts?

What is Faith?

How Can I Study the Bible? (Coming in 2019)

Why is the world so messed up?

Can God forgive my sin?

What is the unforgivable sin?

What is baptism?

What is the church?

What is repentance?

How can I evangelize?

Can I lose eternal life?

Why did Jesus have to die?

Should Christians keep the Sabbath?

What is demon possession?

How can I gain freedom from sin?

What is election and predestination?

Does God love me?

Why did God give the law?

Does God really want blood sacrifices?

What is sin?

What is the best bible translation?

Can I trust the Bible?

If you have a question about Scripture, theology, or Christian living that you would like answered, you may submit it through the contact form at RedeemingGod.com/about/ or join my online discipleship group at RedeemingGod.com/join/.

Several of the "Christian Question" books are available as free PDF downloads to people who join my online discipleship group.

Visit RedeemingGod.com/join/ to learn more and join today.

ACKNOWLEDGEMENTS

All great ideas are formed in the crucible of conflict. So first of all, I want to thank all those who have condemned me to hell for writing a book which challenges the traditional concept of hell. When I deny that the God revealed to us in Jesus Christ could send people to an eternal torture, some Christians eagerly condemn me to such a place for denying its existence. When this happens, I am thankful that God is God, and these people are not.

Without this condemnation, however, I might never have written this book. In writing it, I set out to show these "hellmongers" that it is entirely possible to believe everything the Bible teaches about hell, while *not* believing that people scream and suffer there forever in flames of unquenchable fire. (And no, I am not a Universalist or an Annihilationist either. But more on that later …)

So if you have condemned me or called me a heretic for my views on hell, thank you. You spurred me on to write this book. Hopefully you will now read it and consider the arguments presented within. Maybe, by reading this book, you will come to see that God does not torture people, for God is more loving, kind, gracious, and forgiving than you ever thought or imagined.

I always, of course, want to thank my wife, Wendy, and our three daughters, Taylor, Selah, and Kahlea. These four amazing women provide light, joy, encouragement, help, and support for all the books I write. When life occasionally throws hell at me, they are my heaven on earth.

I must also thank the members of my Advance Reader Team who helped proofread and prepare this book for publication. Nizam Khan, Wesley Rostoll, Mike Edwards, Grahame Smith, Michael Rans, Elaine O'Connor, Pete Nellmapius, Michael Wilson, Wickus Hendriks, David DeMille, Taco Verhoef, Wickus Hendriks, John Flegg, Radu Dumitru, Bernard Shuford, Craig Duncan, and Jim Maus, thank you for your help on my books. Please let me know how I can help you on any books or projects in the future.

Finally, I want to thank *you*, the reader of this book. Thank you for taking the time to consider the ideas and arguments presented within. I hope you are encouraged and challenged by what you read and that your questions about hell are answered. Ultimately, I hope you see that when it comes to what God does with people in hell, even here, God always looks just like Jesus.

FOREWORD

I admire Jeremy Myers' courage. Since our first acquaintance, I've witnessed his willingness to tackle stubborn questions and converse with stubborn critics. I'm especially inspired by his unwillingness to sidestep the difficult biblical texts that were traditionally [mis]used as deal-killers in the conversation about hell. Most recently, I'm impressed by Jeremy's boldness to invite someone who differs with him on key points to write a foreword to this book. Unlike Jeremy, I personally believe in a specific version of ultimate redemption, though I cannot teach it as doctrine. Yet I dare say that my own growth requires clear-minded, cool-headed interlocutors who help me think—discussion partners like Jeremy are gold.

Not that we're on an entirely different page. To begin with, I affirm the great care and detail he's taken to dig deep into the precise meaning of the key Scriptural terms and images that relate to his theme. His diligence is gratifying to those who like to see the data gathered, tabulated and presented with clarity. Others, including me, have attempted this with varying success. Jeremy's orderly version is superb. He's overtly biblical without proof-texting so that the burden of proof lies with those who disagree with his assessments.

In my view, Myers' greatest contribution to the hell debate is his thorough explanation of the already sense of hell—that infernal kingdom of darkness as it appears here and now in this world—and how Christ has already come to rescue those who were *already* enslaved to it. Jeremy cites my article, "Hell as a Kingdom" favorably but then expands on the theme in a way I've not seen elsewhere. He interprets Christ's descent into hell as the story of the Incarnation into "this present darkness" to rescue those who are *already* perishing (cf. John 3). Perhaps we could call Myers' approach an explication of "realized infernalism" along with its "Christovictorious" solution. How similar this is to the *kontakian* prayers of Eastern Orthodox liturgy:

> Having descended to me, even unto hades, and made resurrection a way for all, thou didst ascend again, taking me with Thee on Thy shoulder, and didst bring me to the Father. Wherefore, I cry out to Thee: Hymn the Lord, O ye works, and exalt Him supremely for all ages.

Note how this chorus applies Christ's descent into the earthly life of the liturgist, who has experienced deliverance from hades in this world. Christ's resurrection is a done deal from the hellish predicament of our alienation. The gospel of our Lord Jesus Christ is our way out of hell's now-kingdom into eternal life now in "the kingdom of the Son" (cf. Col 1).

When Bible teachers like Jeremy point out alternative interpretations to ugly, inaccurate, medieval visions of hell, contrarians typically object: "So, you don't believe in hell!" Of course we do! It's not the reality of hell that Jeremy or I contest. The issue is around the *nature* of hell—the where and when and what of hell. Our claim is that the treatment of hell as revealed (or not) in Scripture is not as simplistic as what's been marketed by the status-quo infernalists. Further, it's not to be cavalierly dismissed with a wave of the hand as you see among certain pop-universalists. There is a hell. It's just not what we were told. Then what is it? Jeremy Myers "goes there." Let's go there with him!

FIAT LUX
Pascha 2019

–**Bradley Jersak**
Author of *Her Gates Will Never Be Shut*

PREFACE

Hell is the greatest of all tragedies that can befall a human being. But it is just as tragic to hear what some Christians think the Bible teaches about hell. Though I don't agree with the ultimate conclusion of John Stott about hell (he held to Annihilationism), I do agree with his sentiment when he wrote this:

> I want to repudiate with all the vehemence of which I am capable the glibness, what almost appears to be the glee … with which some Evangelicals speak about hell. It is a horrible sickness of mind or spirit. Instead, since on the day of judgment, when some will be condemned, there is going to be 'weeping and gnashing of teeth' (Matt 8:12, 22:13, 24:51, 25:30; Luke 13:28), should we not already begin to weep at the very prospect? I thank God for Jeremiah. Israelite patriot though he was, he was charged with the heartbreaking mission of prophesying the destruction of his nation. Its ruin would only be temporary; it would not be eternal. Nevertheless, he could not restrain his tears. "Oh that my head were a spring of water and my eyes a fountain of tears! I would weep day and

night for the slain of my people" (Jer 9:1; cf. Jer 13:17; 14:17).

> … I am sorry that you use in reference to God the emotive expression 'the Eternal Torturer,' because it implies a sadistic infliction of pain, and all Christian people would emphatically reject that. But will the final destiny of the impenitent be eternal conscious torment, "for ever and ever," or will it be a total annihilation of their being? The former has to be described as traditional orthodoxy, for most of the church fathers, the medieval theologians and the Reformers held it. And probably most Evangelical leaders hold it today. Do I hold it, however? Well, emotionally, I find the concept intolerable and do not understand how people can live with it without either cauterizing their feelings or cracking under the strain.[1]

John Stott is exactly right. It is shocking to hear some Christians talk about hell as they celebrate the eternal torment of their enemies in everlasting flames. Does this really reflect the heart of God toward His "enemies"? Regardless of what hell "is," I agree with those pastors and Bible teachers who say that if we cannot talk about hell without tears in our eyes, then we should not talk about hell at all. Just as Jeremiah wept over the destruction of Israel, we must weep over the fate of any unredeemed person, whatever that fate may be. N. T. Wright said something similar when he wrote this:

[1] David L. Edwards and John Stott, *Evangelical Essentials: A Liberal-Evangelical Dialogue* (London: Hodder & Stoughton, 1988), 312-329.

As soon as we find ourselves wanting to believe in hell we find ourselves in great danger. The desire to see others punished—including the desire to do the punishing ourselves—has no place in the Christian scheme of things.[2]

But as soon as we, as sinful human beings with calloused hearts and damaged consciences, begin to feel pain, sorrow, and deep sadness about the fate of people who end up in hell, this raises serious questions about God. Does not God, who knows no sin and loves all people with unsurpassable love, feel even greater pain, sorrow, and sadness for the fate of His sons and daughters who find themselves in hell? And if this is so, then we must further ask why God made hell in the first place. Could not God, who is in control of all things, arrange things differently so that His rebellious sons and daughters do not suffer for all eternity? Was there truly no other option for an eternally loving and infinitely creative God?

To ask such questions is to answer them. Of course there were other options! We humans can think of several. So if we humans can think of alternative options to hell, surely God could have done so as well. But if God could have created an alternative option to hell so that He did not have to send people to suffer for eternity in hell, why didn't He?

The answer is that maybe He did.

[2] N. T. Wright, *Following Jesus: Biblical Reflections on Discipleship* (Grand Rapids: Eerdmans, 1995), 92.

Maybe hell as we humans imagine it is not the hell that God created.

Maybe hell as traditional Christian theology presents it is not the hell that actually exists.

Maybe hell as it is presented in many books, sermons, and movies is not actually taught in Scripture.

But if these are possibilities, then what is the alternative? What did God actually make for His rebellious sons and daughters (and even His rebellious angels)? Where will they spend eternity? Will they even *exist* in eternity? How can God honor the free-will choices of His creatures in granting them the freedom to exist without Him, while also not becoming a monster Himself in torturing people for eternity simply because they don't love Him or want to serve Him?

It is these sorts of questions this book seeks to answer. By reading this book, you will take a journey into hell and back. You will discover what Scripture teaches about hell, and what it does not. You will learn what *and where* hell is, how to avoid hell yourself, while also working to rescue people from hell. You will see that hell (as you imagine it) does not actually exist. You will also discover that you should stop talking about "hell" altogether. Ultimately, you will come to realize that hell (which is not hell) is not an expression of God's hate for sinners, but an expression of His infinite love.

The journey begins in Chapter 1 with a survey of the three main views about hell and a short history of the development of hell. Chapter 2 defines eight key terms that are often associated in Scripture with hell and reveals what each term really means. Chapter 3 then takes what we have learned about hell and reveals what *and where* hell is. This then allows us, in Chapter 4, to understand how to avoid hell ourselves and rescue those who are in hell. The book then concludes with some summary thoughts and ideas about hell. I have also included an Appendix on the word "fire" since it is the most common image related to hell. This Appendix defines what the Bible teaches about fire, and considers several key passages from Scripture that contain "fire" imagery.

So are you ready to take the first step on the road to hell? Don't worry, Jesus is on the road to hell also, and with Him by your side, you'll be just fine.

CHAPTER 1

WHAT ARE THE
MAIN VIEWS ON HELL?

The business world has a concept known as "the FUD factor." It is used by a company that wants to influence a potential customer into doing business with them instead of with a competitor. They do this by raising fear, uncertainty, and doubt (FUD) in the mind of the customer about the dangers of doing business with the competition.

The church often follows similar practices as it seeks to gain converts to Christianity and keep these Christians on the "straight and narrow" path of discipleship. When it comes to creating fear in the minds and hearts of both believers and non-believers, the doctrine of hell is the most widely used tool of Christian pastors, authors, and leaders. The fear of hell keeps people returning to church on Sunday morning, following every word the pastor says, trying their hardest to make amends for the sins they have committed, and praying fervently that God might love and forgive them. The underlying implication of much Christian teaching is, "You better do these things, or you might end up in hell."

But is this so wrong? After all, as many pastors like to point out, didn't Jesus teach more about hell than He did about heaven? If Jesus thought that warning others about the threat and danger of hell was a valid approach to ministry and discipleship, should not we follow His example by issuing similar warnings today? Or, as many other teachers say, if people are headed for hell, is it not the loving thing to warn them about where they are headed? If someone was about to drive off a cliff, shouldn't we warn them about the dangers ahead?

The answer to all these sorts of questions is "Yes! … *If* hell is really what we think it is." But if hell doesn't actually exist, *or* if hell is not what many imagine it to be, then our warnings about the threat and danger of hell are misinformed, misguided, and even dangerous. If we are wrong in our understanding about what the Bible teaches regarding hell, and if we use this wrong understanding to create fear and worry in the minds and hearts of other people, then we are not helping or loving them at all, but are actually hindering their understanding of God, their experience of His love, and their ability to follow Him in freedom without fear.

Indeed, in this book, we will discover that Jesus did not, in fact, teach more about hell than He did about heaven. We will discover that while hell is real, it is not what most assume it to be. We will also discover how to teach and warn people about hell, but in a way that does not inspire fear. We will discover a loving way of viewing and teaching about hell, and how Jesus shows us to rescue those who are there. But before we can consider such truths, we must begin with a survey of the three common views about hell.

SURVEYING HELL

In western Christian theology, there are three common views about hell.[1] The first, Traditionalism (sometimes called Eternal Conscious Torment or Infernalism), is the most widely recognized. In this view, the unredeemed dead suffer for all eternity in flames of fire.[2] The traditional view of hell is usually equated with pictures of people screaming in agony for all eternity as they float around in a Lake of Fire while being burned alive but never dying. Such a view is found in many popular books and movies, including Dante's *Inferno*, Bill Wiese's *23 Minutes in Hell*, and the 1997 science fiction horror movie "Event Horizon."

[1] William Crockett, ed. *Four Views on Hell* (Grand Rapids: Zondervan, 1996); Edward Fudge and Robert A. Peterson, *Two Views of Hell: A Biblical & Theological Dialogue* (Downers Grove: IVP, 2000).

[2] Harry Buis, *The Doctrine of Eternal Punishment* (Philadelphia: P&R, 1957), Francis Chan, *Erasing Hell: What God Said About Eternity, and the Things We've Made Up* (Colorado Springs: David C. Cook, 2011), Robert A. Peterson, *Hell on Trial: The Case for Eternal Punishment* (Philadelphia: P&R, 1995).

The second view, Universalism, is the opposite of Traditionalism. In this view, there is no eternal dwelling place for the unredeemed dead. Instead, all people will end up living with God for eternity.[3] Though many people reject God in this life, the Universalist believes that when a person stands before God in eternity, they will see the error of their ways and will gladly choose to be with God for eternity. God, who is defined by love, will accept all people into eternity with Him. In the Universalist view, those biblical texts which seem to teach about people living in eternal fire are either out-right rejected or are interpreted as referring to some sort of divine discipline in this life or next before a person enters eternity with God.

The third common view is Annihilationism (sometimes called Conditional Immortality or Conditionalism). This view holds that all the unregenerate dead will ultimately cease to exist so that only the redeemed will live with God in eternity.[4] This view tends to be the

---

[3] Rob Bell, *Love Wins: A Book About Heaven, Hell, and the Fate of Every Person Who Ever Lived* (New York: HarperOne, 2012); Julie Ferwerda, *Raising Hell: Christianity's Most Controversial Doctrine Put Under Fire* (Lander, WY: VagabondGroup, 2011); Thomas B. Thayer, *The Origin and History of the Doctrine of Endless Punishment* (Boston: Universalist Publishing, 1885).

[4] Christopher M. Date, Gregory G. Stump, and Joshua W. Anderson, eds., *Rethinking Hell: Readings in Evangelical Conditionalism* (Eugene, OR: Wipf & Stock, 2014), David L. Edwards and John Stott, *Evangelical Essentials: A Liberal-Evangelical Dialogue* (London: Hodder & Stoughton, 1988). Alan E. Bernstein, *The Formation of Hell: Death and Retribution in the Ancient and Early Christian Worlds*

"middle ground" view between Traditionalism and Universalism. It recognizes, along with Traditionalism, that choices made in this life have eternal consequences and that some people will continue to rebel against God, even in eternity. Since God cannot force people to spend eternity with Him against their will, something must be done with these people.

When it comes to *what* is done with these rebellious people, the Annihilationist agrees with the Universalist in saying that it would be monstrous for God to torture people for all eternity. The biblical texts which seem to imply an eternal existence in fire are understood as texts that describe an eternal destruction so that those who undergo it simply cease to exist. Some Annihilationists believe that this destruction occurs immediately after a person dies, while others believe that there is first a period of punishment and suffering for sins, until a person is finally consumed.

Although these are the three main views on hell, there are various other flavors and degrees of each. For example, the Catholic teaching of Purgatory contains pieces of both Traditionalism and Universalism. Purgatory teaches that while some will suffer in hell for all eternity, others will have a shortened period of suffering to pay for their sins, after which time they will be able to enter heaven and spend eternity with God.

(New York: Cornell, 1993), 208. Cornell, 199; Edward Fudge, *The Fire That Consumes: A Biblical and Historical Study of the Doctrine of the Final Punishment* (Lincoln, NE: iUniverse, 2016).

Then there is the view known as Ultimate Reconciliation, which, like Purgatory, is also a cross between Traditionalism and Universalism. However, in this view, rather than some people spending eternity separated from God in hell, those who hold to Ultimate Reconciliation teach that eventually all people will end up reconciled to God in heaven.[5] So while Purgatory is closer to Traditionalism, Universal Reconciliation is closer to Universalism. But both include a period of time in which a person undergoes suffering for the sins they committed in this life while they were in rebellion against God.

There are other views as well, but these are the main views on hell. So which of these views is presented in the book? The answer is "None of the above." Technically, my view falls within the stream of Traditionalism, though most who swim in that stream would probably disagree that I am part of their group. However, my view fits within Traditionalism because I agree that Scripture teaches that many people will indeed spend eternity separated from God. However, as I explain later

[5] Brad Jersak, *Her Gates Will Never Be Shut: Hope, Hell, and the New Jerusalem* (Eugene, OR: Wipf & Stock, 2009); Hans Urs von Balthasar, *Dare We Hope "That All Men Be Saved"?* (San Francisco: Ignatius, 1999); Thomas Jay Oord, *God Can't: How to Believe in God and Love After Tragedy, Abuse, and Other Evils* (United States: SacraSage, 2019), 164. Sharon Baker seems to hold to a cross between annihilationism and ultimate reconciliation, so that all will either be redeemed or annihilated. See Sharon Baker, *Razing Hell: Rethinking Everything You've Been Taught About God's Wrath and Judgment* (Louisville: Westminster John Knox, 2010), 117.

in this book, I believe this "separation" is only in a person's *experience*; God will not separate Himself from anyone in eternity.

My view cannot be in the Annihilationist stream, because I believe that all people will live for eternity. I do not believe that God destroys people simply because they rebel against Him or choose to live life without Him. To be honest, I do not believe that Annihilationism is loving toward those who are destroyed, and "it minimizes the scope and power of Jesus' resurrection."[6] Finally, I am not a Universalist because, once again, I agree with Traditionalists that God does not (and cannot) force people against their will to love Him or to believe in Jesus for eternal life. I believe that some people, even if they were given infinite chances in eternity, would still reject God forever.

So since I fall within the Traditionalist camp, what is it that separates my view from that of Traditionalism? I completely agree with many critics of Traditionalism that God does not and will not torture people for all eternity. If it is monstrous for a person to torture another person or an animal for a short period of time on this earth, it is even more monstrous for God to torture somebody for eternity in hell. So while I do believe that many people will spend eternity separated from God (again, in their experience, but not in reality), I do not

[6] Cf. Joshua Ryan Butler, *The Skeletons in God's Closet* (Nashville: Thomas Nelson, 2014), 64.

believe that their eternal conscious existence will be one of torment.

In fact, it is this complete rejection of all forms of torture or torment on the part of God that also causes me to reject the other views of hell. After all, many Annihilationists believe that before a person is destroyed, they will suffer in torment for their sins for a period of time. Many Universalists similarly believe that before God accepts a person into eternity with Him, they must first suffer for the wrong things they have done in this life. According to some forms of Universalism, it is this period of suffering that causes some people to turn from their selfish rebellion against God and turn to Him for love, forgiveness, and acceptance instead.

But again, if it is wrong for humans to torture other creatures for a period of time, is it not also wrong for God to torture people for a period of time? Although "God is God and can do what He wants," it is also true that God cannot sin. God cannot torture people without sinning, which means that God cannot torture people at all. Nor does God *want* to torture people. God is love, and in Him there is no darkness, sin, or violence at all. Any Scripture text which seems to teach that God wants to torture people or that He does torture people (either in this life or the next), is a passage that is misunderstood. This book will consider numerous such passages to show what they *really* teach.

So if Scripture does not teach that God tortures people in the flames of hell for all eternity, how did such an idea come to be the dominant picture of hell for most people? The answer is that just like all other areas of Christian theology, the traditional doctrine of hell has a history of development. To understand what the Bible teaches about hell, you first need to understand the history of hell.

THE HISTORY OF HELL

The commonly accepted modern concept of "hell" has not been commonly accepted for most of human history. To the contrary, it is only in the last few hundred years that people have begun to think of hell as a place of flames and torture for sinners.

In her book, *The History of Hell*, Alice K. Turner provides a summary of the evolution and development of the concept of hell throughout human history. Nearly all ancient concepts of the afterlife do not contain images of fire and torture, but rather "a mountain barrier, a river, a boat and boatman, a bridge, gates and guardians, [and] an important tree."[7] In nearly all records, there is no separation between the evil and the righteous, for all people go to the same place and experience the same events after death. For example, in an-

[7] Alice K. Turner, *The History of Hell* (New York: Harcourt, 1993), 5.

cient Mesopotamian culture, "all people go to the underworld, live in darkness and sorrow, eat clay and are plagued in various ways. There is no fiery torture."[8]

The Egyptians, however, did eventually develop a two-tier system for people in the afterlife. Upon a person's death, they would first stand before Osiris in judgment. If a person was found to be lacking in obedience to the Egyptian gods, they would be eaten up by the monster Ammit, and would cease to exist. But the fate of those who avoided being eaten by Ammit was not much better, for although they received a new body, they were then subjected to numerous trials and travails in the afterlife as they sought to be transformed into a holy bird, such as a falcon or phoenix.[9] So the two-tiered Egyptian system did not consist of heaven and hell, but of something closer to annihilation and purgatory, though neither involved the eternal suffering of all sinners in fiery torment.

There are, however, some Egyptian accounts that do refer to pits of flames and a Lake of Fire. In the Egyptian *Book of Gates* there is a story where the sun god, Ra, instructs another Egyptian deity, Horus, to destroy his enemies in four fire-filled pits. Later in the same book, certain human souls are sentenced to live at a lake of blazing fire, but they live on its shore, not within its

---

[8] R. Laird Harris, Gleason L. Archer, and Bruce K. Waltke, *Theological Wordbook of the Old Testament*, 2 vols. (Chicago: Moody), II:892.

[9] Turner, *The History of Hell*, 13-14.

flames.[10] In both cases, the text appears to teach that the souls in the pits of fire and on the shore of the lake of flames do not dwell there forever in perpetual agony but are eventually destroyed.[11]

While much of Hebrew literature draws upon and alludes to the imagery, mythology, and literary genres of the surrounding cultures—especially those of Egypt and Mesopotamia—"Israel's canonical literature contains no such epics about descent into the underworld or return from it. … [Instead] Israelite faith concerned a living relationship with Yahweh in the present, not speculation about the future."[12] So while there is frequent mention of death and *sheol* in the Hebrew Scriptures, all such concepts carefully avoid any discussion or imagery about what happens to people after they die. As will be seen in the next chapter when the Hebrew word *sheol* is defined, the Hebrew prophetic tradition contributed nothing to the concept of the afterlife as a place of torment and suffering. All such concepts come entirely from extra-biblical sources. So let us consider the Greek contributions to the subject of hell.

The Greek mythology surrounding the concept of Hades lacks many of the modern conceptual elements of hell. It is usually depicted as a gloomy place of darkness

[10] Bernstein, *The Formation of Hell*, 15.

[11] Ibid., 17.

[12] Philip S. Johnston, *Shades of Sheol: Death and Afterlife in the Old Testament* (Downers Grove: IVP, 2002), 69-70.

where incorporeal souls wander around aimlessly. The Greeks also had a two-tiered system, with Tartarus being a lower level of Hades. Tartarus was typically reserved for the defeated Titans of primordial Greek mythology, so that most humans avoided Tartarus and went to Hades. But even in the Greek concept of Hades, while some people are tormented with hunger, vultures, or with endlessly rolling a boulder up a hill, few, if any, are tormented with everlasting flame.[13] In fact, in Greek thinking, most punishment for wrongdoing was meted out by the gods upon humans during *this* life; punishment "was not generally an after-death affair."[14]

The Greek philosopher Plato, through the words of Socrates, describes a three-tiered destiny for the dead. In Plato's construct, it is the good people who go to Hades, which is invisible, pure, and noble. Evil people are reincarnated as despised animals, such as donkeys or wild dogs. The morally neutral people are sent into the Acherusian Lake, where their true nature is revealed over time.[15] If they turn out to be good, then they are reborn as humans to give life another chance. Those, however,

---

[13] Turner, *The History of Hell*, 21-29; Thayer, *The Origin and History of the Doctrine of Endless Punishment*, loc 670f.

[14] Turner, *The History of Hell*, 28.

[15] Cf. Thayer, *The Origin and History of the Doctrine of Endless Punishment*, loc 755, 803.

who turn out to be incurably evil, are sent down to Tartarus forever.[16]

It is interesting to note that when a person is cast into Acherusian Lake, they are given the opportunity to "lift up their voices and call upon their victims that they have slain or wronged, to have pity on them, and to be kind to them, and let them come out of the lake. And if they prevail, then they come forth and cease from their troubles; but if not, they are carried back again into Tartarus."[17] This sounds quite similar to the story of the Rich Man and Lazarus in Luke 16:19-31. But again, the Greek philosophical concept of the afterlife is closer to reincarnation than any modern concept of "hell."[18]

During the Intertestamental and New Testament eras, the concept of the afterlife went through numerous developments.[19] The most significant change was that some Jewish teachers and thinkers began to believe in a future physical resurrection.[20] Prior to this time, most Jewish people believed that when a person died, there was no return from death.[21] Yet Jesus Himself endorsed

---

[16] Bernstein, *The Formation of Hell*, 54-55.

[17] Turner, *The History of Hell*, 32.

[18] Cf. Thayer, *The Origin and History of the Doctrine of Endless Punishment*, loc 791.

[19] Some of these are discussed in Bernstein, *The Formation of Hell*, 136ff.

[20] Ibid., 172ff.

[21] A few Old Testament texts do hint at a developing belief in a future resurrection. See Johnston, *Shades of Sheol*, 218-230.

the idea of the resurrection, as did Paul (cf. 1 Cor 15), who taught that Jesus was the firstborn from among the dead (cf. Col 1:18). A belief in the future resurrection caused some to wonder who would receive resurrection. The biblical answer is that everyone would be raised from death, both the good and the bad (John 5:28-29; Acts 24:15; Matt 25:32; Rev 20:11-15).

But if everyone is raised from the dead, the related questions must also be asked: Would the resurrected experience of evil people differ from that of the resurrected experience of the righteous? Again, the New Testament answer is clearly "Yes." But what are these differences? Though most people answer that the righteous go to everlasting heaven while the wicked go away to everlasting hell, neither statement is taught in Scripture. Heaven is *not* the eternal dwelling place of the resurrected righteous,[22] and hell is *not* the eternal dwelling place of the resurrected wicked. Indeed, as will be seen later, neither Jesus nor Paul ever spoke of "hell" as a place of torment in the afterlife. To the contrary, all New Testament teachers reveal something entirely different about the eternal state of the resurrected dead. Later chapters of this book will explain the New Testament view in more detail.

---

[22] God does not intend for humans to spend eternity with Him in heaven. We were made for earth, and God will create a new earth for us to dwell upon, and He will dwell there with us (cf. Rev 21:1-5). The resurrected righteous will dwell on earth; not in heaven. Cf. Paul Marshall, *Heaven is Not My Home* (Nashville: Thomas Nelson, 2001).

So if Scripture does not teach that the unregenerate dead will spend eternity in a place of unquenchable flames where they suffer in torment for all eternity, how did such a belief enter into Christianity? The answer is found in Christian history and human psychology. Due to their abstention from various cultural practices such as membership with the guilds and attending the Roman religious feasts and celebrations (many of which paid homage to Roman deities), Christians were viewed as threats to Roman society. When Christians refused to declare that Caesar was Lord, they were condemned as traitors to the Roman Empire. And so, by the middle of the first century AD, Christians were actively being arrested, tortured, and killed for their faith. For example, after Nero blamed Christians for the burning of Rome, some sources report that he used Christians as human torches during one of his evening dinner parties.

Similar horrors continued to be practiced during the next couple centuries. The historian Eusebius reports that during the reign of Marcus Aurelius, a young Christian slave girl named Blandina was tortured in prison until her torturers were exhausted and could not continue. She was then tied to posts in the arena to be torn apart by wild beasts. But when the beasts did not touch her for several days, she was whipped, then tied to a red-hot grate, before being wrapped in a net and tossed into the air by the horns of a bull. They finally killed her with a dagger.[23] This sort of torture was common practice in the Roman Empire against Christians until the legalization of Christianity under Constantine in 312 AD (which brought a whole different set of problems).[24]

With this historical picture in mind, and with a basic understanding of human psychology, it is not difficult to understand that some Christians wanted to see their torturers experience the same pain, suffering, and agony that these torturers were inflicting upon the followers of Jesus. But since Christians had no political power, some Christians began to teach that God Himself would be the One to bring retribution, revenge, and punishment upon those who tortured Christians. Such punishment would not come in this life, however, but in the next. Some of the more creative and vindictive Christian writers began to imagine and devise all sorts of tortures and punishments that God might inflict upon those who tortured Christians.

For example, a document from the second century AD called *The Apocalypse of Peter* describes various punishments that will be inflicted on the enemies of Christianity. The unknown author of this text (it is *not* the Apostle Peter) describes blasphemers being hung by their tongues, adulterers being hung upside down with

---

[23] Johann Peter Kirsch, "St. Blandina," *The Catholic Encyclopedia* Vol. 2 (New York: Robert Appleton, 1907). http://www.new advent.org/cathen/02594a.htm

[24] See my "Close Your Church for Good" series of books.

their heads stuck in sewage while their children look on with tears, and usurious money-lenders being forced to roll around on sharp, hot gravel. Though the document does contain some "familiar" hellish imagery such being people roasted over fires or tossed into rivers of flame, the depictions it contains are contrary to Scripture, theology, and the character of Jesus Christ. So while *The Apocalypse of Peter* was widely read and distributed in the early church, and was even included in one of the earliest lists of "Canonical" writings (see the Muratorian fragment), the document was eventually (and rightly) rejected by the church for not properly reflecting Christian theology and practice.

Yet the imagery of God inflicting torture on the enemies of Christians in ways that were similar to how these enemies tortured Christians had taken root. Christians began to feel that just as they were tortured and burned to the cheers of watching crowds, so also, when the roles were reversed in eternity, Christians would watch and cheer as their enemies suffered. In mimicry of the Roman bloodlust, some Christians had trouble deciding which enemy they most wanted to watch suffer. Tertullian (c. 160-230 AD), who was the first church father to write about eternal hell,[25] looked forward with great eagerness to watching his enemies burn and suffer. Here is what he said on the subject:

---

[25] Ferwerda, *Raising Hell*, 52.

What a panorama of spectacle on that day! What sight shall I turn to first to laugh and applaud? Mighty kings whose ascent to heaven used to be announced publicly groaning now in the depths with Jupiter himself who used to witness that ascent? Governors who persecuted the name of the Lord melting in flames fiercer than those they kindled for brave Christians? Wise philosophers, blushing before their students as they burn together, the followers to whom they taught that the world is no concern of God's, whom they assured that either they had no souls at all or that what souls they had would never return to their former bodies? Poets, trembling not before the judgment seat of Rhadamanthus or of Minos, but of Christ—a surprise? Tragic actors bellowing in their own melodramas should be worth hearing! Comedians skipping in the fire will be worth praise! The famous charioteer will toast on his fiery wheel; the athletes will cartwheel not in the gymnasium but in flames ... These are things of greater delight, I believe, than a circus, both kinds of theater, and any stadium.[26]

Most Christians of that time were justifiably opposed to this sort of gleeful expectation of watching sinners suffer in eternal torment. In the early church, the majority of Christians seem to have held to various forms of universalism or ultimate reconciliation.[27] However, due to the influence of St. Augustine (354-430

---

[26] Tertullian, quoted by Turner, *The History of Hell*, 76.

[27] See "Universalism" in Samuel Macauley Jackson, ed., *The New Shchaff-Herzog Encyclopedia of Religious Knowledge* (Grand Rapids: Baker, 1949), 96.

AD), one of the most influential theologians of early church history, the view of hell as a place of eternal suffering for the damned grew in influence. Yet Augustine did not know Greek, and relied heavily upon Jerome's *Latin Vulgate* (a Latin translation of the Bible) for his views. Many of Augustine's writings show the marriage between the vindictive deities of Roman mythology and the Greek concept of Hades with a liberal dose of creative torture thrown in. And since Augustine was so influential, his views formed the foundation for much Christian thinking about the afterlife of the unredeemed.

So although Jesus taught His followers to "Love your enemies" and "Do unto others as you would have them do unto you," several early Christians nevertheless believed that God would instead torture the enemies of Christianity and do unto them as they had done to us. Yet revenge was not the only reason for holding to the concept of hell; others taught it for more pragmatic reasons. The doctrine of hell is extremely helpful "as a means to control the masses with fear."[28] People will do almost anything you say if you threaten them with eternal torture for disobedience.

During the next thousand years of Christian history, the doctrine of hell as a place of suffering and torment was so commonly accepted in Western Christianity that few rejected it. Those who did reject it were often con-

[28] Ferwerda, *Raising Hell*, 52.

demned as heretics and were hastened on their way to the fires of hell by being burned at the stake or some other gruesome death. In one account, a teacher named Johannes Erigena (c. 815-877 AD) had the audacity to tell his students that hell was not a place of fire and torment, and so after being condemned as a heretic, he was killed by being stabbed to death by his own students with their pens.[29]

Even theological giants such as Peter Lombard (c. 1100-1160 AD) and Thomas Aquinas (c. 1226-1274 AD) believed and taught that hell was a place of physical torture and fiery burning for the unredeemed dead. But it was not just the theology of hell which gained popularity during the Middle Ages, but also the imagery and creativity with which hell was described. Some of the most popular preachers, sermons, books, and plays contained garish and graphic portrayals of the sufferings and torments that came upon the poor souls in hell. In fact, the best-selling books during the Middle Ages were those that presented "visions of hell" and described in great detail the twisted delights of the demons who imagined ever more creative ways to inflict pain and agony on the human captives trapped forever in the fiery furnace of hell. Many of these stories borrowed heavily from the violent imagery of ancient Greek mythology and Northern European paganism.[30]

[29] Turner, *The History of Hell*, 89.

[30] Ibid., 91-113.

It is actually not too surprising that the Christian theology of hell incorporated so much imagery and teaching from Greek myths and pagan culture, for after Constantine legalized Christianity in 312 AD, this marriage between Christian and non-Christian theology and practice was carried out in nearly every aspect of Christianity. From clergy and buildings to holidays and rituals, Christianity adopted much of the stories, culture, and traditions that had formerly been considered "non-Christian."[31] So the doctrine of hell was no different. Very little of the hellish imagery with which we are familiar comes from Scripture. The vast majority was borrowed from non-biblical sources.[32]

However, of all the sources that influenced the doctrine of hell, there is none more important than Dante's *Divine Comedy,* and specifically, the *Inferno,* in which he takes a tour of hell.[33] Capitalizing on the widespread popularity of the "vision of hell" genre from the Middle Ages, and writing his account as a beautifully constructed epic poem, Dante's account heavily influenced Christian thinking about hell. "Dante took every theme … philosophic, mythic, Orphic, demonic, repulsive, fantastic, allegorical, grotesque, comic, psychological—and

[31] I cover much of this in my "Close Your Church for Good" series of books.

[32] Baker, *Razing Hell,* 5; Turner, *The History of Hell,* 114-125.

[33] Cf. Baker, *Razing Hell,* 6.

put them together with meticulous care for all time."[34] And not surprisingly, Dante draws most of his hellish imagery, not from Scripture, but from the same mythical and pagan sources that all of his predecessors used as well.[35]

It also appears that the Muslim Qur'an was one of Dante's primary sources for his lurid depictions of hell as a place of burning torment.

> Of all the scriptures in the world to appear before Dante's time, Islam's were the ones that most resembled the vision of Hell in the *Inferno*. The Holy Qur'an and early Islamic teachings were strangely preoccupied with not some vague underworld or indeterminate afterlife, but with an angry, burning, furious Hell. … The parallels between Hell in the Qur'an and what Dante uses to build his vast *Inferno* are stunning at times.[36]

So not only do Dante's depictions of hell have no basis in fact from Scripture, he also draws heavily on the way hell is portrayed in Greek mythology and the Muslim Qur'an. Neither of these should be considered reliable Christian sources for the experience of unregenerate dead in the afterlife.

Nevertheless, Dante's representation of hell was so impressive and imaginative, it dominated Christian

---

[34] Turner, *The History of Hell*, 134-144.

[35] Cf. Jon M. Sweeney, *Inventing Hell: Dante, the Bible, and Eternal Torment* (Chicago: ACTA, 2017), 13, 183.

[36] Ibid., 154, 157.

thinking and theology for the next several centuries. Even today, when most people describe what they imagine hell to be like, the images and terms they use have more in common with Dante's *Inferno* than they do with Scripture, even if they have never read (or heard of) Dante.

Curiously, however, following the Reformation, some Christians began to realize that Dante's *Inferno* was too fantastic and too creative to be taken seriously by a thinking person. Besides, as many scholars pointed out, much of what Dante described could not be found anywhere in the Bible. And so various church scholars and teachers began to strip away all the "unbiblical" imagery of Dante's hellish creation, keeping only the fire, darkness, and worms, though how all three of these could co-exist in one place was still an issue of some debate.[37] However, much of Dante's vivid imagery was later resurrected to much popular acclaim in John Milton's (1608-1674 AD) *Paradise Lost.*[38]

Further support for the traditional doctrine of hell came from the Catholic Church's Council of Trent (1564 AD), which emphatically affirmed the existence of hell as a place of torment for the unregenerate dead. Yet as scientific advances began to make greater strides in understanding the order and organization of the world, the solar system, and the universe, the traditional

[37] Turner, *The History of Hell*, 173.

[38] Ibid., 177-189.

doctrine of hell began to come under attack. After all, where could hell exist, and how did human beings from earth arrive there? In light of these (and many similar questions), the doctrine of Annihilationism began to grow in popularity among Christians.[39] Nevertheless, some tried to use science to discover the location of hell, and while some suggested it was in the center of the earth, others argued that hell was in the center of the sun.[40]

As the Great Awakening swept throughout Great Britain and the thirteen American colonies, many preachers used the threat of hell as a way to spark fear in their audience and encourage mass conversions. Some of the greatest sermons of these revivals include "The Eternity of Hell-Torments" by George Whitefield, "Sinners in the Hands of an Angry God" by Jonathan Edwards, and "Of Hell" by John Wesley. Jonathan Edwards even describes God hanging sinners over the flames of hell like a child might dangle a loathsome spider over a fire. Of all the Great Awakening preachers, the sermons by Edwards tended to be the most vivid and alarming.[41] While all such vivid imagery creates a strong reaction from the listening audience, it is not found in, nor supported by, Scripture.

[39] Ibid., 194.

[40] Ibid., 195.

[41] Cf. Baker, *Razing Hell*, 7-8.

In the last few centuries, more and more Christians, pastors, and theologians have begun to question the traditional doctrine of hell as it has been widely taught for the past 1800 years. While some have moved toward Universalism and others toward Annihilationism, the reactions against hell are mostly fueled by the persistent picture of hell as a place of burning torment and eternal suffering. Others, however, as much as they dislike the concept of hell, are convinced that it is taught in Scripture, and so are forced, against their better judgment, to accept such a damnable doctrine.

Yet as can be seen from the brief history of hell summarized above, the popular view of hell as a place of suffering torment in flames is not primarily drawn from Scripture, but from a variety of other non-biblical sources. These myths then shade our reading of Scripture with flame-colored glasses so that we think Scripture supports the traditional view of hell, when in fact it does not. The texts which often get trotted out to defend "hell" did not mean any such thing to the original author or audience. But due to the tradition about hell and what we have been taught about it through many books, movies, and sermons, we read "fiery hell" into various passages of Scripture, even though such a doctrine of hell was not originally intended by Jesus, Paul, or the authors of Scripture.

Therefore, far from being biblical or godly, hell was "created" by a strange cycle of twisting events whereby humans used pagan mythological imagery to project upon God their own human desire for revenge. When Christians were tortured and mistreated by their enemies (always in the name of a foreign deity), some Christians sought to comfort one another by teaching that these enemies would experience similar suffering at the hands of God in eternity. And there were numerous passages from Scripture which easily lent themselves to such a view, which in turn gave support to the vindictive and violent depictions of hell which became prominent in the centuries that followed.

But what would happen to the doctrine of hell if we could hold firmly to the teachings of Scripture while also recognizing that God does not have a torture chamber in the deepest dungeon of His good creation? Can it really be that one of the central truths of the Gospel of Jesus Christ is "Love God or else He will torture you for all eternity"? What if Jesus and the apostolic writers of Scripture never intended us to hear and read their teachings in light of Egyptian, Greek, Roman, and Northern European mythology? What if the biblical passages that are often used to defend the doctrine of hell were intended to be used for a much more practical and beneficial use than to threaten people into heaven?

If these sorts of questions give you hope that maybe there is some way to accept and believe everything that Scripture teaches *while also* rejecting the idea that some people are tormented in hell for eternity, keep reading this book. You will discover that the passages which often get quoted as the "biblical teaching about hell" are actually teaching something quite different. The next chapter reveals what this "something quite different" is by looking at eight terms in Scripture that are often associated with hell.

CHAPTER 2

WHICH BIBLICAL WORDS
MEAN "HELL"?

Several phrases from Scripture are often used to teach about hell. These words will be considered individually below, but it is important to note that when they are all considered together, it becomes obvious that they cannot all be taken literally. The word *sheol*, for example, refers to a dark and gloomy pit. Also, the "outer darkness" refers to a place of darkness that is away from light. Yet other images, such as the references to "fire" and the "Lake of Fire," seem to indicate the presence of flames. How can a location be *both* a place of burning flames *and* gloomy darkness? Logically, it cannot.[1]

It is better, therefore, to recognize that other options exist for these terms. For example, maybe one or more of these terms are symbolic. Maybe one or more of these terms do not refer to the eternal dwelling place of unbelievers. Maybe one or more of these terms do not refer to "hell." In regards to this last option, the following

[1] Cf. Ibid., 131; Crockett, ed. *Four Views on Hell*, 59.

chapter will reveal that while there are many passages in the Bible that some people use to support the idea that sinners will suffer for eternity in a fiery hell, none of them actually teach such a concept.

The goal of this chapter is to carefully define the eight biblical phrases which often get equated with hell, and then see which of them might be symbolic or refer to something other than an eternal torture chamber for the unregenerate dead. These eight terms are studied in more detail in the lesson on "Hell" in my "Gospel Dictionary" online course, but the summaries below will provide enough information to understand what Scripture teaches regarding these eight terms. The eight terms are: *sheol, abyss, hadēs, gehenna*, fire, the Lake of Fire, the outer darkness, and *tartarus*.

Note that the word "hell" itself is not among these eight phrases. Why not? Because "hell" is not a biblical word. As we will see below, the word "hell" is not a proper English translation of any Hebrew or Greek word in the Bible. Let us consider these eight terms to discover what they actually mean, beginning with the word *sheol*.

SHEOL

The Hebrew word *sheol* is the most common word in the Old Testament that is used in reference to the state of the dead. Curiously, however, "The word does not appear outside of the OT, except once in the Jewish Elephantine papyri, where it means 'grave.'"[2] So when it comes to understanding what the Old Testament authors meant with the word *sheol,* we are limited to its usage within Scripture itself. Thankfully, there are numerous passages which guide our definition of this word. The word *sheol* occurs sixty-six times in the Hebrew Scriptures. A few of these are occasionally translated as "hell" depending on which Bible translation you read. Yet "hell" is not a good translation of any of these occurrences. The Hebrew Scriptures never indicates any form of punishment after death, so this translation is inappropriate.[3] This is seen in a variety of ways.

For example, both good and evil people go to *sheol* (cf. Gen 37:35; Num 16:30; Jon 2:2). Since it is not a place only for wicked and evil people and since even the righteous go to *sheol,* it cannot be equivalent to the modern concept of hell. Some teach, therefore, that *sheol* was a special "holding tank" or "intermediate state" for all people who lived and died prior to the death and resurrection of Jesus, and that after the resurrection of Jesus, people no longer go to *sheol,* but are immediately sent to either heaven or hell. Texts such as Matthew 27:52, Ephesians 4:8-10, and 1 Peter 3:19 are used to defend this idea.

---

[2] Harris et al., *Theological Wordbook of the Old Testament,* II:892.

[3] Johnston, *Shades of Sheol,* 73.

However, when all the references to *sheol* are considered together, it appears that the most likely definition of the word is also the most literal translation. The word itself means "grave" or "pit."[4] When Hebrew authors wrote about *sheol* they were thinking about a literal hole in the ground in which dead bodies were laid. It does not represent any sort of afterlife experience.[5] When adjectives are used to describe *sheol*, it is portrayed as a wet, dank, dark, dusty, musty hole. If you have ever dug a hole into the ground, you know that such terms describe the hole perfectly.

Support for this understanding is found in the fact that the Hebrew word *bor* is often used as a synonym for *sheol*, and *bor* is literally a hole dug in the ground (cf. Isa 14:11-20). And much like any grave, *sheol* is characterized by the presence of worms and decay (Job 17:13-16; 24:19-20). There is not a single Old Testament text which speaks of *sheol* as an eternal place of suffering and torment for the unregenerate dead.[6] Nowhere does *sheol* "indicate anything other than the place in which a body

[4] Cf. Bernstein, *The Formation of Hell*, 140-141. Johnston attempts to raise a few objections to "grave" as a consistent translation, but all of his evidence is drawn from prophetic texts where poetic terms are being used to describe the experience of the dead. See Johnston, *Shades of Sheol*, 74.

[5] Sweeney, *Inventing Hell*, 38. Cf. Ferwerda, *Raising Hell*, 40.

[6] Cf. Fudge, *The Fire That Consumes*, 81, 85.

is laid to rest, except when used metaphorically to indicate depression or despair."[7]

Even when New Testament authors quote Old Testament texts which speak about *sheol,* they do so in connection with the bodily resurrection of people from the grave (cf. Psa 16:10; Hos 13:14; Acts 2:27; 13:35; 1 Cor 15:55). The idea is that the human bodies went into the ground, and at the resurrection, their bodies come up out of the ground and are made whole and complete once again. So even the New Testament supports the idea that *sheol* is simply "the grave." And since all people die and go to the grave, it makes sense for the Old Testament texts to speak about all people going to *sheol.*

The Biblical data about *sheol* "does not give us a picture of the state of the dead in gloom, darkness, chaos, or silence, unremembered, unable to praise God, knowing nothing. Such a view verges on unscriptural soul sleep. Rather, this view gives us a picture of a typical Palestinian tomb, dark, dusty, with mingled bones … All the souls of men do not go to one place. But all people go to the grave."[8]

The Old Testament, therefore, does not have much to say about the afterlife for either the righteous or the wicked. All it knows is that when people die, they are put down into a dark and musty grave, where worms and decay destroy their bodies. As such, the word *sheol*

[7] Turner, *The History of Hell*, 40.

[8] Harris et al., *Theological Wordbook of the Old Testament*, II:893.

has nothing whatsoever to say about "hell" and should not be translated as "hell" in any of its uses (contrary to KJV texts such as Deut 32:22; Psa 16:10; Prov 9:18; Isa 14:9-10). The best way to translate all uses of *sheol* is "grave." It literally refers to a pit or hole dug into the ground into which dead bodies are laid. When used metaphorically, it can refer to depression, sorrow, or loneliness, which are emotions often associated with death and burial. The term suggests a "gloomy existence without meaningful activity or social distinction."[9]

The term, therefore, is the theological opposite of the life that God wants and desires for His people.[10] Since God is a God of the living, not the dead, then *sheol* represents the experience of those who are not functioning as God desires, whether it is because they are dead and buried in the ground, or because they are cut off from community due to loneliness and depression. Unlike those who are alive, there is no meaningful existence for those who are in *sheol*.[11] There is not a single text that describes *sheol* as a place of suffering and torment in the afterlife for the unregenerate dead.

There is no other Old Testament word which can be used as a reference to hell. This helps us realize that if the doctrine of hell as a place of suffering torment is

[9] Johnston, *Shades of Sheol*, 85.

[10] Ibid., 75.

[11] Fleming Rutledge, *The Crucifixion: Understanding the Death of Jesus Christ* (Grand Rapids: Eerdmans, 2015), 399.

correct, then God left humanity completely ignorant and blind to this idea for most of human history. If it is true that the vast majority of people from the days of Adam to the days of John the Baptist will end up in a place of burning torment forever and ever, wouldn't it have been loving for God to at least warn people about such a potential fate? Yet there is not a single such warning in all of the Hebrew Scriptures. In reference to the concept of eternal torment in a fiery hell, Thomas Thayer wrote this:

> It is impossible to believe that, if true, God would have kept His children in the dark all this while; that no hint of it, no allusion to it, should have found place in His revelation to the Patriarchs; that He should never have threatened anything bordering upon it, [not even] in such cases of extreme wickedness as that of Cain, the Sodomites, and the corrupt inhabitants of the old world [at the time of the flood].[12]

> It seems as if no honest mind, no sincere believer in the authority of God's word, could appeal from a testimony so positive and unmistakable as this. There is no room for comment or criticism. In the presence of such an unimpeachable witness, the question is reduced to its sim-

---

[12] Thayer, *The Origin and History of the Doctrine of Endless Punishment*, loc 194.

plest form: either to abandon the Bible argument, or to abandon the doctrine of eternal punishment.[13]

[The word *shĕol*] is never used by Moses or the Prophets in the sense of a place of torment after death.[14]

If hell really exists, then was it just and right for God to not warn a single person prior to the birth of Jesus about the eternal torment that awaited them in eternity? Is it conceivable that the God revealed to us in Jesus Christ could watch billions of humans fall into a pit of eternal suffering and torment while never saying a single word of warning about it to those who were alive? If -kingdom-4.pdf looked or neglected mentioning it in His revelation to humanity for the majority of human history?

People often say that it is loving to warn people about hell, just as it is loving to warn people about driving off a cliff. But if this is so, why did God not warn people about hell for most of human history? Is God unloving? To ask the question is to answer it. God is infinitely loving, and would not have failed to warn the objects of His love about such a potential disaster. Therefore, the only other rational conclusion is that such a disaster does not exist. God didn't warn people because the warning was not needed.

---

[13] Ibid., loc 337.

[14] Ibid., loc 411.

Yet despite the complete silence in the Hebrew Scriptures about eternal conscious torment in hell, people today continue to hold to the doctrine, primarily because they believe it is taught in the New Testament. As will be seen below, nearly *all* the evidence provided for the doctrine of eternal torment in a fiery hell comes from the New Testament. But if the Hebrew Scriptures do not teach the concept of eternal torment in hellfire, it is legitimate to ask whether the New Testament does. Maybe we have misunderstood what the New Testament teaches about hell as well.

The New Testament contains seven terms which are thought to refer to hell. In alphabetical order they are: *abyss*, fire, *gehenna*, *hadēs*, Lake of Fire, outer darkness, and *tartarus*. Let us consider each in turn.

ABYSS

The first Greek New Testament word to consider is *abussos*, which is often translated as "abyss" or "pit." The word means "bottomless" and refers to a hole or pit of immeasurable depth. In the LXX (the Greek translation of the Hebrew Old Testament), *abussos* is often used to translate the Hebrew word *tehom,* which means "the deep" and refers to the deepest parts of the sea (cf. Gen 1:2; 7:11; 8:2, 7; Psa 32:7; 35:7; 41:8; 104:6; Job 38:16; Jon 2:6; Isa 44:27; 51:10; 63:13; Ezek 26:19; 31:4, 15; Dan 3:55).

But the Hebrew concept of "the deep" (*tehom*) is not just equivalent to the deep parts of the ocean. As I taught in my podcast on Genesis 1:2 (and forthcoming commentary on Genesis 1), the word *tehom* was "an ancient, mysterious, and menacing word. To ancient minds, it was an evil word."[15] It carries the idea of powerful forces of chaos arrayed against the order of God's creation.

This imagery and connection with the deep (*tehom*) sea helps explain why Paul changes the original wording of Deuteronomy 30:13 when he quotes this text in Romans 10:7. Deuteronomy 30:13 speaks of "the sea" (*yam*), but Paul changes it to "the abyss" (which should be *tehom* in Hebrew). But this change is allowable, because "the deep" is part of the sea.

Furthermore, when it comes to thinking about the relationship between "hell" and the abyss, we see that since the abyss refers to the deepest parts of the sea on this world, it cannot refer to some sort of afterlife experience where people burn and suffer for eternity. The abyss, the deep, *tehom*, is a symbol of the power of chaos arrayed against God and the order of creation. It is not a place where people go after they die to suffer in flames for all eternity.

The symbolic nature of the abyss is especially significant in the book of Revelation, where the word is used

---

[15] Listen to the podcast episode here: https://redeeminggod.com/genesis_1_2/

most frequently in the New Testament. Since the beast came out of the sea (Rev 11:7; 13:1; 17:8), this symbolizes that the beast brings chaos. And indeed, when the abyss is opened, chaos, in the form of fire and smoke, comes up out of the pit (Rev 9:1-2, somewhat like a volcano that rises from the sea). But ultimately, just as Jesus sent a demonic horde back into the depths of the sea (Luke 8:31), so also, God will send the beast back into the abyss from whence he came (Rev 20:1-3).

So as with *sheol,* the abyss does not represent hell. The abyss is literally the deep waters of the ocean, and it symbolizes chaos and disorder in God's creation. When people go down into the abyss, it symbolizes their death in the depths of the ocean (Ezek 26:19). Similarly, to be delivered from the abyss is to be delivered from death in the sea (cf. LXX Psa 105:9; Jon 2:6; Isa 63:13). No reference to the abyss ever contains descriptions of fire, suffering, or the torture of people for eternity. Therefore, the word abyss cannot refer to a place of everlasting suffering and torment in the fires of hell.

But what about the word "fire" itself? Surely this term refers to hell.

FIRE

The word *fire* is a translation of the Greek word *pur*. Similar words include *burning* (or *burn*, from the Greek words *kaiō* or *katakaiō*). Obviously, the word *fire* in

Scripture most often refers to literal flames where wood, fields, or buildings are consumed and burned by fire. We are not concerned about these references as everyone understands when this type of fire is in view. The passages that do concern us are those that use the terms in a symbolic sense to describe what happens to some people either in this life or the next.

When people read these metaphorical references to *fire* in the Bible, they most naturally think of hell. This is not surprising, since many Christians have been taught from a young age that hell is a place of burning fire where the unredeemed are tortured for eternity. But a careful analysis of the biblical references to *fire* reveals that the term rarely refers to what people think of as hell.[16] Instead, the term and its related imagery usually refer to some sort of divine judgment, which can occur during this life *or* the next, upon believers *or* unbelievers alike. Such *fire* does not necessarily refer to a literal *fire*, but to a symbolic or metaphorical judgment of burning.

In other words, while there are a few texts which use the image of fire to describe the state of the unregenerate dead, the image also refers to the refining fire of God's discipline during this life on earth (Isa 33:10-16; 48:10; Zech 13:9; Mal 3:3; 1 Pet 1:7; Heb 12:29), or to the shame that some believers will experience at the Judgment Seat of Christ (cf. 1 Cor 3:15). The majority

---

[16] Joseph C. Dillow, *The Reign of the Servant Kings: A Study of Eternal Security and the Final Significance of Man* (Miami Springs, FL: Schoettle Publishing, 1992), 412.

of these metaphorical uses of fire and burning, therefore, do not refer to hell at all, and especially not to the eternal suffering of the unregenerate dead.

It is significant to note that Scripture describes God as "a consuming fire" (Heb 12:29). But this does not mean that God is made of literal fire. Instead, this text means that God works to *pur*ify (*pur* is the word for fire) everything and everyone from that which is contrary to His character and purposes. Wood, hay, stubble, and dross get burned away by God, leaving behind only gold, jewels, and precious stones (1 Cor 3:13-15). But this refining fire of God is experienced in different ways by different people (cf. Exod 24:16-18; Mal 3:2-3; 4:1-2). If someone's life consists primarily of sin and rebellion, then the fire of God will be a hellish experience in which all that they are and everything they have done gets burned away. The person who imitates God and follows the way of Jesus, however, will have exactly the opposite experience with the same divine fire. "God is the fire that we experience as either a blessing or a torment, depending on our spiritual state."[17]

> By way of analogy, when the children of Israel fled Pharaoh's army, the presence of God stood between them as a pillar of fire. To God's people, he was warmth, light, and comfort. To his enemies, he was darkness and terror. The same is true of the fiery furnace in the book of Daniel. To Daniel's friends, the fire served to burn only the ropes

[17] Jersak, *Her Gates Will Never Be Shut*, 77.

of their bondage. Meanwhile, it incinerated their cap-
tors.[18]

So the biblical truth about "fire" is that while the
word can be used to refer to the experience of some
people after they die, it does not refer only to the experience of unbelievers, but occasionally to believers as well.
And in every case where the Bible speaks about fire
coming upon people in the afterlife, it is not literal
flames that are in view. Instead, fire is used as a metaphorical symbol of judgment or purification. I know
this is a challenging concept, and I have only briefly
summarized what the Bible teaches about fire. So the
Appendix at the end of this book provides a defense of
this idea by considering numerous biblical passages that
refer to fire.

We are seeing, therefore, that whatever hell is, it is
not a dark and bottomless pit; nor is it a place of burning fire. The words *sheol, abyss,* and *fire* do not refer to
hell as it is typically taught in contemporary Christianity
or imagined in popular culture. But what about *gehenna*? Jesus speaks of *gehenna* more than any other person
in Scripture, and so it is important to consider this term
as well.

[18] Ibid., 78.

GEHENNA

The word *gehenna* is a Greek transliteration from the Hebrew "Valley of Hinnom" (or *Ge-Hinnom*) which was a deep gorge to the southwest of Jerusalem.[19] It was also called the Valley of Tophet. The valley has a sordid history. It was a place of idolatry, injustice, and spiritual infidelity.[20] It was here that child sacrifices to Molech were performed in the days of Ahaz and Manasseh (2 Kings 16:3; 21:6; 23:10).[21] Furthermore, when 185,000 Assyrian soldiers died during their siege in the days of King Hezekiah, the bodies were piled in the Valley of Hinnom and set on fire (Isa 30:31-33; 37:36). Jeremiah built on this history and said that if the Israelites did not turn and follow God, something similar would happen to them (Jer 7:30-34; 19:2-13). And indeed, after the slaughter of the Israelite people by the Roman military in 69-70 AD, this is what occurred.[22]

But it was not just the history of prophecies of this valley which made it a place of horror. In the days of Jesus, the valley was used as the city dump.[23] Yet it was not only filled with garbage, refuse, and sewage, but also with dead bodies that people were trying to dispose of

[19] Bernstein, *The Formation of Hell*, 167-169.

[20] Butler, *The Skeletons in God's Closet*, 36.

[21] *Easton's Bible Dictionary,* "Gehenna."

[22] Fudge, *The Fire That Consumes*, 160.

[23] Wright, *Following Jesus*, 93; Baker, *Razing Hell*, 128-130; Sweeney, *Inventing Hell*, 111.

(due to crime, sickness, poverty, or shame). City officials occasionally sought to get rid of the garbage and also cover the stench by igniting the refuse on fire. But since there was so much garbage, and since more was added every day, the fire never really died. It burned day and night, seemingly forever and ever. Even in places where there was no open flame, the piles of refuse would still smolder for weeks on end, sending constant billows of smoke and ashes into the air.

Yet not everything in *Gehenna* burned. As is the nature of flames, they go where they will, sometimes leaving entire sections untouched. In these areas, worms and maggots went to work on the refuse and corpses that were left behind.

Furthermore, as is the nature of all city dumps throughout the world (even to this day), the sick and poor often scavenged through the garbage looking for things to eat or sell. Some of these were undoubtedly lepers in various states of disease and decay who might have lived in the rock tombs on the lower end of the valley.[24]

With all this in mind, imagine what it would be like to "take out the garbage" on a typical Jerusalem morning. As you haul your cart of trash down the hill into the valley, you first become aware of the smoke that rises

---

[24] Ferwerda, *Raising Hell*, 43. Cf. https://www.that theworldmayknow.com/gehenna and http://www.nbcnews.com/id/3849407/ns/technology_and_science-science/t/ancient-lepersbones-found-jerusalem/

continually from the dump. It is acrid and oily from the burning trash and causes your eyes to smart. But soon, not even the smoke can cover the stench that rises from rotting food and corpses on a hot Middle-Eastern day. The smell is so bad, you struggle not to vomit and retch.

But the smoke in your eyes and the smell in your nostrils are not the worst of it. As you descend down into the pit, it becomes harder to see. The sun turns blood red due to the smoke and there is a constant gloomy haze that surrounds you. But this is a blessing in disguise, for what you do see is difficult to forget. On your left there is a mangled corpse. It is missing some limbs and is half-burned from the fire. The remaining half is crawling with maggots and buzzing with flies. You avert your eyes, only to see a ragged leper stumbling through the smoke while eating a moldy piece of fruit he has pulled from the trash. He is missing his nose and an arm and appears to be a walking corpse.

Horrified, you decide you have traveled far enough into the pit. You dump your trash as quickly as possible before retreating back up the slope toward Jerusalem. As the smoke recedes and the sun brightens above you, you peer back over your shoulder at where you left your trash, only to see half a dozen walking corpses shuffling toward your pile of garbage as fast as their mangled feet will carry them. They are eager to be among the first to dig through what you have left behind, hoping to find a bit of food or clothing that will get them through another day. You shudder and pick up your pace to leave the nightmare valley behind and return to the land of the living.

In the days of Jesus, this is what came to mind when someone used the word "Gehenna." The term conveyed "a sense of total horror and disgust. … Gehenna was a place of undying worm and irresistible fire, an abhorrent place where crawling maggots and smoldering heat raced each other to consume the putrefying fare served them each day."[25]

Therefore, since Gehenna was a literal place outside the walls of Jerusalem, the word should not be translated in our Bibles. We do not translate "Jerusalem" as "City of Peace," "Bethel" as "City of God," or "Gilgal" as "circle," even though that is what those place names mean. So also, we should not translate Gehenna as "hell" or any other word. It should be left as it is, thereby alerting the reader to the fact that the text is referring to the valley called Gehenna outside the gates of Jerusalem. Translating it as "the Valley of Hinnom" would also be fine.

But even if we leave *gehenna* as "Gehenna," we are still faced with the question as to whether Jesus had something more in mind than the physical and literal Valley of Hinnom when He taught about *gehenna.* In other words, when Jesus spoke about *gehenna,* was He only speaking about the Valley of Hinnom, or was He

[25] Fudge, *The Fire That Consumes*, 161-162.

using the imagery, history, and inherent horror of this valley to teach His listeners about the experience of some people in the afterlife?

When the various texts are considered (cf. Matt 5:22, 29, 30; 10:28; 18:8-9; 23:15, 33; Mark 9:43-47; Luke 12:5; Jas 3:6), the answer becomes obvious. Jesus (and James, who is the only other person in the New Testament to speak about *gehenna*), is indeed using the Valley of Hinnom in a symbolic way, but not to teach about what happens to some people in the afterlife, but rather to teach about what can happen to some people in *this life.* People who are sent to the Valley of Hinnom (usually because of crime or leprosy) lose their friends and family, and face a life filled with horror, decay, and destruction.

The warnings about *gehenna* are given by Jesus so that we do not destroy our health, life, family, friendships, and reputation in this life. Rather than live in the Valley of Death, God want us to enjoy everything He has given to us in this life. In his book, *Surprised by Hope,* N. T. Wright says this about *gehenna*:

> When Jesus was warning his hearers about Gehenna he was not, as a general rule, telling them that unless they repented in this life they would burn in the next one. As with God's kingdom, so with its opposite: it is on earth that things matter, not somewhere else.
>
> His message to His contemporaries was stark, and (as we would say today) political. Unless they turned back from

their hopeless and rebellious dreams of establishing God's kingdom in their own terms, not least through armed revolt against Rome, then the Roman juggernaut would do what large, greedy and ruthless empires have always done to smaller countries (not least in the Middle East) whose resources they covet or whose strategic location they are anxious to guard. Rome would turn Jerusalem into a hideous, stinking extension of its own smoldering rubbish heap. When Jesus said "Unless you repent, you will all likewise perish," that is the primary meaning He had in mind.[26]

Therefore, a word that is commonly translated as "hell" in the New Testament, does not in fact refer to a place of burning torture or torment in the afterlife. Instead, the word refers to a literal place outside the walls of Jerusalem. Jesus uses the history and imagery of this place to warn His disciples about what can befall them in this life if they do not follow His teachings and take steps (sometimes drastic) to protect themselves and their loved ones from the devastation of sin. When Jesus speaks about *gehenna,* He is not warning about hell in the next life, but a hellish existence in this life.

So we still have not found a word in Scripture which properly refers to "hell" as a place of otherworldly burning and suffering for the unregenerate dead. But we have four words to go, and so there is hope (or no hope,

[26] N. T. Wright, *Surprised by Hope: Rethinking Heaven, the Resurrection, and the Mission of the Church* (New York: HarperOne, 2008), 176.

since we're talking about hell) that we can find a word which teaches about hell. The next word, *hades,* is a likely candidate.

HADES

One of the Greek words that is commonly translated as "hell" in the New Testament is *hadēs.* But the word *hadēs* is the Greek equivalent to the Hebrew word *sheol.*[27] In the Greek translation of the Hebrew Bible (the LXX), the Hebrew word *sheol* is most often translated as *hadēs.*[28] And since we have already seen that *sheol* is best translated as "grave" or "pit," then this hints that the word *hadēs* should be understood in a similar fashion (cf. 1 Cor 15:55).[29]

However, in the days of Jesus and the apostles, Jewish teachers were rethinking the concept of the afterlife. The idea of a future resurrection was gaining prominence, and with this idea, people were beginning to speculate about what might happen to humans after they died but before resurrection. So while most Old Testament texts which refer to *sheol* can be understood as only referring to a grave in which dead bodies were laid, the New Testament texts about *hadēs* seem to show

[27] Cf. Rutledge, *The Crucifixion*, 400.

[28] Gerhard Kittel, ed. *Theological Dictionary of the New Testament*, 10 vols. (Grand Rapids: Eerdmans), I:146.

[29] Cf. Thayer, *The Origin and History of the Doctrine of Endless Punishment*, 1094.

an evolution in thinking about what happens to humans after they die.

Those who did not believe in a future resurrection (such as the Sadducees), continued to teach that after death, all people went to the grave (*sheol* or *hadēs*) and that was the end. But those who believed in the resurrection (such as the Pharisees), began to think that there was some sort of conscious existence for the dead as they awaited the future resurrection.[30] For example, the apostle Peter quotes David (Psalm 16:8-11) as saying that God would not allow his body to see corruption in *hadēs,* but would raise Him up (Acts 2:26-27, 31). Peter used these texts to defend the idea of the resurrection, and to explain why God raised Jesus from the dead.

Therefore, those who believed in life after death also believed that people continued to exist somewhere and somehow after death while they awaited resurrection. But they did not have a "heaven and hell" concept as many do today. Instead, people in the days of Jesus believed that all the dead went to the same place, though with different "compartments" for the righteous and the wicked (Josephus, *Antiquities,* 18.14). This concept is seen in the story of the rich man and Lazarus in Luke 16:19-31. Jesus' use of this imagery should not be seen as an endorsement of it. Just as someone today might

---

[30] "The notion of 'soul sleep' is just as foreign to the NT as to Judaism; the image of the sleep is introduced (Mark 5:39 and par.; 1 Thess 5:10; John 11:11-12; etc.) simply as an euphemistic description of death." See Kittel, ed. *TDNT*, I:148.

tell a story about meeting Peter at the Pearly Gates without believing that this is *actually* what will happen, so also, Jesus could tell a story about Abraham's bosom in *hadēs* (Luke 16:22-23) without actually endorsing the concept.

Yet those who believed that *hadēs* was an actual realm in which the dead consciously existed, also believe that the dead would not exist there forever. Instead, *hadēs* was a "holding tank" for people while they waited for the resurrection. At some point in the future, when the resurrection occurred, *hadēs* would be emptied because all of the dead within it would be raised to life. But this was not an endorsement of Universalism. Though *hadēs* would be emptied through the resurrection of all people, the righteous would go away to everlasting life with God, while the rest would go away to everlasting death with the devil (cf. Rev 20:13-14). This idea does not match the modern concept of hell, for in this first-century way of thinking, the people who go to *hadēs* do not stay there forever.

So what is the New Testament concept of *hadēs*? What did Jesus and the apostles have in mind when they taught and wrote about *hadēs*? Several texts provide a shocking insight into the nature and location of *hadēs*. For example, Jesus indicates that *hadēs* is set in contrast to heaven. In Matthew 11:23, Jesus says that while Capernaum was exalted to heaven, it will be brought down to *hadēs* (cf. Luke 10:15). Does this mean that all the citizens of Capernaum were headed for eternal suffering in the pit of hell? No, it cannot mean this, unless the citizens of Capernaum were all previously in heaven. Such an idea makes no theological sense. Even those who believe that it is possible for a person to lose their eternal life do not think that those in heaven can still be sent to hell.

Therefore, it is better to see that Jesus is speaking of both heaven and *hadēs* in symbolic ways. In these texts, Jesus is speaking of heaven as a reference to the apparent blessing of God upon a city in this life and on this world. The city of Capernaum had great fame, honor, glory, wealth, power, and respect in the minds of most people. Going down to *hadēs*, therefore, symbolizes the opposite. The city would lose its power, privilege, and position and would become weak, poor, and desolate, much like Tyre and Sidon (Luke 10:13) or Sodom and Gomorrah (Matt 11:23-24). The "day of judgment" to which Jesus refers in these texts does not refer to some future judgment when all the people of these cities are condemned to eternal punishment in hell, but rather to the historical events which cause the physical destruction of the cities. So when Jesus teaches about *hadēs* in Matthew 11:23 and Luke 10:15, He is speaking about the destruction of cities on this earth in history; not about the torment of human souls in fiery flames for all eternity.

The greatest insight into what Jesus believed about *hadēs* is found in Matthew 16:18. In the preceding context, Peter has just declared that Jesus is the Christ, the Messiah. In response, Jesus states that it is on this declaration from Peter that He will build His church. Jesus then says that the "gates of *hadēs*" will not prevail against the church. Since the church Jesus is building exists here and now, on this earth, in and through our lives, this means that *hadēs* also is here and now, on this earth, and it is set against the church. Furthermore, the church is on the offensive against the gates of *hadēs*, rather than the other way around. But the gates will not prevail, or stand, against the attacks of the church.

When many people read Matthew 16:18, they imagine that the church exists behind a gleaming white wall, and that hell is on the outside, trying to batter down the gates. But the imagery is actually the opposite. Jesus says that the "gates of *hadēs* will not prevail" against the church. In other words, it is *hadēs* that is behind a wall, and the church is attacking the gates. And in order for the church to attack these gates, they must exist in this life and on this earth. This further means that humans are imprisoned by these gates, so that the *way* Jesus builds His church is *by* attacking the gates of *hadēs* to rescue and deliver those within.

It appears, therefore, that in the mind of Jesus, *hadēs* is not a dwelling place for evil people in the afterlife, but is the experience of many people in this life, which is characterized by everything that is opposed to the ways of Jesus Christ and the will of God on earth. So rather than life, light, liberty, and love, those who are trapped behind the gates of *hadēs* live in bondage, corruption, despair, and destruction. Jesus leads His church to help free these people from their hellish life. *Hadēs* is here and now, and Jesus leads the church to set free those who trapped behind its bars. This revolutionary and shocking idea about *hadēs* will be developed further in the next two chapters.

The book of Revelation also contains several references to *hadēs* and while many people are most familiar with the reference in Revelation 20:13-14 where *hadēs* is emptied and its inhabitants are cast into the Lake of Fire, we must first understand the previous references to *hadēs* in Revelation (Rev 1:18; 6:8) before we can understand what John is talking about in Revelation 20. In Revelation 1:18, we read that through His death and resurrection, Jesus gained the keys to death and *hadēs*.

What is interesting about this is that the Greek god *Hadēs* was occasionally depicted in Greek mythology as carrying a key to the gates of the underworld. He kept the gates forever locked so that nobody who was within could ever escape. But in Revelation 1:18, we see that Jesus now carries the keys, and He plans to throw the gates of *hadēs* wide open. When Revelation 1:18 is read in connection with Matthew 16:18, we discover that when Jesus storms the gates of *hadēs* with the church, there is no battle waged. Jesus simply walks up to the gates and unlocks the door, calling those who are within to "Come forth!" The task of the church is to show people how to be free and live life.

Death and *hadēs* are once again paired together in Revelation 6:8. Death is depicted as riding a pale horse, though the "greenish-yellow" color of a corpse is probably a better translation for the Greek word used here. Of the four horsemen in the context, this fourth rider is the only one who is given a name (i.e., "Death"), and is also the only one who does not have a tool or weapon. However, in place of a weapon, Death has *hadēs.* This means that while the other horsemen accomplish their devastation through an instrument, death accomplishes its task through *hadēs.* In other words, *hadēs* is not a place to which people go after they die; instead, *hadēs* is the tool by which the rider on the pale horse brings death and destruction upon the world. Death comes upon this world through the instrument of death, namely, *hadēs.* Once again, this shows that *hadēs* is a present experience for some people; not a future place of existence.

Near the end of Revelation, in 20:13-14, we read that death and *hadēs* are thrown into the Lake of Fire. If we believe that *hadēs* is a place, then this description make little sense. But when we recognize that death and *hadēs* are the powers that destroy and devastate life on this earth, then it comes as no surprise that before Jesus restores all things to the way God wants and desires them to be, He does away with death and destruction (*hadēs*) by throwing them into the Lake of Fire. And as we will see in the next term, this doesn't mean that death and *hadēs* go to hell, for the Lake of Fire is also not "hell."

So "hell" is not a good translation for the Greek word *hadēs*. While the most basic meaning for *hadēs* is similar to *sheol*, the grave, further development in the New Testament era reveals that *hadēs* can primarily be understood as the power of despair, decay, and destruction that enslaves human beings in this life. It operates in direct contradiction to the kingdom of God and the power of life, light, and love that accomplishes the will of God on earth. *Hadēs* is not a place of burning suffering for the unregenerate dead. It is instead a destructive presence here on earth that ruins what God wants for our lives. And in the end, just as with everything else that is arrayed against God, *hadēs* will be cast into the Lake of Fire. But what does this mean? Let us look at the term "Lake of Fire" to see.

LAKE OF FIRE

The image of the Lake of Fire in the book of Revelation has caused much consternation about the living conditions for the unredeemed dead. And while the image is thought to depict the eternal torment of non-Christians in hell, it has also been used to psychologically torment lots of people in this life. The thought of swimming around forever in a molten lake of lava is extremely distressing. The Lake of Fire may be "the most troubling image in the New Testament."[31]

So what is the Lake of Fire and how can we understand it? There are a wide variety of views, some more outlandish than others. I read one scholar who argued that the Lake of Fire was the sun at the middle of our solar system. I once talked with a seminary professor who argued that since all humans around the earth talk about "going down" to hell and the Lake of Fire, this means that all their concepts of "down" converge at the magma core of the earth, which is the Lake of Fire. (I am not making this up.)

Most concepts of the Lake of Fire, however, teach that it is a place created by God where He sends the unredeemed dead to suffer and burn in torment for all eternity. A somewhat less horrific view is found among some Universalists who argue that the Lake of Fire is a temporary torture chamber where sinners have all their impurities burned out of them before they are allowed entrance into heaven. Another view I have recently encountered argues that the Lake of Fire refers to the temporal destruction of Jerusalem in 70 AD.

But whether we are talking about unending torture or a shorter period of time, many people are (rightly) concerned with the idea of God torturing and burning

[31] Butler, *The Skeletons in God's Closet*, 273.

anyone. Does God want us to torture people? No! We are called to love and serve. So is it okay for God to do what He forbids us from doing? Some think so, but I do not. I believe God's commands to humanity are based on His own character and nature, and He sets the example for us to follow. But if this is the case, then we must understand what John meant when he wrote about the Lake of Fire in Revelation 20:10, 14-15, and 21:8.

Thankfully, when John wrote about the Lake of Fire, he was not thinking about tortured souls screaming in agony from being boiled in lava for all eternity. We know this because of the symbolic nature of the book of Revelation. Very little in the book of Revelation is to be understood "literally." Yes, the book should be read and studied seriously, giving careful attention to its words, images, and ideas, but we must never forget that nearly every picture and event in the book of Revelation is full of allusions to the Hebrew Scriptures, Christ-centered theology, Roman politics, and ancient Mediterranean culture.

When we begin to study the symbolism of Revelation and look for clues in the first century Mediterranean world about what John might have been referring to when he wrote about the Lake of Fire, it does not take long to discover that there was an actual "Lake of Fire" in his day that he was referring to. This lake still exists today and you can go swim in it if you would like. But do not worry, for while you might get a sunburn, the lake itself will not burn you. But more on that in a bit.

To help us understand the imagery that John is using, as well as the identity and location of the Lake of Fire, imagine if someone today told you that they were going to live in Salt Lake. Would you think that this person would be floating around all day in the salty water of a Utah lake? No, you would understand that they were moving to the city called "Salt Lake" which is on the shore of a salty lake, and that it would be possible to live in Salt Lake for their entire life without ever setting foot in the lake of salt.

Or, to use another example, what if you heard that someone was going to visit the Valley of Fire on their vacation. Would you think that they were going to visit a place where they would get incinerated and tortured in flames? This would not be much of a vacation. Instead, if you were not familiar with the Valley of Fire, you might look it up online, and discover that it is a popular tourist destination about one hour from the city of Las Vegas. It would be foolish to assume that just because it mentions "fire," this means that anyone who visits the Valley of Fire will be tormented or tortured in flames while they were there. It means no such thing. About 300,000 people go into the Valley of Fire each year, and they all come back, none the worse for wear.

A nearly identical situation occurs with "the Lake of Fire." It was (and is) a literal place on planet earth. And since many people today (and throughout church history) do not know where this location is, they have wrongly assumed that John was describing an eternal place of fiery torture in the afterlife for the unredeemed dead.

So what and where is the Lake of Fire? In the days of Jesus and John, what we now call the Dead Sea was referred to by some as the Lake of Fire, or the Fiery Lake.[32] The Dead Sea sits on a fault line, and during the several thousand years prior to the first century AD, it used to regularly erupt, spewing forth tar, pitch, bitumen, asphaltites, smoke, sulphur, and flame. As a result, the Greeks even named it the "Lake Asphaltites."

But the Greeks were not the only ones to describe the sea in such a way. The Wisdom of Solomon also records that Lot "escaped the fire that came on the Five Cities, cities whose wickedness is still attested by a smoking waste" (*Wisdom of Solomon* 10:7). Diodorus Siculus, a first century BC historian, wrote this about this region: "The fire which burns beneath the ground and the stench render the inhabitants of the neighboring country sickly and very short lived" (Diodorus Siculus, *Bibliotheca Historica,* Volume II:48.6).[33]

---

[32] Cf. Jersak, *Her Gates Will Never Be Shut*, 82-87; Stephen John Spencer, *The Genesis Pursuit: The Lost History of Jesus Christ* (Longwood, FL: Xulon, 2006), 185-212.

[33] This text can be read here: http://penelope.uchicago.edu/Thayer/E/Roman/Texts/Diodorus_Siculus/2B*.html

Philo, writing in the days before the ministry of Jesus, said that the valley of the Dead Sea was filled with fires, which were very difficult to extinguish, and that many of these fires had been smoking and burning for a very long time, even to his own day (*On Abraham,* XXVII:141). When Josephus was writing his history of the Jewish wars, he said that one could still see the burnt remnants of the five cities, and that fruit from the region dissolves into smoke and ashes if plucked (*The Wars of the Jews*, IV:8.4.483-484). The first century geographer Strabo called the valley "a land of fires" because there were frequent boiling outbursts of fire in the region, and the entire area smelled of sulfur and brimstone (*The Geography of Strabo,* XVI:2.42-44).

Even in more recent times, others have noted similar things about the valley. When the explorer Volney visited the region in 1787, he reported that "this valley [is] the seat of subterranean fire, which is not yet extinguished. Clouds of smoke are often observed to issue from the lake" (*Travels,* I:281-282). In 1848, a scientific investigation of the region by a man named Lynch reported that the valley held a strong smell of sulfuret hydrogen (*Journal of Royal Geographical Society,* XVIII: 127). He also wrote that he witnessed a purple vapor rising above the Dead Sea, "contrasting strangely with the extraordinary color of the sea beneath and, where they blended in the distance, giving it the appearance of smoke from burning sulfur. It seemed a vast cauldron of metal, fused but motionless. In the afternoon of the same day, it looked like molten lead" (Ibid, 276, 324).

Some modern scholars and commentators have noted this as well. For example, John Gill, in his *Exposition of the Entire Bible,* in the section on Revelation 20:14-15, points out that the Dead Sea was also called the sulpherous lake, the lake of asphaltites, and the bituminous lake. The Jewish people understood that the lake sat in the valley which used to be home to the cities of Sodom and Gomorrah, and so whatever idolatrous or sinful thing the Jewish people wanted to get rid of, they would cast it into the Salt Sea. Gill quotes the Babylonian Talmud as saying that "any vessels that had on them the image of the sun, or of the moon, or of a dragon, 'let them cast them into the salt sea'" (Avoda Zara, 42.2; 49.1; 53.1; 71.2; Nazir 24.2; 26.1-2; Bava Metzia 52.2; Temura 22.2; Meila 9.2; 10:1). This image of being cast into the salt sea is very similar to what John writes in Revelation 21:8.

Even the PBS documentary called "A Naked Planet Special" said this about the Dead Sea: "Geologists have discovered large pockets of gas trapped under the sediment … in the southern Dead Sea. [When these bubbles escape or are] released into the atmosphere by an earthquake, it would only take a spark to ignite a giant inferno; a vast ball of flame raining down." One wonders if such a scenario ever occurred as people traveled along the edges of the Dead Sea, thereby causing it to also be named the Fire Sea. Indeed, Stephen Spencer suggests that the lake itself occasionally caught on fire.[34]

It is also critical to remember that the ancient site of Sodom and Gomorrah are beneath the southern edge of the Dead Sea, where, on the western shore, there sits Mount Sodom and a rock formation called "Lot's wife." These images and memories of the destruction that came upon the cities of this valley help explain the list of sins that John mentions in Revelation 21:8.

So there is much historical evidence to see that in the first century, when people heard about the Lake of Fire, they understood this to be a symbol for the region that we now call the Dead Sea.

But how are people cast into the Lake of Fire? After the destruction of Jerusalem in 70 AD, the bodies of over one million Jews were thrown into the Valley of Hinnom outside of Jerusalem, where they were then burned. When the rains come, much that is in the valley is washed down into the Dead Sea through the Wadi an-Nar (Streambed of Fire).[35] So it is a historical fact that as a result of the destruction of Jerusalem, over a million people ended up being cast into the Lake of Fire, also known as the Dead Sea. Furthermore, many Jews of that time believed that if a body was burned to ashes and did not receive a burial, then that person would not be raised from the dead in the future resur-

[34] Spencer, *The Genesis Pursuit*, 197.

[35] Cf. Ibid.

rection.[36] Therefore, if a person was cast into the Lake of Fire via the Streambed of Fire because their ashes were carried from *Gehenna* down to the Dead Sea, that person would remain in the Lake of Fire forever, never being able to experience the resurrection. (We know from Scripture, however, that everyone will be resurrected. See John 5:29; Acts 24:15; cf. Dan 12:2.)

With all of this in mind, how then are we to understand the references to the Lake of Fire in Revelation 20:10, 14, and 21:8? Bradley Jersak sees these statements as an "apocalyptic threat of being leveled by the fire of God's wrath, historically fulfilled through obliteration by foreign armies. In Revelation, the threat is specific to Jerusalem."[37] Indeed, passages like Isaiah 1:7-10 equate the city of Jerusalem with the cities of Sodom and Gomorrah, indicating that they will share similar fates. Other cities that behaved in similar ways also experienced similar ends (cf. Isa 34:8-10; Jer 49:17-18; Dan 7:9-11).

But the destruction of Jerusalem was not the end of Jerusalem. Jerusalem was "resurrected" from the ashes, so that one can go and visit it today. Furthermore, Jerusalem will play a significant and prominent role in the future, including in eternity when a New Jerusalem comes down out of heaven from God (Rev 21:2). In this way, the restoration of Jerusalem appears to be a fore-

[36] Ibid.

[37] Jersak, *Her Gates Will Never Be Shut*, 87.

shadowing, or firstfruits, of the restoration of other cities that also experienced fiery judgment and destruction. For example, the description in Ezekiel 16:53-55 and 47:1-12 seems to indicate that the Dead Sea valley, along with the cities that are in them (which would include Sodom and Gomorrah), will also experience a restoration to fruitfulness, life, and fertility when Jesus returns and brings healing to this world.

It seems, therefore, that there is something unique in eternity about being cast into the Lake of Fire. Though the cities of Sodom and Gomorrah were burned with fire and brimstone, they will be restored. Though Jerusalem was brought to ruin through fire and war, it too will be restored. But the things that are cast into the Lake of Fire do not seem to experience restoration. Being cast into the Lake of Fire is not about the wrath of God, invading armies, or even destruction by fire in this life or the next. Being cast into the Lake of Fire is not about being tortured in any way. Instead, those that are cast into the Lake of Fire are never heard from again. They have no more influence, power, or sway on this earth. This seems to be the symbolic significance of the Lake of Fire.

And this indeed fits with what we read about the Lake of Fire in the book of Revelation. When Jesus comes again, He will banish the spirit of accusation and scapegoating (the devil), the idolatry of science and money (the beast), human religion (the false prophet), all useless and destructive ways of living (death), and the reign of hell on earth (*hadēs*). These are the five primary enemies of humanity, and Jesus sends them all away into the Lake of Fire, never to be heard from again. (cf. Rev 21:4 where they are not even named, but are simply called "the former things." After this, they are never heard from again. "Death" is mentioned in 21:8 for the last time, but only as the second death.) There is no possible restoration or redemption for accusation, idolatry, manmade religion, destruction, or the reign of hell. These are sent away into the sea of forgetfulness and have no more place on earth.

The fact that intangible concepts or powers such as death and *hadēs* are cast into the Lake of Fire strongly indicates that the Lake of Fire itself is also intangible. That is, one cannot put an immaterial idea, concept, power, or force into something material. When we say that we have "love in our heart" we do not literally mean that the immaterial feeling of "love" is literally being stored in the blood-pumping organ of our body. Instead, since "love" is intangible and immaterial, this means that the word "heart" is also understood as symbolic, intangible, and immaterial. So also with throwing the immaterial death and *hadēs* into the Lake of Fire. "Death and hell, or death and the grave, are not something tangible you can just pick up and throw into a lake."[38]

[38] Spencer, *The Genesis Pursuit*, 188.

Some might object that since I have just shown that the Lake of Fire was originally a literal place, namely, the Dead Sea, then the items thrown into it must also be literal, material objects. But it works the other way. Much like the symbol of *gehenna,* the literal place, cultural history, and theological significance of the Dead Sea provides insight into what it means to be cast into the Lake of Fire. Again, to use the analogy of love, if I say that my love for my wife extends higher than the moon, I am using a literal place (the moon) as a symbol to describe the extent of an immaterial concept (my love). The same is true with casting death and *hadēs* into the Lake of Fire.

This imagery of things that are contrary to God being cast into the Lake of Fire would have been immediately identifiable to John's reading audience. In the first century Jewish culture, people often made the journey to the Dead Sea to cast things into it which they considered to be sinful or idolatrous. In his *Commentary on the New Testament from the Talmud and Hebraica,* John Lightfoot records that "The Talmudists devote 'to the sea of Sodom' anything that is destined to rejection and cursing, and that by no means is to be used."[39] Lightfoot goes on to cite several quotes from the Jewish Talmud which describe this practice being carried out.

[39] John Lightfoot, *A Commentary on the New Testament from the Talmud and Hebraica*, 4 vols. (Ada, MI: Baker, 1859, 2003), 15.

But John not only writes about things that are contrary to God being cast into the Lake of Fire, he also says that such things will be "tormented day and night forever and ever." The word for "torment" (Gk., *basanizō*) literally means "to rub on a touchstone." A touchstone (Gk., *basanos*) was a stone that was used to test the quality of metals, especially gold and silver coins. It was usually a fine-grained dark schist or jasper stone that was used to determine the purity of gold and silver coins by the streak left on the stone when rubbed with the metal. A *basanos* helped discover whether or not a coin was counterfeit.

When used in reference to people, the verb form of the word can refer to physical suffering (Matt 8:6; Rev 9:5), hard toil (Mark 6:48), and the pain of childbirth (Rev 12:2). When used of inanimate objects, it has the idea of being buffeted and battered, like a ship in a storm (Matt 14:24). In the Gospels, the demons often ask Jesus if He has come to torment them before the set time (Matt 8:29; Mark 5:7; Luke 8:28).

But in Revelation, the word only applies to the devil, the beast, and the false prophet (Rev 20:10), which are not "people," but institutions or powers that had been twisted and perverted away from God's will and design. These "things" will be "tormented" in that, like a counterfeit coin, they will be discarded and thrown out, having no more value, power, or influence in this world. They will be shown to be false and fake forgeries, twisted perversions of what God wanted and desired. Death, after all, does have a role in God's good creation, as does religion (Jas 1:27), and the proper use of judging between right and wrong (accusation is a perversion of judgment). But the perversions of these are done away with in eternity. This is a judgment of ungodly structures and institutions; not primarily a judgment upon people.[40]

But doesn't the text say that people are cast into the Lake of Fire? Revelation 20:13-15 says that the sea, and death, and *hadēs* gave up the dead that were in them, who are judged at the Great White Throne Judgment, before being cast into the Lake of Fire. And then Revelation 21:8 seems to list the sorts of people who are cast into the Lake of Fire, such as the cowardly, unbelieving, murderers, sexually immoral, and liars. If this judgment is not specifically upon people, then what is happening to the people who are described in these ways?

Some scholars try to argue that John is referring only to a past historical event here, in which cities and nations were destroyed by fire. For example, since Sodom and Gomorrah were characterized by the sorts of behaviors described in Revelation 21:8, and since these cities were destroyed by fire, and since the "ruins" of these cities likely lie at the bottom of the Dead Sea (the Lake of Fire), some scholars say that this is what John is referring to in this text. But this cannot be the case, for when

[40] Butler, *The Skeletons in God's Closet*, 277.

people died in those historical events, this was their first death. Revelation 20:13-15 says that people are resurrected and brought back to life to face judgment, and are then sent to the Lake of Fire.

But note that the text does not say that the humans who end up in the Lake of Fire will be tormented *by* the Lake of Fire (Rev 20:15). Unlike the devil, the beast, and the false prophet, humans are not tormented *in* the Lake of Fire. They are actually sent there to *escape* torment. A careful reading of Revelation shows how this works.

Earlier in Revelation, John wrote that the people who worship the beast and his image will "be tormented with fire and brimstone … and the smoke of their torment ascends forever and ever" (Rev 14:10-11). The word used for "torment" in Revelation 14:10-11 is the same word used in Revelation 20:10. But the torment that these people experience in Revelation 14:10-11 does not come from the Lake of Fire, because they are not there yet. They do not get sent to the Lake of Fire until after the Great White Throne judgment. The torment these people experience comes from "fire and brimstone," which is what brought the initial destruction of Sodom and Gomorrah. The fact that the smoke ascends forever would remind the readers that the smoke of Sodom and Gomorrah was still ascending in the region of the Dead Sea to that very day.

So is John saying that humans will get tormented after all, but in a different way? No, for John subverts the violent imagery of Revelation 14:10-11 in a subtle way. When people think and teach about the torment that people receive in the fires of hell for all eternity, they usually also teach that such people are completely separated from the presence of God. But Revelation 14:10 says that the torment these people receive is "in the presence of the holy angels and in the presence of the Lamb." Isn't this strange? They are only tormented when they are in the presence of Jesus (the Lamb) and the holy angels (which might represent the spirits of the church; cf. Rev 1:20). But does this mean that our entertainment in heaven will consist of watching people burn and suffer? It cannot be, for this would be less than restful (Rev 14:13).

Quite to the contrary, it appears that John is saying that as long as these people worship the beast and his image (whatever they may represent), it is torment for them to be in the presence of Jesus and His righteous church. How is it torment? Earlier, in Revelation 11:10, John wrote that these same people were tormented by the preaching and presence of the two witnesses. This does not mean that the two witnesses were burning people alive with their sermons. It refers instead to the inner conviction one feels when they are presented with something that is contrary to their spirit or nature. Righteous people have this same experience when they are in the presence of wickedness (2 Pet 2:8). Therefore, the "torment" (Gk., *basanizō*) of humans in Revelation is not physical torture in fire, but refers to the spiritual vexation that unrighteous people experience when they are presented with the truth or when their behavior is challenged (Rev 11:10).

In Revelation 11:10, the people who experienced this torment, tried to escape it by killing the two witnesses, but John writes in Revelation 14:10 that they will continue to experience the torment of the truth as long as they are in the presence of Jesus and the holy angels. Therefore, since Jesus knows that the life of those who worship Him is not compatible with the life of those who worship the beast, and that each group is tormented by the other, Jesus separates them so that *neither group is tormented.* In Revelation 20:14-15, out of love for the people who do not want to hear the truth, Jesus sends them to be with the beast, the false prophet, death, and *hadēs* in the Lake of Fire. They are not sent to be tormented, but to escape the convicting and "tormenting" presence of Jesus and the church.

So what will their existence be like? What will they do? How will they live? The truth is that we do not know. But it won't be torment or torture. It won't be burning and screaming in agony for all eternity. Scripture does not say what their existence will be like, or if it can even be called "existence."

It seems that the life in the Lake of Fire (which is not a literal place of burning and flame) is a place where people are allowed to live as they want. It is a place where they will be given true human freedom apart from God, which is what many people think they want, but which is actually not freedom; it is slavery. It will likely be similar to life on this present earth, but without physical death. While this initially sounds like heaven, such an existence will end up being hell. People who try to live life apart of from God, live life in a way that God never intended it to be lived. This way of living does not build loving relationships, but ruins and destroys them. It is a selfish, hateful, broken way of living.

A truly hellish existence is having no way out of this sort of "living." It cannot even be called "living," but is rather an ongoing experience of dying. True hell is an eternal existence in a sin-filled world without the blessed escape through death. Currently, we have a "way out" through death and resurrection. But if there is no death, there can be no resurrection, and so those who experience the eternal second death (living in the realm of death, but never dying) are living in a hell of their own making. Their eternal existence will be a life dominated by the sins mentioned in Revelation 21:8. In eternity, where there is no death to deliver a person from the devastation they have brought into their lives, this ongoing death will simply continue forever and ever.

C. S. Lewis' theological fantasy book, *The Great Divorce,* depicts what this sort of everlasting death might look like. In this life, as we destroy our families, friendships, and health, we draw into ourselves and become more and more separated from others over time. Death stops this process of separation so that we can finally see ourselves and others as we really are. Death and resurrection provide reconciliation, so that we can forgive and be forgiven, and begin to live in eternity with the love and grace that God desires. But in an eternal existence without God, where physical death is not an option, people will continue to separate themselves until eventually, they cut off all contact from everyone, and live solitary lives of self-centeredness and complete separation. For people who were created for community and relationships, this truly is a living hell. But it is a hell constructed by their own choices.

So what is the Lake of Fire? It is literally the Dead Sea, into which all things are cast that are contrary to the will and ways of God. As a symbol, therefore, it refers to an existence without God. People who are sent to "the Lake of Fire" for eternity will not be tortured in flames for all eternity, but will be given the freedom they think they want, so they can live life as they please, apart from the guidelines and instructions of God. This way of living is not really "living," however, and such people will ultimately find themselves separated, not only from God, but also from all other people. The Bible calls this the second death (Rev 21:8).

The Lake of Fire is not traditional hell where people suffer and burn for eternity. They are not in torment there, but are sent there to escape their torment. It is there that they can live according to their sinful desires, which only lead them into an eternal existence and experience of ongoing death.

But what about the outer darkness, where people wail with weeping and gnashing of teeth? This sounds like torment, doesn't it? Let us consider the term in Scripture to see.

OUTER DARKNESS

There are three passages in Scripture which refer to "the outer darkness" (Gk., *to skotos to exōteron*) and all three are recorded as teachings of Jesus in the Gospel of Matthew (Matt 8:12; 22:13; 25:30). In all three instances, the phrase is further described as being a place of "weeping and gnashing of teeth." Due to these descriptive terms, many have equated *the outer darkness* with hell. If this were true, however, then it would be impossible for hell to be *both* a place of burning flame *and* darkness, for the two are mutually exclusive. One or both of the descriptions must either be figurative or not referring to hell at all. We have already seen that the descriptions of fire in the Bible are not describing hell, so what about the description of outer darkness? If hell is not a place of burning, is it a place of darkness and gloom?

The answer is "No." A careful consideration of each passage that refers to *the outer darkness* reveals that Jesus was not teaching about hell in these texts, but rather about the initial experience of some Christians at the beginning of the physical reign of Jesus Christ on earth in the future. In other words, when Jesus physically returns in the future to finally and completely restore justice and peace upon this world, some Christians will not experience His coming with joy, gladness, and celebration, but with regret, grief, and sadness. They will not experience the initial party of the Wedding Feast of the Lamb, but will instead be left outside in the darkness, because they were not ready for the arrival of their King. When Jesus returns, He will throw a party full of lights, music, feasting, and dancing. But not all Christians will get to experience this party. Some will be left outside the celebratory circle of lights in the darkness. They will be on the outside looking in. They will still have eternal life, and will still enter into the new heavens and the new earth, but they will miss out on the initial inauguration party, and will instead be in the darkness outside the party (the outer darkness).

To see this, let us briefly consider the three texts that refer to *the outer darkness.* The first reference to *the outer darkness* is in Matthew 8:12, where Jesus teaches that while many from all corners of the earth will sit down with Abraham in the kingdom of heaven, "the sons of the kingdom will be cast into outer darkness" where there will be "weeping and gnashing of teeth." Jesus said these things after seeing the great faith of the Gentile centurion, stating that He had not even found such great faith in all of Israel (Matt 8:5-10). So Jesus is contrasting the faith of the centurion with the faith of many of the people of Israel.

The image of people sitting down with Abraham in Matthew 8:11 refers to the kingdom of heaven arriving in all its fullness and glory. While the kingdom of heaven was inaugurated during the first coming of Jesus, it will not fully arrive or be experienced by people on this earth until His second coming. Jesus is saying that when this future event happens, and the citizens of the kingdom are invited to sit down with Abraham at the celebration feast, it will be people like the Gentile centurion who had great faith that will participate in the celebration. There will be other "sons of the kingdom" however, such as many among the Israelite people, who will not participate in the feast. They will instead be in the outer darkness, which simply means that they will be excluded from the light and joy of the inauguration party.[41]

Note that if Jesus was referring to unregenerate people who were going to spend eternity in hell, He would

---

[41] Zane Hodges and Robert Wilkin, *What is the Outer Darkness?* (Denton, TX: GES, 2016), 43f.

not have referred to them as "sons of the kingdom." The "sons of the kingdom" are those who are members and citizens of the kingdom. But the fact that the "sons of the kingdom" are in the outer darkness does not mean that they lose eternal life and spend eternity in hell, but that they miss out on the initial celebration at the full arrival of God's rule and reign on earth. Some "sons of the kingdom" fail to participate in this party because they did not have the right beliefs and behaviors to warrant a seat at the table. They will instead stand outside the glow of the joyful celebration, watching from the darkness with profound regret and shame for how they lived their life on earth. Hell is not in view in Matthew 8:12, but rather describes the experience of some Christians who miss out on the initial inauguration party when Jesus returns to rule and reign on earth.

The second reference to *the outer darkness* is found in Matthew 22:13. This text makes it clear that the reference to *outer darkness* has exclusion from the Wedding Feast in view rather than hell, for Jesus specifically tells a parable about who gets to participate in this future celebration. In the Parable of the Wedding Feast (Matt 22:1-14), many people are initially invited to the celebration, but are too busy to attend. So the king sends out his servants into the highways to invite anyone and everyone they find. As a result, many people attend the feast, both good and bad. Yet one man shows up at the feast who is not wearing a wedding garment, and so the king has him thrown out of the party into *the outer darkness,* where there is weeping and gnashing of teeth.

Some have wondered how the man should have known what to wear to the wedding celebration, or if he was poor, how he could have afforded the proper attire. But many scholars point out that it was a common practice in the Middle-Eastern and Mediterranean cultures for the host to provide proper garments for the guests (cf. Judg 14:12).[42] So regardless of this man's background or social position, he would have been provided with a garment to wear into the celebration. But for some reason, the man did not put on the clothing he had been given. He came wearing his own clothes. He thought the clothes he had on were just fine, and that he didn't need the clothes provided to him by the king. Yet he was wrong, and so he is removed from the celebration, and sent outside, away from the lights and feasting of the party, where he experiences shame and regret.

The fact that this man is at the wedding feast proves that he is a genuine believer, for only believers are welcomed into the feast. If he was an unbeliever, then how did he get into the wedding celebration in the first place? He could not have even entered. Therefore, he is a believer, which granted him access to the feast. But he

---

[42] This cultural insight is found in nearly every commentary on Matthew. Several sources are cited by Gregory Sapaugh, "A Call to the Wedding Celebration: An Exposition of Matthew 22:1-14" *JOTGES 5:1* (Spring:1992). https://faithalone.org/journal/1992i/Sapaugh.html

didn't come wearing the proper clothing, and so he is removed from the feast. His removal from the feast is not a removal from heaven and eternal life so that he ends up in hell, but is simply a disciplinary process in which the man is not allowed to participate in the inauguration celebration.

So what is symbolized by the man's lack of proper clothing? As Gregory Sapaugh writes, "The wedding garment is a figure for righteous living. Therefore, this man did not faithfully perform the good works that are necessary to be present at the wedding banquet. … Eternal salvation is not an issue in this passage."[43] The man represents a person who believes in Jesus for eternal life, but who fails to put on the righteous garments that God provides, and instead lives selfishly and sinfully throughout their life. Such a person still has eternal life, but they might miss out on the initial inauguration banquet when Jesus returns and sets up His earthly kingdom. Joshua Ryan Butler argues similarly:

> When the King shows up, the prodigals and prostitutes are running into the kingdom while the self-righteous and self-made are weeping outside the party. The sick, poor, blind, and lame are partying it up at God's Wedding Feast while those who thought their own clothes were good enough are cast out into the darkness.[44]

---

[43] Ibid.

[44] Butler, *The Skeletons in God's Closet*, 113.

Here again, the outer darkness is not hell, but instead describes the initial experience of some unfaithful Christians at the beginning of the future rule and reign of Jesus Christ at His second coming. The second coming of Jesus Christ will begin with a great time of celebration. But those who did not look for the return of Jesus, or prepare for it with their lives, will miss out on the joy and excitement of this event. Like Scrooge in "The Christmas Carol" who stands in the cold and darkness out in the street while he peers through the window at a happy and warm Christmas celebration inside, some Christians will only be able to watch the party from the darkness outside. Scrooge missed out on the celebration because of his behavior, and so will some Christians. Such a person is represented in this parable by the man who attends the feast without the proper garments.

> Matthew 22 doesn't say there were a bunch of torturers out there in the darkness who suddenly take this poor man who is tied up hand and foot and start torturing him. The imagery is one of exclusion and limitation on activity. That's what being tied hand and foot means. [He] can't really do anything. Exclusion from the lighted banqueting hall is a synonym for co-reigning with Jesus Christ.[45]

---

[45] Hodges and Wilkin, *What is the Outer Darkness?*, 28.

The third and final reference to *the outer darkness* is found in Matthew 25:30, near the end of the Parable of the Talents (Matt 25:14-30). Most Bible teachers believe that the Parable of the Talents refers to God's gifts to believers, and our responsibility to use those gifts wisely in this life. If this view is correct, then the experience of the unprofitable servant at the end of the story can be understood in a similar way as seen in both Matthew 8:12 and 22:13. As in both of those previous situations, the unprofitable servant of Matthew 25:30 would represent a believer who failed to live as God wanted and desired during this life, and so is cast into the outer darkness during the initial stage of the earthly reign of Jesus. Rather than experience the joy of this celebration, they only experience regret for how they lived their life and shame for missing out on the greatest celebration in all of celestial history.[46]

However, I think there is a better way of understanding the Parable of the Talents. Though many assume that this parable describes the return of Jesus and how He judges Christians at His return, this is not what Jesus says. While most Bible translations do include the words "the kingdom of heaven" in Matthew 25:14, these words have been added by the translators and do not exist in the Greek. Jesus *is* describing the kingdom of heaven in the preceding parable, the Parable of the

---

[46] Note that several of the following paragraphs are copied from the discussion of Matthew 25:41 in the Appendix on Fire Texts at the end of this book. I hope you don't mind!

Wise and Foolish Virgins (Matt 25:1-13), as well as in the following parable, the Parable of the Sheep and the Goats (Matt 25:31-46), but He is not describing the final arrival of the kingdom of heaven in the Parable of the Talents. Instead, this middle parable is a contrast with the other two, in which Jesus shows His followers what life will be like for them if they try to live in the kingdom of this world.

Numerous lines of evidence support this view. Chief among them is the fact that the actions of this man who travels to a far country would have been understood as quite evil in the first century Mediterranean world. They not only closely follow the actions and behaviors of King Herod and how he went to Rome to become the king of Israel, but the values of this man also reveal the opposite of what Jesus taught and encouraged.

The first century Mediterranean world was guided by the cultural values of honor and shame. Modern western culture is guided by materialism. Today, we value any activity which gets more money and gains more possessions. Yet in an honor-shame culture, such activities were great sins. They believed that money and possessions were zero-sum commodities, which meant that the only way for one person to gain more money and possessions was by taking it away from someone else.[47] This was very shameful behavior. "Anyone who

[47] Bruce J. Malina and Richard L. Rohrbaugh, *Social-Science Commentary on the Synoptic Gospels*, 2nd ed. (Minneapolis: Fortress, 2003), 124, 385-386, 400.

suddenly acquired something 'more' was automatically judged to be a thief."[48]

Therefore, in light of these cultural values about money, the first two servants, like their master, were exploiters. "They both use the same exploitive economy to increase the plunder that constitutes the master's wealth."[49] This means that "from the peasant point of view … it was the third slave who acted honorably, especially since he refused to participate in the rapacious schemes of the greedy, rich man."[50]

So Jesus is saying that if one of his disciples does not look with anticipation for the coming of the kingdom of heaven, their only other option is to participate with the kingdom of this world, by imitating its greedy ways. If a person does not follow the way of Jesus, they will either behave very shamefully in stealing from their brethren, or will receive harsh judgment and punishment from the rulers of this world for not participating in their greedy game. The rulers of this world expect and demand their subjects to follow their twisted, thieving ways to enrich themselves at the expense of others. Those who refuse to follow these marching orders will

---

[48] John J. Pilch, *The Cultural World of Jesus, Cycle A* (Collegeville, MN: Liturgical, 1995), 164.

[49] William R Herzog II, *Parables as Subversive Speech: Jesus as Pedagogue of the Oppressed* (Louisville, KY: Westminster John Knox, 1994), 161.

[50] Malina and Rohrbaugh, *Social-Science Commentary on the Synoptic Gospels*, 125.

be punished by the rulers, and will be banished to "the dark world of poverty, misery, and certain death."[51] But when followers of Jesus experience such treatment at the hands of the rulers of this world, they should not despair, for the punishment of worldly rulers is not the end of the matter.

So in this interpretation, the Parable of the Talents is not about the second return of Jesus, but about life in this world now and the two ways that people can live. If we help the rulers steal from others, we ourselves will gain recognition and reward from those greedy rulers. But if we refuse to play their evil game, we will gain only condemnation from them, and they will even steal from us what we have and give it to others who do not need it. But Jesus surrounds this parable with two others about what it looks like to live life in light of the kingdom of heaven.

Zacchaeus is the perfect example of the two kingdoms at work. Indeed, the Parable of the Talents in Luke 19:11-27 immediately follows the story of Zacchaeus. Prior to meeting Jesus, Zacchaeus operated according to the principles of the kingdom of this world and became very rich as a result. Yet his actions were extremely shameful as he stole from the poor to gain wealth for himself. So when Zacchaeus started to follow Jesus, he adopted a new set of values and behaviors, which caused him to give away all of his accumulated

[51] Herzog II, *Parables as Subversive Speech*, 166.

wealth. His new behavior, however, likely cost him many rich friends, powerful politicians, and invitations to fancy parties. He also likely lost his job, and along with it, his house, servants, possessions, and status in Roman society. Those who continued to live within that system likely looked upon Zacchaeus' new behavior with shock and disdain, thinking that he would eventually regret his decisions.

This is also what the lord of the servants in Matthew 25:14-30 thinks of his unprofitable servant. The rich landowner commands that the man be cast out into outer darkness where there is weeping and gnashing of teeth (Matt 25:30). This is not a reference to hell, and in this case, is also not a reference to Christians missing out on the Wedding Feast of the Lamb. Here, the imagery represents the perspective of the rich lord. Since the third servant didn't use his talent to steal from others, nor did he even gain usury with the bankers (Matt 25:27), this servant can no longer join the human party where there is light, laughter, feasting, and dancing. Instead, he is sent out of the palace into the dark alleyways where there is only poverty and problems. In Matthew 25:30, the master is essentially saying, "Since this servant didn't play by my rules, he doesn't get to enjoy the privileges of my household. Kick him out into the street where he will experience profound regret that he didn't do what I wanted. He passed up the deal of a lifetime, and will live to regret it."

But this is not the end of the story. Jesus now goes on in the final parable of Matthew 25 to show His disciples that even though they might be rejected by the kingdoms of men and miss out on the parties of men, they will not be rejected or despised by the kingdom of God. Since the values and behaviors of the two kingdoms are diametrically opposed to one another, the consequences for actions are different as well. While a lack of greed brought punishment from the kingdoms of the world, this same behavior brings praise and honor in the kingdom of heaven. With the Parable of the Sheep and the Goats (Matt 25:31-46), Jesus shows the distinctive characteristics that separate the two kingdoms, and calls His disciples to choose which kingdom they will serve. The parables represent the choice Jesus laid out earlier in His career, when He stated that no man can serve both God and money (Matt 6:24).

So once again, *the outer darkness* does not refer to hell, nor does the accompanying description of *weeping and gnashing of teeth.* Instead, both terms are symbolic ways of referring to "missing out on the party" and "expressing profound shame and regret" as a result. It is an image of loss.[52] The phrase "weeping and gnashing of teeth is an oriental term for extreme sorrow."[53] The imagery can be used of believers missing out on the inauguration ceremony of the kingdom of heaven when Je-

[52] Butler, *The Skeletons in God's Closet*, 325.

[53] Hodges and Wilkin, *What is the Outer Darkness?*, 50, 82, 89f.

sus returns to rule and reign on earth, but it can also be used of the experience of believers who get neglected and forsaken on this earth by worldly rulers for not living according to the rules of the kingdom of this world. But those who miss out on the party here can expect to enjoy a better party when Jesus returns.

The truth that Jesus reveals is that believers will experience *outer darkness* in one form or another. If we seek the praise of kings and the riches of men now, we will lose out on such things when Jesus returns. If, however, we seek first the kingdom of God and His righteousness (Matt 6:33), then while we might be reviled and hated by men now, we will receive a warm and rich welcome by Jesus when He returns to rule and reign.

So what is *the outer darkness,* and why is it described as a place of weeping and gnashing of teeth? The outer darkness is a term which describes the place of darkness outside the lights of a party or celebration. It can describe our experience here on earth when we do not live according to the ways and rules of this world, and it can also describe the experience of some Christians at the beginning of the next life if they do not live according to the rules and ways of Jesus. If Christians do not live in light of the kingdom of heaven, and so experience *the outer darkness* at His return instead of the inner light of the party, this does not mean they will spend eternity in hell. They still have eternal life, and they will still participate in the eternal rule and reign of Jesus Christ on earth and throughout the universe, but they will miss out on the initial inauguration celebration when Jesus sets up His throne on earth.

The people who miss out on this party experience profound shame and regret. They miss out on the party of the ages! So they weep and gnash their teeth in shame and disappointment at how they lived their life here on earth before Jesus returned. The phrase "weeping and gnashing of teeth" is not a description of suffering torment in hell, but is a Middle-Eastern idiom describing the expression of sorrow and lament for missing out on a great blessing or opportunity. The people who weep and gnash their teeth at the return of Jesus do so because they are in the darkness outside the lights of the party, looking in at the great joy and celebration taking place inside, knowing that if they had just lived with greater obedience and expectation, they could have been participating in the party as well.

Such sadness will not last forever, of course. For after the Wedding Feast of the Lamb (Rev 19:6-9), every tear will be wiped away (Rev 21:4) so that all children of God will be welcome to participate in the never-ending joy and peace of the new heavens and new earth, where there will be no more death, sorrow, mourning, or pain.

So like every other term we have considered, *the outer darkness* also does not refer to hell.[54] There are no

---

[54] Cf. Michael G. Huber, "The 'Outer Darkness' in Matthew and Its Relationship to Grace" *JOTGES* 5:2 (Autumn 1992).

passages in Scripture which describe hell as a place of darkness where people are tormented for eternity as they wail and gnash their teeth. Jesus' teachings on *the outer darkness* are a warning for believers to watch how we live our lives now, looking for the soon and blessed return of our Lord and Savior Jesus Christ.

This only leaves one more term to consider, which is also quite rare in the New Testament. It is the word *tartarus*.

TARTARUS

The final word from Scripture which might possibly refer to hell is the word *tartarus*. The word is only used in 2 Peter 2:4 (in the verb form, *tartaroō*), where Peter describes God's action of casting the angels who sinned down into hell, delivering them in chains of darkness while they awaited judgment. To understand Peter's words, it is important to identify the symbolism of Tartarus, and also the event to which Peter refers. Let us first consider the symbolism of Tartarus.

Since the Bible nowhere else speaks of Tartarus, we must assume that Peter had the Greek and Roman mythology of Tartarus in mind when he wrote of it. In Greek mythology, the word *tartarus* spoke of two things. It was first of all the name of one of the original primordial deities. However, the word *tartarus* also speaks of a place. In this way, the word *tartarus* is like *hadēs,* which also refers to a place and a god in Greek mythology.[55]

As a place, *tartarus* was thought to be a dungeon of suffering and torment for the Titans. The Titans were the second generation of primordial deities, and ruled during the legendary Golden Age of humanity, but were eventually defeated by the third generation of gods, the Olympians, which are the Greek and Roman gods that most people are familiar with (Zeus, Hades, Poseidon, etc.).[56] When the Olympian deities defeated the Titans, the Titans were sent to Tartarus to suffer. Humans typically went to Hades rather than Tartarus, though later mythology describes how some of the "worst" humans were sent to Tartarus, such as King Sisyphus for violating the rules of hospitality, and King Tantalus for killing and eating his own son.

So by referencing Tartarus, is Peter endorsing the Greek and Roman mythology about this place?[57] While Peter is certainly alluding to this myth, we cannot accept that he is endorsing the idea of multiple generations of deities waging war with each other in primordial history. Peter is referring to the myth to make a point, without endorsing the myth itself. "Concepts from the cultural background may be taken up without ac-

---

[55] Cf. Butler, *The Skeletons in God's Closet*, 326.

[56] Cf. Richard J. Bauckham, *Jude, 2 Peter, Word Biblical Commentary* (Waco: Word, 1983), 249.

[57] Bernstein, *The Formation of Hell*, 251.

ceptance of their underlying ideology."[58] Even today, Christians might talk about Achilles' heel or Cupid's arrows, reference the days of the week or the months of the year, and even celebrate Christmas, Easter, and Halloween, all without any sort of endorsement of the pagan mythology that lies at the roots of all these terms and holidays.[59] Peter is likely doing exactly the same thing with Tartarus.

However, having said that, the Greek and Roman myths do bear some resemblance to various events recorded in Scripture. So maybe in referring to *tartarus* in which angels were bound with chains as they await judgment, Peter is pointing his readers to one of these biblical events. There are two possible candidates.

Some believe that Peter is referring to the angelic rebellion which is purportedly described in Isaiah 14:12-21 and Ezekiel 28:1-19 (cf. Luke 10:18; Heb 12:22; Rev 9:1; 12:3-9). As to the timing of this event, some believe it occurred before Genesis 1:1, others believe it occurred in a "gap" of time that might exist between Genesis 1:1 and Genesis 1:2, while a third group thinks it occurred sometime after the final day of creation in Genesis 2:3, but before the serpent comes to tempt Eve in Genesis 3:1. So in this view, regardless of *when* the angels rebelled against God, He bound them with

---

[58] Johnston, *Shades of Sheol*, 25.

[59] Or maybe as a redemption of them. See my book, *Christmas Redemption* (Dallas, OR: Redeeming Press, 2011).

chains of darkness and sent them to a place called Tartarus to await judgment.

A second view is that Peter is referring to the flood which came upon the earth as a result of the sons of God having children with the daughters of men (Gen 6:1-4). The offspring of this union is referred to as the Nephilim, which might have also been the "giants" among men (Gen 6:4; Num 13:33; Deut 3:11; Josh 11:21-22; 1 Sam 17). Support for this view is found in 1 Peter 3:19-20, where Peter indicates that Jesus preached to the spirits who were in prison, who sinned in the days of Noah. Jude 6 also speaks about angels who did not keep their proper abode being bound by God with chains of everlasting darkness until the day of judgment. As a result of what happened in Genesis 6:1-4, God may also have restricted or limited the actions and behavior of the angels so that they could not sin in such ways again.

Both views, however, suffer from one significant problem. If the angels who sinned (either during a rebellion or preceding the flood) were all bound with chains of darkness and sent away into Tartarus, how is it that Jesus encountered evil spirits during His earthly ministry? Furthermore, how is it that Satan still prowls about like a roaring lion, seeking whom He may devour (1 Pet 5:8)? Satan was, after all, one of the angels who rebelled. If all the demons and evil spirits are already bound, then why are we instructed to stand against principalities and powers, against the rulers of the darkness of this age, and against the spiritual hosts of wickedness in heavenly places (Eph 6:12)? If fallen angels are already bound, how is it that Satan can be bound again for a thousand years (Rev 20:2)?

It appears, therefore, that nearly all of the imagery in 2 Peter 2:4 is symbolic for something other than a literal chaining of angels in a place called Tartarus. Support for this idea is found in Wisdom of Solomon 17:17, which describes the ninth plague of darkness that came upon Egypt (Exod 10:21-29) as a "chain of darkness."[60] In fact, the entire chapter of Wisdom of Solomon 17 seems to be referenced by Peter. The chapter speaks of captives of darkness and prisoners of a long night who engage in secret sins and suffer from a self-kindled fire (17:2-6). The chapter says that the darkness came upon them from Hades (17:14), and so they were kept in a prison not made of iron (17:16). All of this imagery describes the ninth plague of darkness that came upon Egypt. Literal chains and prisons were not involved at all. The imagery instead refers to the oppressive darkness that struck the people of Egypt with fear and caused them to be immobilized, as if they were bound with chains.

This appears to be the meaning of 2 Peter 2:4. Since fallen angels have always been active after they rebelled against God, and have apparently not been literally bound with chains in some mythical Tartarus, Peter's

[60] Bauckham, *WBC: Jude, 2 Peter*, 249.

words must be understood symbolically as referring to the fear of God that fallen angels feel as they wait in trembling for the judgment of God to come upon them (Jas 2:19). The rebellious angels are immobilized in some sense by the fear (the chains of darkness) of the judgment that will come upon them from God.

Even if this view is not accepted, and someone wants to think that God truly did lock away fallen angels with chains of darkness in some mythological location called Tartarus, it is still important to note that Peter's description says nothing about humans being sent there. So even if Tartarus truly is a prison for fallen angels as they await judgment, Scripture does not teach in any way that humans are sent there.

Whether Tartarus is a literal spiritual prison for fallen angels or a symbolic way of referring to the fear of God that fallen angels feel and the judgment of God that is coming upon them, it is not describing a hellish place of suffering and torment for human beings. There is no passage in Scripture which says that humans will be sent to Tartarus.[61] Therefore, just like *sheol, abyss, fire, hadēs, gehenna,* and the *outer darkness,* the word *tartarus* does not teach about a place called "hell" where humans will be sent to suffer and burn for all eternity. Whatever Tartarus is, humans do not experience it at all.

---

[61] Cf. Butler, *The Skeletons in God's Closet*, 326.

CONCLUSION

Having looked at all the terms in Scripture which sometimes get translated as "hell" or thought of as referring to hell, we see that the traditional concept of hell is not taught in Scripture. There is no word or idea in the Bible which is properly translated as "hell." The traditional concept of "hell" is not biblical. And as long as we are on the subject, "hell" is also not in view in any reference to wrath, destruction, judgment, death, perishing, or punishment (2 Thess 2:12; Rom 2:5, 8-9; 5:9; Gal 1:8-9; Col 3:6; 1 Thess 1:10; 5:9; 2 Thess 1:8-10; 2:10).

This means, therefore, that "Most of the passages in the New Testament which have been thought by the Church to refer to people going to eternal punishment after they die don't in fact refer to any such thing."[62] Aside from the fact that God does not torture anyone, Scripture does not teach that the unredeemed dead will be sent to a place of eternal conscious torment.

As we learned in the previous chapter, the modern concept of hell as a place of torture and suffering of wicked people does not come from Scripture, but from pagan mythology that was incorporated into western Christian theology during the Dark Ages. Therefore, since the word "hell" causes most people to think of a place where people are burned and tortured for eternity, and since none of the words and phrases defined above

[62] Wright, *Following Jesus*, 92.

refer to this idea, it might be best to get rid of the word "hell" altogether.

However, maybe it is best to keep "hell" in our theology, not as a place where some people go after they die, but as a way of describing some of the experiences all people face while they live. Maybe hell does not come in the afterlife, but in the present life. Maybe hell is best discussed, not by asking "Where is hell?" or "When will people go there?" but rather "What is hell?" and "How is it experienced?" These are the questions about hell that are considered in the next two chapters.

CHAPTER 3

WHAT IS HELL?

We now find ourselves in a strange situation. The previous chapter revealed that none of the terms in Scripture which are typically understood as references to hell actually say anything about the state of the unregenerate dead. Furthermore, all the ideas and images we have about hell as a place of suffering in the afterlife come from pagan mythology rather than Scripture. So everything we think we know about hell as a place of suffering for the dead comes from non-biblical sources, while the Scriptures themselves say nothing about such a place. *So what then is hell?*

To answer this question, it must first be clarified. On the one hand (and at the risk of appearing to contradict everything I wrote in the previous chapter), I am fine with translating words such as *hadēs* and *gehenna* with the English word "hell" as long as we understand that these words do not refer to a place of suffering and torment in the afterlife, but to something else instead. So in this case, when we ask "What is hell?" we are asking

"What is the 'something else' to which *hadēs* and *gehenna* refer?"

But on the other hand, when most Christians ask "What is hell?" what they are actually asking is "What happens to unbelievers after they die?" We have already learned that the state of unbelievers after they die cannot be described with the word "hell." But certainly the afterlife state of the unregenerate dead must be described somewhere in Scripture, right? In other words, if the words *sheol, gehenna,* and *hadēs* do not refer to the place that unbelievers go after they die, then what words, terms, or ideas in Scripture *do describe* the state of unregenerate people after they die? What, if anything, do we know about the state of afterlife existence for the unbelieving dead? If the unregenerate dead are not tormented in the flames of hell for all eternity, then where do they go and what happens to them?

So these are the two separate and unique questions that can be drawn from the single question "What is hell?" On the one hand, we can seek clarification about what and where "hell" (as *hadēs* and *gehenna*) actually is and how it is experienced, and on the other hand, we can ask what Scripture teaches about the eternal state of the unbelieving dead. This chapter seeks to answer both questions. We begin with the one that is most clearly answered in Scripture: What is "hell" when it is used as a translation for *hadēs* and *gehenna*?

HELL IS A KINGDOM

Once we free our minds from thinking about hell as a place of torture and torment in the afterlife, and study Scripture with new eyes about the nature and identity of hell, we are immediately presented with a surprising truth. We discover that our belief in the existence of a divine torture chamber has blinded our eyes to the truth about hell. But once our eyes are open, we see that Scripture is quite clear on the nature and identification of hell. And what does Scripture say? It reveals that hell is a kingdom; it is a power that rules and guides the way some people experience life. Hell is a kingdom on this earth which has tentacles into nearly all aspects of every person, and is diametrically opposed to the kingdom of heaven that was introduced and inaugurated by Jesus. In other words, when Jesus and the apostles teach about fire, *gehenna,* and *hadēs,* they are not referring to a torturous, afterlife existence for unbelievers, but rather, to a way of living in this life that is governed by death and destruction, rather than love and liberty. Hell is a way of living life which is exactly opposite to the way of living that God wanted and intended for us. While many people live according to the kingdom of hell, "hell" is not exactly a way of life, but a way of death.

In his insightful article "Hell is a Kingdom: the Missing Motif Reconstructed," Brad Jersak shows that the imagery about fire and *gehenna* in James 3:6 serves as a guiding light for understanding all the other "hellish" passages in the New Testament.[1] James writes that the tongue sets our lives on fire, because it itself is set on fire by hell (Gk., *gehenna*). Outside of the Gospels, this is the only other time the word *gehenna* is used in the New Testament, and since the letter of James was likely written before any of the four Gospels, it is helpful to consider how James uses the word so that we can also understand the images of fire and *gehenna* elsewhere in Scripture.

Note first of all that the images of fire and *gehenna* are entirely symbolic. A tongue does not literally burn with flame, nor does a tongue ignite literal fires in our lives. Instead, James 3:6 is teaching that the words we say can destroy our lives, and that these destructive words have their source in *gehenna*. And though *gehenna* was a garbage dump outside of Jerusalem, it too is used symbolically in this context. It is not that our literal tongues are empowered by a garbage dump, but that just as the garbage dump was filled with nothing but death, decay, and destruction, so also, our words can bring death, decay, and destruction into our lives, rather than life, light, and love. So the images of fire and *gehenna* in James 3:6 do not refer to a literal fire or a place of torment for people after they die, but symbolically point to the destruction that comes upon our lives when we are not careful with the words we say.

[1] Sinner Irenaeus, aka Brad Jersak, "Hell is a Kingdom: The Missing Motif Reconstructed" Online Article. http://www.clarion-journal.com/files/hell-is-a-kingdom-4.pdf

Based on this symbolism in James 3:6, Brad Jersak argues that Jesus used the images of fire and *gehenna* in similar ways. He points to Matthew 23:15 and John 8:44 as examples of Jesus speaking about *gehenna* "not so much as a destination [but] as a shadow-kingdom."[2] This kingdom of darkness is set in direct contrast to the kingdom of heaven which Jesus revealed and inaugurated through His life and ministry. Jersak argues something similar for the word *hadēs*. When Jesus speaks of hell, He is not using the calamities of this life to illustrate the horror that awaits some people in the next life. Instead, He is using the imaginary horrors of the *hadēs* myths and the dreadfulness of the *gehenna* valley as illustrations for the actual condition of some people in this world during their life here and now.

What this means, then, is that there are two kingdoms at work on this earth. There is the kingdom of heaven, which is full of life and liberty for those who reside within it, and there is the kingdom of hell, which is full of death and bondage for those who are entrapped within it. The kingdom of heaven is not just a *new way* of doing things, but a way of living that is starkly opposite to the way this world is typically run. Jesus brought the kingdom of heaven to help liberate people from the kingdom of hell, which had ruled and reigned upon this earth since Adam and Eve relinquished control of the

---

[2] Sinner Irenaeus, aka Brad Jersak, "Hell is a Kingdom: The Missing Motif Reconstructed" Online Article. http://www.clarion-journal.com/files/hell-is-a-kingdom-4.pdf

earth in the Garden of Eden. Hell is a kingdom of darkness and destruction that is set against God's kingdom of heaven in this life.[3] The two kingdoms are at war with each other, and while one brings light and life, the other brings death and devastation.

So rather than ask, "What is hell?" the real question is "Where and when is hell?" And the answer to this question is that hell is a kingdom of darkness that rules and reigns upon on this earth. It is the way of living that humans are sadly accustomed to as "normal," but which Jesus came to rescue and liberate us from. Hell is here, on this earth, and many people are living in it.

Here is Brad Jersak's account of his visit to hell:

> I know hell exists, because I've been there. It's just west of Thailand. The horrors of Burma rival anything from Dante's tour of the netherworld. The apocalyptic fires, dismemberments, and everlasting tortures in Burma inspire belief in the reality of Gehenna—or worse, they evoke a bitterness that incites one to hope for it.

> I have not yet recovered (*should I?*) from interviewing the victims of torture by gasoline, fire, and salt in the Karen refugee camps on Burma's borders. I remember my sacred visits to the thatched hospice for those whose limbs, faces, and eyes had been taken by the click-*boom* of landmines. Testimonies of emergency amputations performed on-site amidst razed villages by amateur relief-

---

[3] Sinner Irenaeus, aka Brad Jersak, "Hell is a Kingdom: The Missing Motif Reconstructed" Online Article. http://www.clarion-journal.com/files/hell-is-a-kingdom-4.pdf

workers wielding only a Leatherman tool. Abduction and rape of children by soldiers who were themselves kidnapped as children and crafted by others into instruments of horror. I can relive the late night conversations with aid-workers—eyes red with frustration, tears, and whiskey from the trauma. Yes, I've been to hell. And I feel the guilt of thanking God that I was only visiting.

And Burma is just one tiny corner of hell on earth. One has only to survey the historical landscape of the twentieth century to see how hell can reign on earth. The litany of hellfire's lament circles the globe: The genocides of African colonialism and tribalism; the holocausts of Nazi Germany, Stalinist Russia, and Maoist China; the killing fields and napalm saturation of Southeast Asia; the superpower driven civil wars of Central America; the disappeared of South America; from the war crimes of former Yugoslavia to the "extraordinary rendition" and suicide bombers of the Middle East.[4]

Hell is not an experience reserved solely for some people in the afterlife; hell is a real and horrifying experience for many people in this life. Some people bring this hell upon themselves, while many bring hell upon others. For example, war is hell. So is rape and addiction. Sickness, poverty, famine, and disease are all hell.[5] Physical, emotional, and mental abuse bring hell. The kingdom of hell is all around us. It is within us and

[4] Jersak, *Her Gates Will Never Be Shut*, 151-152.

[5] Cf. Butler, *The Skeletons in God's Closet*, 19-27.

among us. Hell is *not* an afterlife experience for the damned who deserve it; it is a this-life experience for far too many innocent people.

> Since trench warfare in World War I, a century ago, can we still read of sinners dying slowly in fiery pits [in Dante's *Inferno*] as God's divine punishment as opposed to our own horrible mistake? Since Auschwitz, seventy-five years ago, can we read of tearing and sizzling human skin and believe that it could ever be just? Can anyone read [Dante's *Inferno*], where devils chase and gleefully torture shades, without thinking of Hutus chasing Tutsis in Rwanda or what is going on in Syria or the Sudan as I write these words? What sorts of devils are chasing shades today in Iraq? Afghanistan? North Korea?[6]

Hell is real, and hell is here. It is on earth, in human history, wrought and sustained by human hands as we engage in hateful and hurtful activity against one another. The history of the world is the history of hell because hell is a kingdom that rules and reigns upon this world. When Jesus spoke about hell, He "was talking about a literal hell in *this* life."[7]

As such, it is not necessarily wrong to say that Christians can go to hell and even live in hell in this life. William Paul Young writes this about hell:

---

[6] Sweeney, *Inventing Hell*, 186.

[7] Brian Zahnd, *Sinners in the Hands of a Loving God* (New York: Waterbrook, 2017), 124.

> Hell is not outside of Jesus. All things were created in Him and through Him and by Him and for Him. Nothing can possibly exist apart from or outside of Jesus; John and Paul are emphatic on that. So hell is real, but it has to be understood in relationship with Jesus. I think hell is what we experience, now and hereafter, when we live in rebellion and alienation to who we really are in Jesus. But Jesus has met us in our hell and intends to deliver us from our own evil.[8]

Once this idea of hell is introduced, we begin to see life and Scripture through new eyes. We start to understand that the New Testament everywhere describes the differences between these two kingdoms, and what life looks like in each. God, in Jesus Christ, is calling us out of the kingdom of hell and into the kingdom of heaven. As Joshua Ryan Butler describes it, in Jesus Christ, "God is on a mission to get the hell out of earth."[9] Hell is here on earth, and Jesus brought the kingdom of heaven as the antidote and cure for the kingdom of hell. Jesus is seeking to replace the kingdom of hell on earth with the kingdom of heaven on earth.

So it is not surprising that the way of the kingdom of heaven is exactly the opposite of the way of the kingdom of hell. If you want to understand what hell is, all you need to do is look at how Jesus lived and described the kingdom of heaven, and then think of its opposite. But

[8] Wm. Paul Young, in an interview with Baxter Kruger. See https://www.perichoresis.org/william-paul-young-orthodox-novelist/

[9] Butler, *The Skeletons in God's Closet*, 15.

there are numerous images and ideas from Scripture that also describe the kingdom of hell. The following chart shows some of the terms and imagery from Scripture which fit with both kingdoms.

Kingdom of Heaven	Kingdom of Hell
Everlasting Life	Everlasting Death
Exemplified by Jesus	Exemplified by Satan
Walking in Light	Walking in Darkness
Life Guided by Love	Life Guided by Hate
Abiding in the Truth	Abiding in Lies
Practicing Righteousness	Practicing Wickedness
Hope and Healing	Despair and Destruction
Fruitfulness and Creativity	Fire and Corruption
Fellowship and Unity	Separation and Fighting

Forgiveness and Grace	Accusation and Grudges
Fulfilling our Divine Purpose	Neglecting our Divine Purpose
Revealing the Image of God	Hiding the Image of God
Living Fully Human Lives	Living Sub-Human Lives

Note that all of the terms on both sides of the chart are available options for people here and now in this life. The two columns describe the two options we face in our *present* life, not in a future life after death. How we respond to the instructions and commands of God determine what sort of life experience we have here and now.

> The sinner goes to sheol, but in reality *he is there already* … Where there is darkness, there is also the nether world; for the nether world is wherever there is a nether world nature. He who is struck by evil, by unhappiness, disease, or other trouble *is* in sheol, and when he escapes from the misery and 'beholds the light,' then he has escaped from sheol.[10]

Christopher Barth (the son of Karl Barth) argued similarly, that hell (which he referred to as *sheol*) is primarily

---

[10] Johannes Pedersen, quoted by Johnston, *Shades of Sheol*, 89.

experienced in *this life*. Philip Johnston writes this about Barth's view:

> Life is characterized by time, freedom of movement, community, sustenance, health, light, and water, and death by the lack of these. Any reduction of vitality is a form of death, of coming under the power of death. For Barth, sheol is more a power which invades life than a place to go after life. … He asserts repeatedly that the individual in any form of affliction, whether illness, captivity, enmity, poverty, or sinfulness, has a real experience of sheol.[11]

So where is hell? It is here, on this earth. When is hell? It is now, in our lives. And what is hell? It is the experience of life that is diametrically opposed to the life God wants for us. It is sickness and pain, death and disease, pestilence and famine, rape and murder, abuse and neglect, fear and loneliness, greed and lust. A person experiences hell to the degree that they experience such things.

This insight about the present reality of hell raises a startling truth. The fact that the kingdom of hell exists here and now on earth rather than as an afterlife experience, means that any theological system which thinks of hell as *only* an afterlife experience is actually helping and aiding the kingdom of hell grow in power on this earth. In other words, those who only think that hell is an afterlife experience for unbelievers will not be working to

[11] Ibid., 91.

rescue and liberate people from the kingdom of hell that is here *now*. And when the kingdom of hell goes unchallenged, it grows in power and influence. The three main view of hell, which were summarized at the beginning of this book (Traditionalism, Universalism, and Annihilationism), are all guilty in this regard. Far from rescuing people from hell, by thinking that hell is only something that happens to people after they die, such views actually help keep people in hell. The religious belief that hell exists only in the afterlife is the first step in creating hell here on earth for those whom the "religious" people think deserve to go there.

You might have heard it said that the greatest lie of Satan is that he does not exist. Yes, and the second greatest lie of Satan is that hell exists only in the afterlife. This lie causes Christians to ignore and neglect the many billions of people who live in hell right here on earth. We walk by them every day, ignoring their cries of pain and calls for help. Hell is here and hell is now, and until we recognize this truth, we will not work to rescue and liberate those who are trapped behind its gates.

Indeed, the traditional Christian doctrine of hell (especially Traditionalism, or Infernalism) is almost solely responsible for creating a spiritual and psychological hell in the minds of those who hear and believe it. The traditional views of hell end up creating hell in the minds of those who hear them. "No single belief has done more to undercut the spiritual journey of more Western people than the belief that God could be an eternal torturer of people who do not like him or disobey him."[12] How can a person worship a God who sends all non-Christians (including those who never heard the gospel), along with children, mentally handicapped, and possibly our own family members to suffer forever in burning flames?

In a twisted perversion of the gospel, Christians who seek to rescue people from eternal hell end up consigning people to a living hell, as people tear themselves up spiritually and psychologically by living in fear of God, fear of sinning, and fear that they have not believed in the right things or performed enough good works to please and appease God. And even if some are convinced that they themselves are headed for eternal bliss with God, such Christians are often in emotional and psychological distress about the eternal suffering of their loved ones. A belief in eternal conscious torment does not lead to the deliverance of people from hell, but leads instead to the creation of hell in the minds of countless millions.

> If there is a proper, though difficult, biblical doctrine of hell in terms of final individual human destiny, there is an equally proper and yet more necessary biblical doctrine of hell in terms of human social and corporate life on this earth. And, indeed, if we were to concentrate on

[12] Richard Rohr in Sweeney, *Inventing Hell*, 5.

the former—the question of personal destiny—we might easily slip into the dangerous position of ignoring the latter. … As Christians, we look for the marriage of heaven and earth, not their separation; and in that light we must look with Christian realism at the possibility of a different, and disastrous, marriage, which has become all too real a possibility in our own day: a marriage of hell and earth. That is what Jesus warned about in His own day. We can do no less in our own.[13]

When we neglect the work of bringing heaven down to earth, we allow hell to rise up on the earth. There is no middle ground. There is no neutral way of living. If we are not expanding the rule and reign of God upon the earth, then we are allowing the rule and reign of hell to remain instead.

Grahame Smith is a professional counselor in Australia. He helped prepare this book for publication and is an active member in my online discipleship group. While reading an early copy of this book, he sent the following message:

A person recently came through my door for counseling. He was referred to me by his employer for failing a drug test. He had tested positive for crystal meth. A trauma he experienced when he was much younger pushed him to into the drug culture, and now, seeing the destruction that drugs were bringing in his life, he sought to find a way out.

[13] Wright, *Following Jesus*, 96.

As we talked, he said that meth was destroying his life, family, marriage, and career. His brother overdosed on meth in front of him, and he spent thirty minutes doing CPR on his brother to no avail, and then had to call his parents and tell them what happened. They wanted to know why he hadn't acted sooner to stop his brother from using drugs. This greatly damaged their relationship.

But that wasn't the end. His former partner went crazy from the same drugs and ran away leaving him with young children to take care of. And now his job was being threatened for drug abuse. If he didn't find a way to break the hell of addiction, he would lose his job and his family, which would then likely lead to the loss of his house, his money, his health, and maybe even his life.

Hell was staring me in the face, and I was trying to rescue this man from its dark chains. He is on his last chance at home and at work. He is looking for hope. I think I was able to show him a way to find it, but there is a lot more work to do.

That same day I helped a divorced couple rescue their 16 year-old from a plan to commit suicide, and a fellow who couldn't go to work anymore because of panic attacks and imminent financial disaster. This is just a snap shot of one of my days. And this experience is not rare for counselors. I clinically supervise other therapists who all report having similar experiences day in and day out. Magnify all this misery across the world, add war and natural disasters, and what do we get? The kingdom of hell. People are living in hell right now and we are at war with it.

Hell is all around us, next door, and even in our families. We see it in our neighbors across the road and in the politics and violence across the world. Christians need to get a handle on this and not turn away.

Hell is a power on this earth, and it lives and resides within each one of us. As long as we restrict hell to an afterlife experience for wicked people, we will never see hell in our own world or how we ourselves contribute to it. We also never learn to follow Jesus in bringing heaven down to earth to oust the kingdom of hell from our midst. But once we see that hell is here, that hell is now, and that hell is within us and amongst us, we then start to look to Jesus for how we can lower hell's flag over this earth and raise the flag of heaven.

This world is a battleground, where two kingdoms are at war. Politics, economics, racism, sexism, and all other –isms are manifestations of the ongoing battle between heaven and hell. There truly is a battle raging around us, and it is not hidden. It is fought in plain sight. You read about it in the newspapers, hear about it around the water cooler at work, and feel it when you walk your dog around the block. It is present when you talk with your neighbor, interact with your spouse, and read your favorite novel. You experience the struggle between heaven and hell (in the words of Morpheus from the movie "The Matrix") "when you look out your window or when you turn on your television. You can feel it when you go to work ... when you go to church ... when you pay your taxes."

And in every case, whether you recognize it or not, the question is the same: "For which side are you fighting?" Are you working, and talking, and spending, and living to help advance the kingdom of heaven … or the kingdom of hell? All of this will be dealt with in the next chapter. The next chapter will explain how to avoid the true hell, the hell of a hellish life on this earth, and also how to rescue and deliver people who live within this hell. But first, we must answer the second question of this present chapter. When people ask "What is hell?" they are either thinking "What does Scripture mean when it talks about *hadēs* and *gehenna*?" or "What happens to unbelievers after they die?" We have answered the first question; let us now turn to the second.

WHAT HAPPENS TO THE UNBELIEVING DEAD?

Before we can understand what happens to unbelievers who die, we must first understand what happens to unbelievers who live. In other words, Scripture occasionally describes life lived outside the will of God as a life filled with death (cf. Rom 7:24). The unbeliever is one who lives in the realm of death, darkness, and decay (cf. 1 John 2:11). Understanding what this means for the person who is alive on the earth helps lay the foundation for seeing what life might be like for those who are no longer alive on the earth.

Since the life of the unbeliever is a life of death, we must understand what death really is, how death works, and why death comes upon humanity. It is first of all important to recognize that the word "dead" never means "non-existent." A dead body still exists; it can be seen and touched. So "dead" doesn't mean "non-existent;" it means "lifeless" or "useless." That which is "dead" is ineffective or useless for the purpose to which it was intended. It does not accomplish the task or function for which God created it. That which is "dead" is not fulfilling its design or purpose.[14]

We see this from the very beginning when Adam and Eve "died" in the Garden of Eden. God told Adam to not eat fruit from the Tree of the Knowledge of Good and Evil, "for in the day that you eat of it you shall surely die" (Gen 2:17). Yet when Adam and Eve did eat from the Tree, they did not immediately die physically. Yes, Adam physically died 930 years later (Gen 5:5), but is this what God meant when He said they would "surely die"? Partly, yes, but most Christians believe that God meant something else as well.

Many Christians believe that in the moment Adam and Eve ate from the forbidden tree, they also died spir-

[14] See the lesson on the word "dead" in my "Gospel Dictionary" online course at RedeemingGod.com

itually. This might be true, but Scripture does not fully endorse the concept of spiritual death, so the theological concept of spiritual death is debated. But regardless of whether or not spiritual death is a reality, the text of Genesis 3 goes on to explain what *did happen* to Adam and Eve, and in this way, helps define "death."

After eating from the forbidden tree, God shows up and tells Adam and Eve what will happen to them. He says that their life will now be filled with problems and frustrations. Though God had instructed Adam and Eve to perform certain functions on the earth (Gen 1:26-31), since they had decided to disobey God, these activities would be accomplished with great difficulty and frustration. This was, as God describes it, the "death" of their divinely-ordained purpose. They were now no longer able to perfectly fulfill the plan or design which God had given to them.[15]

We see from this what "death" is. God created this world and the humans upon it to live in harmony with each other, and to live with satisfaction, joy, fulfillment, peace, and pleasure. But going our own way destroyed much of that created balance, and introduced pain and hardship instead. This is how Genesis 3 defines "death." It is toil by the sweat of the brow, rather than toil with joy and satisfaction. It is bringing forth children with pain, rather than bringing up children with peace. It is

[15] All of this is explained in greater detail in my studies of the "One Verse Podcast" on Genesis 1–3.

living life in ways that are contrary to what God intended or desired.

But there is another form of death which God also introduces to humanity, and it is physical death. Interestingly, this physical death was provided as a way of escape from this life of death and frustration. Since God created humans to do certain things, and since they were now no longer able to fulfill these functions, God *blessed* them with physical death so that they would not have to live forever with these frustrations. Physical death, then, was not a curse for rebelling against God, but was instead the *cure*. When we rebelled, and death came upon us in the form of frustration, dissatisfaction, and a lack of fulfillment in life, God allowed physical death to overtake us so that we might be rescued and delivered from an eternal life of living in the realm of death.

Physical death brings rescue because physical death is not the end. We know from Scripture that in the future, God will raise every person from death. It is not just believers who will be resurrected from death, but all people (John 5:29). Every single person who has ever lived will experience resurrection. Through resurrection, we who have God's life within us are able to break free from these sinful and death-filled bodies so that with our new, glorified bodies, in the new heavens and new earth, we might be able to finally live the way God desired and intended. In eternity, we will live up to our full potential, experiencing love and harmony with God, with each other, and with all of creation. Death and resurrection are the means by which God accomplishes the restoration and redemption of all things.

But if physical death is the means by which people can escape the life of death and frustration, if physical death is the cure for living life as God never intended it to be lived, then what happens to those people who are resurrected but who resolve to remain in rebellion against God for eternity? If, after God has raised every person from death, some people prefer to continue in rebellion rather than follow the way of the living God, what happens to them?

The answer from Scripture appears to be that God will let them go their own way. God will let them continue to live in eternity, but within the realm of death. Of course, since they have been raised from death, there will be no more physical death, and so they will continue to live in the realm of death. Since they physically died and were resurrected, they cannot die again, and so instead continue to live a life in eternity which is much like this life, but without any end. This isn't torment upon humans any more than this life is torment. Life in eternity for the unredeemed will be much like life would have been on this earth if God had not blocked our way back to the Tree of Life in the Garden of Eden. A sin-filled life that never ends will be like the life we now live, but for eternity. Yes, this can be called "hell," but only in the same sense that our current life is hell, as defined previously in this chapter. This is the eternal state of the unregenerate dead.

Their existence in eternity will be very much like their existence in this life. While those who exist within the eternal kingdom of heaven live lives of fulfillment, significance, and satisfaction, many who exist within the eternal kingdom of hell live lives of frustration, emptiness, and dissatisfaction. The images of fire and hell in Scripture do not refer only to a future existence of the damned, but also to a present reality that can be experienced when life is lived outside of the will of God. And this present reality can carry on into eternity. "Since our lives truly mean something, the seeds of our existence today will sprout, blossom, and inevitably bear eschatological fruit, whether heavenly or hellish."[16]

At the risk of speaking where Scripture does not, I imagine there likely will be some elements of joy and happiness in that life, but, as in this life, all such experiences will be marred with aspects of fear, frustration, and a lack of fulfillment. There will probably be activities and adventures as in this life, but they will be overshadowed with hardships in relationships, goals, and plans. This is not because God sends such things upon people, but because when a person refuses to live life as God intended, fear and frustration are the natural con-

---

[16] Sinner Irenaeus, aka Brad Jersak, "Hell is a Kingdom: The Missing Motif Reconstructed" Online Article. http://www.clarion-journal.com/files/hell-is-a-kingdom-4.pdf

sequences. This is not divinely-inflicted suffering and torment, but is instead the mournful agreement of a God who allows His wayward children to go their own way in an empty attempt to live life without Him.

And just as this present life is described as "death," the life apart from God in eternity is known as the second death (Rev 21:8). It is a life of ongoing death. Jesus often describes His way of life as "everlasting life." Everlasting life is a way of life that begins now and will continue on into eternity. The same can be said about the second death, or everlasting death. The life governed and ruled by hell is the life of everlasting death. It begins now and can be experienced in this life, and it has the potential to continue forever, even after physical death. This is why it is referred to as "the second death." It is existence in everlasting death. It is ongoing existence that is filled with all the problems and frustrations of this life, but without any end. The first death is a blessed escape from the frustrations of this life, but the second death has no end. It is an eternal existence without end, while facing the frustrations of life lived without God.

Just as being "born again" does not mean that a person starts their life all over again, but instead refers to the transformation of a person's life so that they head in the direction God wanted, so also, to "die again" does not mean that a person dies a second time, but that a person's life goes in a direction that is even further away from what God wanted and desired. The "second death" therefore, is not annihilation, or the death of the eternal soul. Instead, it is the ongoing experience of being entrenched or solidified in the way of rebellion against God. It is an irreversible step on a path that leads away from what God wanted and desired.

In the previous section, we learned that hell is a kingdom which rules and reigns upon this earth, and which entraps people in ways of living that are contrary to God's design and purpose for them. As such, it is a kingdom of death. But now we see that this kingdom of death can also continue into eternity. It is not just a temporal kingdom of this earth. Just as eternal life, or life in the kingdom of heaven, begins now and continues on into eternity, so also, eternal death, or life in the kingdom of hell, begins now and can continue on into eternity. Just as the kingdom of heaven is God's activity of bringing heaven down to earth so that the rule and reign of God spreads over the earth here and now and then on into eternity for those who are part of it, so also, the kingdom of hell is Satan's activity of bringing hell upon the earth so that his rule and reign spreads over the earth here and now and on into eternity as well.

But does this mean that those who start their life in eternity in the kingdom of death will stay there for all eternity as well? I used to think so, based on passages like Hebrews 9:27, which says that humans are appointed once to die and after that face judgment. But such texts only disprove reincarnation; they don't say that the judgment itself only occurs once or is a final, once-for-all-time judgment. Furthermore, "judgment" itself is a word that simply refers to "naming things as they really are," and so when "the way things really are" changes, the judgment of God can change as well.[17]

So from a biblical perspective, there does not seem to be any reason that God cannot allow people who have never heard the gospel to respond positively to it once they stand before Him in judgment. This would not only include tribes of people that never heard the gospel, but also those who lived prior to the days of Jesus. Children and mentally handicapped would also be given a chance. So might those who were presented with a false gospel, or believed in a god who was not truly the God revealed in Jesus Christ. When people stand before God, and their eyes are finally opened, and they see God for the first time for who He really is, it goes against everything we know about God to think that He would turn people away who, in that moment, believe in the revelation they receive and want to love and worship Him for eternity. If there are such people on that day, I believe God will grant them eternal life and welcome them into His Kingdom. And I am not certain that this

---

[17] See the lesson on "judgment" in my "Gospel Dictionary" online course at RedeemingGod.com

is a one-time offer. Maybe this offer stands for all eternity.[18]

Yet it would still be only an offer, for God cannot
(and will not) force anyone to love Him and follow His
ways. While "God doesn't punish those who refuse
[His] loving relationship, God can't prevent the natural
negative consequences that come from saying "no" to
love. God never sends anyone to hell, never annihilates,
and never gives up calling us to embrace love."[19]
Though the gates of heaven may never be shut for all
eternity (Rev 21:25), this does not mean that all will
eventually walk through them. While Scripture does
contain hints that God wants all to be reconciled to
Him, and even redeems broken areas of His creation (cf.
Ezek 47:1-12; Zech 14:6-9), this does not mean that
everybody and everything will be redeemed. (For example, will Satan and the fallen angels ever be redeemed?
Origen thought so, but most Christians disagree.) Furthermore, the current situation with Satan (and even
our own current human condition) reveals that some
will choose to go their own way for eternity, even if they
were continually given a choice for eternity. Why would
people choose to live separated from God for eternity?
For the exact same reasons they (and Satan) choose to
live separate from God right now. They would rather

---

[18] See Brad Jersak's book, *Her Gates Will Never be Shut* for a
compelling argument of this view.

[19] Oord, *God Can't*, 164.

rule over their own broken life, than submit to God and follow His ways. Since God has given humans a degree of free will, this means He does not control them, and therefore, must let humans go their own way, if they so choose.

Some use passages like Revelation 21–22 to argue for the ultimate reconciliation of all people. However, it seems more likely that the restoration and redemption of the nations in Revelation 21–22 is not about the resurrection of all who were dead and sent to the Lake of Fire … but is about the redemption and restoration of the nations *as a function* of ruling this world. It is not that all who were part of those nations are now brought back to life and placed within those nations again and then invited into the gates of heaven. It is the nations themselves, and what they represent and what role they serve on this earth, that are redeemed and welcomed. Their culture, traditions, and ways of ruling are brought under the authority of Jesus. Jesus redeems the nations, and gives them their rightful role within His rulership of the world, but this is not the same thing as redeeming all the people who ever lived within those nations. "The best of all cultures, now redeemed and transformed into respective 'glory,' will become part of the eschatological joy."[20]

---

[20] Michael L. Westmoreland-White, "War of the Lamb: Violence and Non-Violence in the Book of Revelation," *The Baptist Peacemaker* (Nov-Dec:2005).

But regardless of what actually happens, I agree that God's arms will always remain open and welcoming to anyone who would come to Him, whenever that might be. Nevertheless, it seems doubtful that *all* will eventually be reconciled to God, regardless of how much time passes. The longer people live, the more set in their ways they become. People make their choices, and then their choices make them. The longer a person lives without God, the less like God they become, and therefore, less human. And the less human they become, the less likely they are to be in a position to accept God or welcome a relationship with Him. The path we set in this life prepares us for how we begin the next life, and if a person starts their next life in a state of open rebellion against God and wants to continue walking down that path, they will likely come to a point of no return and will remain forever in a rebellious life of their own choosing.

So there will be many who dwell in eternity who refuse to worship God or submit to His glorious rule. For them, their life in eternity will not be light and glory, but will be characterized by corruption and devastation, as symbolized by the worm and fire. They will live in everlasting death. This means that since they cannot die, their existence is one of eternal futility and frustration, as they continually watch their endeavors fail and their plans come to nothing. Their existence in eternity contains "absolutely no longing for God. The damned person wills himself as he is, and hell as it is."[21] Their sin does not live eternally, but it "fixates man in such a way that he is trapped in an unchangeable rigidity that no longer desires conversion and no longer seeks forgiveness."[22]

God does not and cannot force people to love Him against their will, for this would not be love. If God tried to force people to love Him against their will, He would be guilty of spiritual rape. While God never gives up on anyone, nor will He ever stop loving any person for all eternity, God cannot force people to love or accept Him. Some, I believe, will continue to reject His advances of love for all eternity. So Universalism is not an option.

But Annihilationism is not a viable option either. Since God is not a destroyer, He cannot annihilate humans who do not love Him. The only thing God can do is what He has always done. He can let the objects of His infinite love continue to live forever in whatever way they want. He allows them go off into a far country to squander their inheritance on riotous living.

> There is nothing in the Bible or in Christian tradition to deny the possibility that individual humans can progressively choose to be less and less genuinely human, until they eventually cease to be human at all. ... If it is possible ... for human beings to choose to live more and more

---

[21] A. Winklhofer, cited in Balthasar, *Dare We Hope*, 101.

[22] Otto Betz, cited in ibid.

out of tune with their divine intention, to reflect the image of God less and less, there is nothing to stop them from finally ceasing to bear that image, and so to be, as it were, beings who were once human but are not now. … We sometimes say, even of living people, that they have become inhuman, or that they have turned into monsters. Drugs can do that to people; so can drink. So can jealousy. So can unemployment. So can homelessness, or lovelessness. … I see nothing in the New Testament to make me reject the possibility that some, perhaps many, of God's human creatures do choose, and will choose, to dehumanize themselves completely.[23]

This idea is exactly what C. S. Lewis presents in *The Great Divorce,* a fascinating story of a man who gets on a bus in hell to take a trip to heaven. In the second chapter, Lewis describes what life is like for those who live in hell. When people first arrive, they find themselves in the center of a vast, sprawling town, which is very much like any town you might find on earth, except that everything is free and nobody has any needs. So people move into any house they want, and start living in their new existence. But within a few days or weeks, they have a quarrel with one of their neighbors, and rather than forgive the other person or seek to work things out (for these are characteristics of the kingdom of heaven), they decide to move to a different street. Lewis writes that this process of separation continues forever, until some people get to the point where they live millions of miles

[23] Wright, *Following Jesus*, 94-95.

away from anybody else. In hell, each person is allowed to be as selfish and as mean as they want, and this causes them to eventually separate themselves from everyone else so that they finally live in complete isolation for all eternity, wrapped up in their own thoughts of everybody else's faults and failures.[24]

Lewis claims that what he wrote was only a fantasy, an imaginary tale with a moral about how human selfishness leads to ruin, and how, as he wrote elsewhere, the doors of hell are locked from the inside. People are in hell because they want to be there, and because their preferred way of living cannot allow them to live in community with God or others. Yet there is likely more truth to Lewis' imaginary tale than he wanted to admit. If God does not torture people in a fiery furnace for eternity, and if God allows people to make their choices and live with the consequences for eternity, then it seems entirely possible that life in eternity for the unregenerate dead might end up being very similar to what Lewis describes in his book.

God cannot force people to love Him and spend eternity with Him, but neither can He force people to change their behavior. The only thing God can do is let people live the way they want. When people live outside the will of God, their existence becomes full of frustration and eternal insignificance. Their eternal existence

---

[24] C. S. Lewis, *The Great Divorce* (New York: HarperCollins, 1946), 9-12.

might be full of failed relationships and empty pursuits for pleasure and fulfillment. Though they are not separated from God (for God is truly omnipresent), they might become separated from each other, and even from themselves. It might be that the longer they live in such a state, the less human they become.

Joshua Ryan Butler, in his book, *The Skeletons in God's Closet*, writes that since God does not torture or destroy people for rejecting Him, and since He cannot force people to love Him, the only option left is that, in love, God allows rebellious people to go their own way for eternity. But since He cannot let them ruin eternity for everyone else, "He simply hands them over to the life … that they desire. He hands them over to themselves. … Hell is the absence of God, found in the presence of our own autonomy."[25] This will not be a fiery place of torture, but a life in which a person eternally lives however they please.

Now, can any of this be proven from Scripture? It cannot. Once we have seen that all the passages about *sheol, hadēs, gehenna,* and fire are not talking about the next life, but primarily about this life, then we also discover that Scripture is mostly silent on the subject of the afterlife for the unredeemed. We know that people will

[25] Butler, *The Skeletons in God's Closet*, 65-66, 90. I would argue that God is in this "hell" as well, but the people who reside there have chosen to ignore and neglect Him for so long, that they cannot feel or sense His presence. Though God is always with them, they have cut themselves off from His activity, and so are blind and deaf to His eternal love and call.

not cease to exist, for they too will have been raised from the dead. But beyond that, everything is speculation. But we do know the character of God, that God is like Jesus, and we know that Jesus would never destroy people and would never torture people. Jesus also never forces people to believe or act against their will. He loves, forgives, and woos, but He does not force. So it is logical speculation that life in eternity for the unredeemed might be like life on this earth, except that it never ends and nobody ever dies.

Some people will be upset by such a notion, for it doesn't sound so bad. But why should it? Why do we want God to torture people? Do we think God really wants people to suffer for eternity? No, He does not wish or desire suffering and torment on anyone, even upon those who wish to go their own way. Hell is not God's hatred toward sinners; it is "refusing to receive and be transformed by the love of God."[26]

And yet, it will be a form of torment, will it not? Once we begin to imagine what life on earth might be like if everyone did whatever they wanted, and nobody ever died, we begin to see that such an existence might well be described as "hell" after all. Just read the book of Judges to see what sorts of things occur when "everybody did what was right in their own eyes" (cf. Judg 17:6; 21:25). Again, as discussed earlier, the only reason God allowed death to come upon humans in the first

---

[26] Zahnd, *Sinners in the Hands of a Loving God*, 137.

place is so that He could provide a way for human to escape an eternal existence of self-centered living on this earth.

> Sartre was wrong. Hell isn't other people. Hell is you, all by yourself, eternally removed from all that reminds you of God—and everything points to Him. So there you are, exponentially worse off than Gollum, tormented in your own skin because everything good hurts and everything ugly is all you have left. You are the worm and the rotting meat, the fire and what it consumes, and the worm does not die, and the fire is not quenched. In life, you failed to recognize the divine grace that kept you from that state; in death, you have no illusions about the extent of that grace, and have rejected it all.[27]

But if there is no escape, then eventually, an eternal existence in selfishness will ultimately lead to a separation from all that is good and healthy. It is what C. S. Lewis described in *The Great Divorce.* This is the "everlasting destruction" that Paul writes about in 2 Thessalonians 1:7-9 (cf. Dan 12:2; Matt 25:46). It is a life where nothing works out, and all human plans, goals, and dreams come to nothing. Is that life truly worth living for eternity? Wouldn't it be better to live in eternity fulfilling your divine purpose and finding satisfaction, completeness, and success in everything you do?

[27] Tim Nichols, "Knowing Who You Trust." https://fullcontactchristianity.org/2018/05/29/knowing-who-you-trust/

Yes, of course. But as Butler points out, "hell is preferable from the inside for those who live there."[28]

It must be emphasized again that this form of living is not inflicted on people by God. Those who persist in unbelief and rebellion throughout eternity will live a life of self-separation from God, but they do so by their own choice. God does not separate Himself from them. "Whatever else hell may be, it is not where God isn't."[29] God is omnipresent, which means that wherever the unregenerate dead spend eternity, God is there with them. But it is likely that they will have so conditioned and trained themselves to live life without God, they will not see or feel His loving and accepting presence.

Some people live without the experience of God's love, but this is not because they are not loved, for nothing in creation can separate us from the love of God (including hell; cf. Rom 8:35). The people who live in eternal rebellion against God are not hated, despised, or rejected by God. Quite to the contrary, they are loved and forgiven by God just as much as the saints. But when people live without regard for God or anyone else, they face the ongoing consequences of these choices, and God lets them go their own way. God is not too weak or too unloving to stop them, but is rather too strong in His character and too loving to stop them.

[28] Butler, *The Skeletons in God's Closet*, 98.

[29] Robert Farrar Capon, *Kingdom, Grace, Judgment: Paradox, Outrage, and Vindication in the Parables of Jesus* (Grand Rapids: Eerdmans, 2002), 507.

Out of love for us, God does not stop us in this life from going our own way, and He will not stop people in eternity from doing the same thing.

> Hell begins with a grumbling mood, always complaining, always blaming others … but you are still distinct from it. You may even criticize it in yourself and wish you could stop it. But there may come a day when you can no longer. Then there will be no *you* left to criticize the mood or even to enjoy it, but just the grumble itself, going on forever like a machine. … In each of us there is something growing, which will BE Hell unless it is nipped in the bud.[30]

How then can God allow people to live this way for eternity? Because that's what love does. Giving freedom to the object of your love is the second greatest expression of love. The first is to lay down your life for them, which God did in Jesus. But when God lays down His life for His enemies, and they still choose to reject Him, then God, in love, lets them go their own way. Love can do nothing else. Allowing people to go their own way for all eternity is an expression of God's love, not the absence of it. When they go their own way, God does not abandon them or stop loving them, but in love, continues to walk with them into their pain, rebellion, and darkness, but it nevertheless is "their own way" rather than His.

[30] C. S. Lewis, cited by Butler, *The Skeletons in God's Closet*, 79.

This separation is in their own experience and perspective; not God's. They will *feel* separated from God, even though God has not separated Himself from them. They will definitely not exist in a state of burning flames and tortured suffering in lakes of lava. Instead, their eternal existence will be somewhat like life on this world. This eternal existence will be an expression of God's love; not the absence of it, for God will freely grant them the desire of their heart to live without Him. God will not stop loving them, but they will not exist in eternity with the knowledge or experience of this never-ending divine love.

Hopefully, you want something better for yourself and for others. Hopefully, you desire to experience the love of God now and for all eternity, and to also help others experience the same thing. The next chapter reveals how to accomplish this. In it, you will learn how you (and others) can avoid hellish living in this life and the next.

CHAPTER 4

HOW CAN I AVOID HELL?

Many people want to know whether or not they are going to hell, and more importantly, how to make sure they don't end up in hell. But as we have seen, the question "How can I avoid hell?" is not actually a legitimate question. At least, not in the way people are asking it.

When most people ask about how to avoid hell, they are thinking about hell as a place of everlasting torture in the afterlife. Yet we have seen in this book that such a place does not exist. "Hell," as it is defined in Scripture, is actually in *this* life. "Hell" is a kingdom of death and destruction that is arrayed against God and which seeks to imprison and enslave humans to selfish passions so that they do not live up to their God-given purpose in life. It is not a place of everlasting torment in the afterlife.

So when people ask, "How can I avoid hell?" the biblical answer is, "You are already in hell, but you can work to bring heaven down to hell by following the ways and teachings of Jesus." Yet such an answer doesn't actually answer their question. For although almost everybody recognizes that "life is hell" to some degree, when a person asks "How can I avoid hell?" what they *really* want to know is, "How can I make sure I end up in heaven with God for all eternity?"[1]

Therefore, when someone asks, "How can I avoid hell?" our first task is to explain to them what Scripture teaches about how to receive everlasting life. After this truth is made clear, we can then move on to the discipleship truths of how to avoid hell in the life. Both answers are considered below.

HOW TO RECEIVE EVERLASTING LIFE

The Scriptural offer of eternal life is quite simple: God gives eternal life to anyone who believes in Jesus for it (John 3:16; 5:24; 6:47; etc.). That's it. No fine print; no strings attached. There are no secret steps, hidden requirements, or extra conditions. A life of good works and obedience are not a requirement to earn or keep eternal life, nor do they prove that one has eternal life. Eternal life is the absolutely free gift of God to anyone and everyone who simply and only believes in Jesus for it.[2]

So when a person asks how they can avoid hell, and by this question they mean that they want to know how

---

[1] We will not spend eternity "in heaven" either, but on the new earth in the new creation. See Marshall, *Heaven is Not My Home*.

[2] I cover all of this in much more detail in my online course, "The Gospel According to Scripture."

to receive eternal life so they can spend eternity with God, the main point to impress upon such a person is that they can have eternal life from God by believing in Jesus for it. It is important to use something similar to the phrase "believe in Jesus for eternal life" because the concepts of saying a prayer, committing your life to Christ, and asking Jesus into your heart, while very common in some church circles, are not found within Scripture as a means of gaining eternal life. If Jesus invited people to believe in Him for everlasting life, there is no good reason to modify or change the terminology that Jesus Himself consistently used.

It is usually quite common for people who hear this free invitation of eternal life to offer up various sorts of objections. Statements such as "But you don't know how badly I've sinned" or "Are you saying that after I have eternal life I can just go sin all I want?" are two examples. In all such cases, the person who voices these objections is doubting the extent of God's grace and the truth of Jesus' promise. So the proper response to such objections is to emphasize God's grace, and point people to the truth of Jesus's words.

For example, in response to the first objection, you might say, "You are right. I don't know how badly you have sinned. But God does. And He still loves and forgives you. When Jesus came to this earth, He did not come for the good people, but for all people, which includes you. You are forgiven and loved by God more than you can ever possibly imagine." Then you could turn again to the promises of Jesus about eternal life.

The second objection can also be answered by magnifying the grace of God. Does God's free offer of eternal life mean that a person can just go sin all they want? The answer is yes. Grace, by definition, can be abused in such a way.[3] But once a person understands God's grace, and how sin damages and hurts *us*, then we come to see why God instructs us not to sin. It is not because He is a killjoy, or wants to threaten us with hell if we don't obey Him. No, He tells us not to sin because He loves us, and He doesn't want to see us get hurt. But if we decide we want to hurt ourselves, then He lets us learn about the pain of sin through experience. So can a person who has eternal life go out and sin all they want? Sure, just like they can stab a knife in their leg all they want. But why would anyone *want* to? After answering this objection in such a way, you could once again return to the promises of Jesus.

Such a focus on grace and truth will never lead a person astray. This is important, because one of the reasons a person is afraid about burning forever in hell is because they do not understand the grace and goodness of God and they do not believe the truth revealed in Jesus. People only believe that God can torture people for eternity because they do not believe that God is truly

---

[3] Yes, I am aware of Romans 6:1-2, and have written and taught on this text elsewhere, including in my online course "The Gospel According to Scripture."

good and gracious or that Jesus means what He says. Only as people begin to understand the grace of God and the truth of Jesus will they begin to understand the gospel.

So when a person asks how they can escape hell and go to heaven when they die, the easiest answer is also the biblical answer: They can be invited to believe in Jesus for eternal life. It would not be helpful to correct them right away about the nature of hell or where the unregenerate will spend eternity. Save that discussion for discipleship later on. Instead, simply tell them that God will give them everlasting life if they believe in Jesus for it. (By the way ... do *you* believe this?)

HOW TO AVOID HELL IN THIS LIFE

As we have seen in this book, "hell" is not primarily a place that people go after they die. Yes, there is a place where the unregenerate dead will spend eternity, but the Bible does not refer to this place as "hell" and it will not be a place of eternal suffering and torture. So when the Bible talks about "hell," it is referring to an existence right here and now in this life. "Hell" is a way of living that is completely opposite and contrary to life lived under the rule and reign of God. Many people do not bring such a hellish existence upon themselves, but are instead victims of a hellish life because of the decisions and actions of others. For example, people who live in war-torn countries experience the hell of war, as do children or women sold into sex slavery. These people live in hell, and they need to be rescued and delivered from it.

So when it comes to the biblical teaching about hell, it is important for Christians to understand how to avoid hell in this life for themselves, and then also how to help rescue those who are living in a hellish existence. The answer to the first question is relatively simple. We avoid living in hell during this life by following Jesus. Jesus introduced the kingdom of God through His teachings and example, and then inaugurated it through His death and resurrection. Jesus showed us how to live in this world so that we can escape the kingdom of death and darkness and live in God's kingdom of light and love.

By following the example and teachings of Jesus, we will avoid living in hell during this life. The kingdom of hell is the spiritual opposite of the kingdom of heaven, and so when we live in the light of the rule and reign of God, we will not be living in the darkness of the rule and reign of death.

The opposite is also true. If we forsake and neglect the instructions from Jesus about how best to live this life, then we can expect to experience the destructive and damaging consequences of sin to come into our life. God does not send such suffering upon us, for God does not punish people for their sin. Instead, these painful and hellish consequences of sin come upon us because sin bears its own punishment with it. God does not send "hell" into our lives when we disobey; sin brings "hell" with it. Life can become hell for Christians, but when it does, it is because we bring it upon ourselves.[4]

It is important to note, however, that when a Christian is following and obeying Jesus, this does not mean that bad things will not happen to them. Bad things can and will occur, even to Christians who are seeking to follow Jesus. The effects of the kingdom of hell in this life can be felt and experienced by all, even by those who are seeking to live within the rule and reign of the kingdom of God. The kingdom of hell is at war with the kingdom of heaven, and as in all war, there is collateral damage that often hurts innocent people and bystanders. When we are following Jesus and yet bad things still happen to us, we may assume that these hellish experiences are simply due to the fact that we still live in a war-torn land.

Nevertheless, the fact that we are following Jesus and seeking to live within the kingdom of God means that even when hell drops upon us, we can live with light, love, forgiveness, and peace toward others. We can also know that God will work to bring good outcomes from our hellish experiences (Rom 8:28). God can redeem the hell that comes into our lives. Even though Paul was unjustly sent to prison, he wrote that such a terrible ex-

---

[4] Bernstein, *The Formation of Hell*, 135-136, 146-153.

perience had provided opportunity to spread the gospel (Php 1:12-14). Whether he was abased or abounding, hungry or full, Paul knew that the light of the glory of the gospel would shine through him so that even in the darkest of nights and the deepest of dungeons, the kingdom of heaven would win out over his temporal experience of the kingdom of hell (cf. Php 4:10-13). Paul encouraged the Philippian Christians to view their suffering in a similar fashion (Php 1:29; 2:5-11).

So how can you escape hell in this life? Seek to follow, love, and serve Jesus so that you might live within and bring to pass the rule and reign of God in your life and on this earth. And when you still experience hellish situations in this life, know that God will rescue and deliver you from such experiences, and will even redeem them for His own glory and purposes. Indeed, maybe one of the purposes of God in letting you experience hell on earth is so that you might work with Him to rescue others who are in the pit of hell. In fact, this is why Jesus came to earth … so that He might enter into the hell of this life and rescue those who are here. This is also why Jesus experienced His hellish death on the cross.

WHY DID JESUS DIE?

When some people hear that hell is primarily a form of existence in this life, rather than an eternal torture chamber in the next, they ask, "Then why did Jesus die? If there is no hell, then there is no reason for Jesus to die!" While this objection is primarily directed at people who hold to universalism (which I do not), it has been leveled at me as well. So it is worth responding to this objection before moving on.

Note first of all that I am not saying there is no hell. There is a hell, and it is in this life. Second, unlike people who believe that everyone goes to heaven no matter what, I believe that many will ultimately reject God forever, and as a result, will spend eternity living as if God has no say or sway over how they live. So when Jesus died, I believe He sought to rescue and deliver humans from both forms of existence. Jesus died to rescue humanity from the living hell here on earth, and He died to call us into eternal life with Him, so that we can live in eternity as He always wanted.

But it is primarily the hellish existence of this life that the death of Jesus sought to rescue us from. (Deliverance from eternal death has always been by God's grace alone, through faith alone. Blood sacrifice was never needed for God to offer the free gift of eternal life to humanity.[5]) Jesus died to rescue and deliver us from the kingdom of hell here on earth. How did this occur? The crucifixion of Jesus is simultaneously the greatest revelation of God and the greatest revelation of hell.

---

[5] See my books, *The Atonement of God* and *Nothing but the Blood of Jesus,* for a detailed explanation of this view.

The loving, forgiving, and self-sacrificing actions of Jesus on the cross show us perfectly what God is like and how God has always behaved. At the same time, the accusing, condemning, torturing, and murdering actions of the humans show us what hell is like and how we humans cause it.

The death of Jesus on the cross shows us what hell does, what hell is like, and how hell causes us to accuse, condemn, and kill others in God's name. The death and resurrection of Jesus reveals the gruesome reality of hell to us, and calls us away from it. Through His crucifixion, Jesus said, "Here is what hell does to humanity. You become monsters. So stop living in hell, and follow My ways into the kingdom of heaven." In this way, the death of Jesus sets people free here and now from the blindness of sin and the chains of captivity that keep us enslaved to the kingdom of hell.

In one of His first sermons, Jesus Himself said that He came to "heal the brokenhearted, proclaim liberty to the captives, and recovery of sight to the blind, to set at liberty those who are oppressed" (Luke 4:18). He was not just speaking about mental, emotional, and physical deliverance from depression, sorrow, blindness, and oppression, but also from the spiritual blindness and chains that had come upon us from the kingdom of hell. Jesus said that He descended into the hell of this earth to rescue, deliver, and set free all of us who were imprisoned, chained, and sitting in darkness.

Note that there is no mention in Luke 4:18-19 about how He came to rescue us from the eternal flames of everlasting torment. "Not a word of His being sent to save from a future endless hell; and yet He professes to tell the very object for which God did send Him!"[6] This is not an oversight on the part of Jesus. Quite to the contrary, He specifically and intentionally discards and rejects any hint of divine punishment or retribution, in this life or the next. We see this because Jesus stopped reading from Isaiah in mid-verse. Jesus stopped reading right before Isaiah spoke about "the day of vengeance of our Lord" (cf. Isa 61:1-2). If Jesus had wanted to warn His listeners about the possibility of eternal torment in hell, and if He had wanted to declare that He came to rescue and deliver people from such a place, this would have been the perfect opportunity with the perfect proof text to make such a claim.

But Jesus does no such thing. Instead, He stops reading halfway through a verse, and then sits down to teach. In this way, He not only fails to endorse the doctrine of divine punishment; He intentionally repudiates it instead. By stopping where He did, Jesus shows that He does not support or condone the common view of His day (and ours) that God punishes and torments people for their sins, either in this life or the next.

---

[6] Thayer, *The Origin and History of the Doctrine of Endless Punishment*, loc 1064.

This repudiation by Jesus was not lost on His listening audience. They heard what He said, and were so offended and shocked that He would deny that God punishes sinners, that they decided to take divine retribution into their own hands and kill Jesus. They thought Jesus was a heretic and a blasphemer, and took it upon themselves to silence Him and warn others about the dangers of His "false" teachings. But such is the response of all religious people when someone suggests that God always loves and only forgives.[7]

This reveals the point even more clearly, which Jesus perfectly unveiled on the cross: All "divine retribution" in Scripture is actually human retribution carried out in God's name. God doesn't kill and punish His enemies, for He has none. It is we humans who have enemies, and when God seems to be doing nothing about our enemies, we take it upon ourselves to punish and kill them, and we do it in God's name. This is hell, and Jesus died to bring an end to all such ways of living.

The apostles understood the message of Jesus, and taught much the same thing. Peter said that God sent

---

[7] Let me make a prediction before this book is even published ... If you want a modern example of this same activity today, just go read some of the 1-star reviews of this book on Amazon. The religious rule-keepers will call me a heretic and a false teacher, and will condemn me to hell for writing a book that challenges their fear-based doctrine of hell. Religious people love a vengeful deity, and will try to stop anyone who teaches that God is not like that. If we all lived in a previous century, these people would likely try to burn me, stone me, or crucify me, just as they did to Jesus.

Jesus to bless us by turning us away from our iniquities (Acts 3:26). Again, there is not a single word here about rescuing us from the flames of eternal conscious torment in hell. Jesus came to bless us by showing us why we sin and how we can stop sinning. Paul taught the same exact thing in Galatians 1:4. Jesus came, not to rescue us from eternal hell, but to rescue us from this present evil world and the hell that rules upon it.

And of course, since the apostles saw fit to carry on the message and purpose of Jesus, this means that we also will seek to help proclaim freedom to the captives, and set free those who are oppressed by the kingdom of hell. Just as Jesus came to this earth to set the captives free, and the apostles went into the hellish places of earth to do the same, so also, when we follow Jesus, He will lead into hell to set people free from hell as well.

This is a shocking idea for some Christians, but it is essential that we understand this important point. When we follow Jesus, we should not expect Him to lead us to soft and gentle places where blessings fall from heaven with every step we take. Instead, we can expect Jesus to lead us into hell so that we can break the chains of bondage on those who are there. Just as Jesus entered into our living hell to give us light and love and set us free, so also, when we follow Jesus, He leads us to storm the gates of hell with Him, to break down the walls and proclaim liberty to the captives. Jesus shows us that to rescue people from hell, we must enter into hell with Him.

STORMING THE GATES OF HELL WITH JESUS

In my book, *The Death and Resurrection of the Church*, I point out that the very first time Jesus talked about the church, He said that the gates of hell would not prevail against it (Matt 16:18). We also discussed this above when we looked at the word *hadēs*. When most Christians read Matthew 16:18, they imagine the church as an impregnable fortress, with huge, white, granite walls, behind which all the people of God huddle together in safety as the forces of evil attack from outside. Many believe Jesus is saying that the church He builds will be a safe place for Christians to wait out the onslaught of the invading legions of hell. Though the hordes of hell attack our gates, we are safe within the walls.

But in reality, Jesus says the exact opposite. In Matthew 16:18 Jesus says that the gates of hell will not prevail against the church. Jesus is not saying that His followers will be safely protected against the invading army of hell, but that the church itself will invade hell. Jesus is saying that His church will go to hell. That when the church follows Jesus, He will lead us to storm the gates of hell.

When Jesus describes the church He is building, it is not the church which has the high walls and thick gates, but hell. It is not the church that cowers in fear within a fortified castle, but it is Satan and his minions who huddle behind their blackened walls hoping the gates will hold. And it is not the devil and his forces that attack the gates of the church, but the church which attacks the gates of hell. It is the church which goes to hell to break down its gates and rescue those who are trapped within. The gates of hell are under siege by Jesus and His church.

And Jesus says the gates will fall before us. The gates of hell will not prevail. They will not stand. The gates of hell will fall to the invading church. All of this presupposes, of course, that the church is actually on the offensive. That the church is invading hell. That the church hears our marching orders and follows Jesus to hell.

But this also reveals the truth of what we have seen in this book. If the church is here in this world, and if Jesus is leading the church to attack the gates of hell now, then this means that hell is here and now as well. Hell is a kingdom on this earth, and Jesus launched His attack on the gates of hell by inaugurating the kingdom of God on earth. We are now in the middle of a struggle between two kingdoms, and Jesus has promised that the gates of hell will crumble and fall before us, so that His rule and reign will cover the earth, until every knee bows and every tongue confesses that Jesus Christ is Lord (Rom 14:11; Php 2:10).

When Jesus "descended into hell," it was not into the burning hell of afterlife myths, but into the hell that ruled and reigned upon this earth. He entered into hell to spark a great rebellion. He did this by ushering the kingdom of heaven into this world. Jesus did not "go to hell" after He died, for, like us, He lived in the midst of the kingdom of hell with all humanity. He entered into our hell to defeat it from within. And now He is calling us to do the same. We live in the belly of hell, and Jesus is calling us to set the captives free. In Jesus, God not only brought heaven down to earth; He also brought heaven down to hell, and the church is on the front line of this divine assault.

In his excellent article, "Hell is a Kingdom," Brad Jersak writes this:

> Jesus aims the church at the gates of *hadēs*, not heavenward. The movement is a downward arrow, from heaven down to hell on earth. What are the gates? Where are the gates? When the church does not know, it has lost its way. But at the foundation of his movement, Christ lays out his purpose: to overcome *hadēs* and rescue its prisoners.

> In this model, 'hell' or *hadēs* is a kingdom, located wherever people are imprisoned and oppressed by 'the powers' and death-dealers of 'this *present* darkness'—whether it's the military-industrial complex, corporate and political beasts, or any personal affliction, addiction, or obsession of choice.

Jesus is not calling the death-snares of this world *hadēs* metaphorically in anticipation of the actual subterranean post-mortem *hadēs*. Just the opposite: the afterlife mythology of *hadēs* is a metaphor for the actual human condition 'here above.' The rhetoric of hell is less about the eschatological future and more about educating us in the 'two ways' or 'two kingdoms' competing for our allegiance here on earth.[8]

The message of the kingdom of God and the mission of the church must be read in light of the idea that hell is a present reality.

It is to the humans caught in the kingdom of hell that Jesus said, "The Kingdom of God is at hand" (Matt 4:17) This is not a promise to claim as we wait to die so we can go to heaven and spend an eternal bliss with God. This is a war cry. It is the declaration of Jesus, the thief, entering into the strongman's house, to tie him up and steal his possessions. What possessions? This world and the human beings who live upon it (Matt 12:29).

The terrible, tragic reality about hell is that while the church gets so caught up in the debate about who goes to hell, and how long they will be there, and whether or not hell is a place of eternal suffering or temporary purification, we are ignoring the people who live in hell on

---

[8] Sinner Irenaeus, aka Brad Jersak, "Hell is a Kingdom: The Missing Motif Reconstructed" Online Article. http://www.clarion-journal.com/files/hell-is-a-kingdom-4.pdf I argued something nearly identical in my book, *The Death and Resurrection of the Church* (Dallas, OR: Redeeming Press, 2013).

earth all around us. The debate about hell keeps us from helping those who are suffering in the kingdom of hell here and now. Isn't that sadly ironic? We strengthen and enable hell by discussing and debating hell.

The great problem with much of Christian theology is that we have consigned both heaven and hell to the afterlife, thereby ignoring the present hell in which many people live. We are supposed to be the agents of heaven on this earth, storming the gates of hell, rescuing captives, and setting prisoners free. But instead, we fold our hands in prayer while we wait for the rapture or the day that we die so we can "go to heaven and be with God." We pass the time by burying our noses in the pages of Scripture, and filling our lives with debates about heaven and hell. Meanwhile, God is out walking the sin-darkened streets, hugging the prostitutes, feeding the hungry, and giving shelter to the homeless. And He is saying, "You want to be with Me? Then come follow Me into hell so we can turn it into heaven."

So where do you see the gates of hell in the lives of your family members? Where do you see the influence and power of hell in your neighborhood? Where do you see hell in your town or city? Where do you see people living in addiction, bondage, guilt, shame, and fear? Where are people abused, maligned, neglected, forgotten, overlooked, abandoned, and forsaken? Where they sold? Where are they starving? Where are they seeking love? Wherever you see such things, you see the gates of hell.

Now that you have seen hell, what can you do to go to hell and rescuing those who are there? What is the plan of attack to charge these gates and tear them down? With Jesus at your side, these gates will not prevail. So charge the gates of hell with Jesus, with the battle cry of love and grace on your lips.

And have no fear; He will not leave you alone in this battle. "Those who have known hell in their own lives may sense with gratitude that Jesus came into the worst place imaginable, the place where we sometimes are, to rescue us."[9] When you experience pain, suffering, and torment, know that Jesus is "God with us." He is with you in your pain. He is walking by your side. He will not leave you alone. He will never forsake you, but will walk with you through the valley of the shadow of death with an arm around your shoulder and word of comfort in your ear.

There are two kingdoms at war in this world, the kingdom of heaven and the kingdom of hell. Jesus is calling you to participate in one by storming the gates of the other. Will you answer the call of Jesus and go to hell with Him?

[9] N. T. Wright, *How God Became King: The Forgotten Story of the Gospels* (New York: Harper Collins, 2012), 262.

CONCLUSION

It turns out that pretty much everything we have been traditionally taught about hell is wrong. Hell is not a place of fiery torture and suffering for the unregenerate dead. While the Bible has a lot to say about hell, we have learned that hell is not a place where people scream in agony for all eternity. Instead, hell is a kingdom of death and destruction that is ruining lives right now here on earth, and Jesus is leading us to destroy the gates of hell and rescue those within.

We have also seen that Jesus does not talk about hell more than heaven. Quite to the contrary, Jesus talks about heaven much more than He talks about hell, and He talks about the Kingdom of God more than either (or both combined). He is more concerned with our experience of life *in this life* than our experience of life in the next. And when it comes to this life and the next, He does not scare people into living the way God wants, but loves and liberates them instead.

The surprising conclusion to this study is that when an atheist or an agnostic says "I can't believe in a God who tortures people for all eternity," you can now nod your head in agreement with them, recognizing that this sentiment is put into their hearts by the Holy Spirit. Those who hold to the traditional doctrine of hell as an everlasting torture chamber for the unredeemed are not listening to the Spirit of God. Atheists and agnostics who reject the traditional doctrine of hell are closer to the heart of God than the Christian who believes and teaches it. On this issue, it is as Jesus said to the religious leaders about the sinners and prostitutes: "Assuredly, I say to you that tax collectors and harlots enter the kingdom of God before you" (Matt 21:31).

The traditional doctrine of hell creates an atmosphere of fear, whereby people never fully see the heart of God, nor experience the rule and reign of God in their lives now. But once we see that hell is a kingdom of fear that rules and reigns on this earth here and now, and that the traditional doctrine of hell is part of this kingdom of fear, we are then free to liberate people from hell by showing them that God has always loved them, will always forgive them, and wants only what is best for them in this life and in eternity.

When we share this vision of God with others, they will no longer cringe before Him in fear, but will run to His open and outstretched arms, finally receiving the love and acceptance they have longed for, but have never found in this world. Hell is real, but it is here and it is now. So let the light of God's love so shine in your life, that others may see God for who He really is and will glorify God when the chains of darkness fall away and they are set free to follow Jesus in liberty, light, and love.

Have you been set free? If so, follow Jesus so that you can go to hell and set others free as well.

APPENDIX ON FIRE

The following Appendix is drawn from the entry on "Fire" in my Gospel Dictionary online course (which will eventually be made into a book as well). This course looks at 52 key words of the gospel by defining them and addressing several key passages which contain the word. The texts discussed below are the passages found in the Gospel Dictionary entry on "Fire."

ISAIAH 33:10-16

You shall conceive chaff, You shall bring forth stubble; Your breath, as fire, shall devour you. And the people shall be like the burnings of lime; Like thorns cut up they shall be burned in the fire. … The sinners in Zion are afraid; Fearfulness has seized the hypocrites: "Who among us shall dwell with everlasting burnings?" (Isa 33:11-12, 14).

Scores of passages from the Hebrew prophets could be considered which provide insight into what a Jewish person thought when they heard someone teach about everlasting fire. Isaiah 33:10-16 is representative of many of these prophetic texts, and provides perfect insight into what the Bible means when it refers to fire that comes upon people who disobey God. There are three key insights to note from this text which help guide our understanding of all the others.

First, Isaiah writes that the people of Zion will "conceive" chaff and "bring forth" stubble. Isaiah uses terms of conception and childbirth to speak of the works that these sinners produce. It is not their *lives* that are chaff, stubble, and thorns, but what they *produce* with their lives. Of course, when your entire life's work is destroyed, it may seem as if your life is destroyed as well. Indeed, when other prophetic passages (and later New Testament texts) talk about the destruction that comes upon people for their worthless way of living, it sometimes refers to the people *themselves* being destroyed, rather than the work of their hands. This is how it feels when, at the end of your life, you discover that everything you have worked for has amounted to nothing.

This is not to say that many prophetic passages (including those in the New Testament) do not have the death and destruction of actual human lives in view. Many of them do, as we shall see. But in each case, the passages are always referring to physical death and temporal destruction rather than to everlasting death or eternal physical torture in flames of fire. Some of the physical death and destruction during this life does indeed happen with literal flames when war comes upon a nation or its cities, and in such wars, many human beings do die. But once again, it is physical death that is in view; not eternal death in an everlasting place of torment.

But some point to Isaiah 33:14 as evidence that everlasting burning in the pit of hell is indeed what Isaiah has in view. This is the second important point to note from this text. While the term "everlasting" can indeed refer to a period of time that never ends, it can also refer to an event of limited duration which has effects that never end. This second explanation provides the proper understanding for Isaiah 33:14. In this text, people who are alive are saying that the works of their lives have been destroyed, and nobody in the future will know or hear of them. They are afraid because they have lived hypocritical lives, and see that all they have lived and worked for will be consumed by fire, and will have no lasting value, significance, or remembrance for all eternity. The fire that consumes these people and the works of their hands did indeed go out. It came upon them in 586 BC (when King Nebuchadnezzar invaded and destroyed Judah, along with Jerusalem and the temple) and has long since burned out. But none of their work remains. It burned to ashes long ago and has forever been forgotten.

Note that even though Zion was destroyed with "everlasting fire," the nation, its capitol city Jerusalem, the temple, and even the people of Zion rose again from the ashes. In 538 BC, the Persian ruler, King Cyrus, allowed the Hebrew people to return to their land where they eventually rebuilt the city and the temple. Though the everlasting fire prophesied by Isaiah destroyed many of the people and the works of their hands, this was not the end of the Hebrew people themselves, or their influence upon this world. They rebuilt and regained much of their former glory.

Furthermore, of the people who died in 586 BC, nothing is said by Isaiah or anyone else regarding their eternal state or destiny. It is only the work of their lives which was burned away into nothingness. In fact, it is possible that many of them are already with God, and will spend eternity with Him. We see evidence of this in the fact that Isaiah calls them "hypocrites." A hypocrite is someone who acts in ways that are contrary to their stated identity. As such, anybody can be a hypocrite. Jesus often called some of His followers hypocrites (Matt 15:7; Luke 13:15), and Paul once referred to Peter and Barnabas as hypocrites (Gal 2:11-13). Obviously, if someone is a hypocrite, this does not automatically mean they are truly part of the family of God, but it also does not necessarily mean that they will spend eternity in hell. It just means that they claim one thing about themselves but behave in ways that are opposite. This was true of the people in Isaiah's day, and many of these hypocrites will spend eternity with God.

The third and final thing to note from Isaiah 33:10-16 is that the fire comes from the people themselves. Isaiah writes, "Your breath, as fire, shall devour you" (Isa 33:11). While numerous passages in Scripture indicate that the fires of judgment comes from God, a look behind the curtain reveals that the fires of judgment that come upon human beings for their sinful ways are always self-inflicted. Sin bears its own punishment; rebellion carries within it the flames of ruin. Actions have consequences, and when we live in ways that are contrary to the will of God, these actions lead to destruction and devastation.

This is why God warns us against sin in the first place. God warns us against sin, not because He is a killjoy and wants to ruin our fun with arbitrary laws, but because He knows how best to live this life and get the most out of it. He also knows what happens when we do not live this life as He intends and seeks to warn us against such ways of living. When we sin, we hurt others and we hurt ourselves. And since God loves all of us, He does not want to see us get hurt, which is why He warns us about sin. Yet we often sin anyway, and so destruction comes. This is what Isaiah is teaching. The people were warned by the prophets, including Isaiah himself, about their sinful and hypocritical ways. But they continued to sin, and so the fire of judgment that comes upon them is a fire they lit themselves.

And while it is not always words that spark the flame, words are often the culprit, as Isaiah indicates. He says it is their "breath" that is the fire, which is a way of referring to the words that they speak. Indeed, near the end of Isaiah's life, King Hezekiah said some foolish words to the ambassadors from Babylon. He boasted to them about the treasures of the temple and showed them the riches that were within it. As a result, Isaiah told Hezekiah that because he had said and done these things, Babylon would come against the city and destroy it (2 Kings 20:12-19), which is exactly what happened (2 Kings 24:1-16). Eventually, the entire city, with the temple, was burned with fire, and its inhabitants were carted off into captivity (2 Kings 25:1-21).

So Isaiah 33:10-16 is a guiding paradigm for helping us understand all the passages in Scripture about fire. As we will see below, just as in Isaiah 33:10-16, none of the passages which teach about the destruction of people in fire are referring to the everlasting torment of people in flames where they scream and burn for all eternity. Instead, such texts refer to the worthless work of human hands that gets burned away by destructive forces in this world. All the work of their hands is turned to ash. When lime is burned in a fire or thorns are put to flame, nothing is left but a fine, white powder which blows away with the first puff of wind. So it will be for everything that some people have worked for in this life. As we keep this paradigm in mind, many of the New Testament passages which speak of fire make much more sense.

MATTHEW 3:10-12 (LUKE 3:16-17)

"And even now the ax is laid to the root of the trees. Therefore every tree which does not bear good fruit is cut down and thrown into the fire. I indeed baptize you with water unto repentance, but He who is coming after me is mightier than I, whose sandals I am not worthy to carry. He will baptize you with the Holy Spirit and fire. His winnowing fan is in His hand, and He will thoroughly clean out His threshing floor, and gather His wheat into the barn; but He will burn up the chaff with unquenchable fire."

This is a message from John the Baptist to the Jewish people who came to be baptized by him in the Jordan River. The words of John are sometimes used by modern teachers who want to defend the idea that those who don't have good works will end up in hell. They argue that all true Christians will prove the reality of their new birth by having good works. If someone doesn't have the necessary good works, they will lose their eternal life (or prove they never had it in the first place) and so will end up in hell. This misapplication of the text arises primarily from thinking that the fire John speaks about refers to hell.

In the context, John the Baptist is not talking about hell, but about impending temporal judgment on the people of Israel if they fail to repent. In verses 7-8, John warns the religious leaders that wrath was coming upon them, but they could escape this wrath if they bore fruits worthy of repentance. Scholars have always understood this as a prophecy about the destruction of Jerusalem in 70 AD. There is no thought of hell here, but only of temporal judgment on the nation of Israel and the people who are part of it.

The references to fire in Matthew 3:10-12 must be understood in light of this context. When John speaks of the ax being laid at the root of the tree, he is saying that the judgment is imminent. The ruling class of Israel was often compared to a tree (cf. Isa 11:1), and so John is saying that the rulers of Israel (such as the religious leaders) will be cut down unless they repent. But it was not just the rulers. While the *root* of the tree represents the leaders of the nation, from whom the teaching and direction of the nation comes, the tree itself represents the rest of the nation.[1]

Similarly, when John uses the image of the wheat and the chaff, he is describing the common practice of farmers gathering the harvest into their threshing floor where the wheat was separated from the chaff with a winnowing fan. A winnowing fan was a cross between a rake and a shovel so that large scoops of grain could be tossed into the air while also creating a bit of breeze.

---

[1] Craig S. Keener, *A Commentary on the Gospel of Matthew* (Grand Rapids: Eerdmans, 1999), 123.

The heavier grain would fall back to the ground, while the lighter chaff would get blown off to one side, where it would pile up against a low wall of the threshing floor. Once the wheat and chaff had been separated in this way, the grain would be taken away for storage, while the chaff would be set on fire. Since chaff is light and insubstantial, it burns quickly, leaving almost no ash behind and very little evidence that it ever existed. John says that this is what will happen to the Jewish leaders and those who follow their teachings if they do not all repent and turn to follow God.

This was a challenging teaching, for while most Jewish people expected God to judge the surrounding Gentile nations, few believed or taught that God would judge the nation of Israel itself. But this is what John preached. He was speaking to them as if they were Gentiles in need of repentance.

Repentance, of course, is not a necessary condition for receiving eternal life, but is an actual turning from sin toward obedience. We receive eternal life by believing in Jesus for it, not by repenting, or turning, from sinful activities. Such turning is extremely helpful in experiencing the blessings that God wants for us in this life. But those who do not repent will experience the devastating and destructive consequences of their sinful choices. This is what John warns the leaders about and the nation of Israel as a whole. John uses the image of fire to refer to this destruction.

When John says they will be "thrown into the fire" (Matt 3:10), he is not talking about being thrown into the fires of hell, but is using the imagery of cutting down a tree which then gets burned. Many trees are cut down and then used to make planks of wood for building and construction. But John says that Israel's leaders, and those who follow their teaching with a lack of repentance, will be symbolically cut down and burned. They will not be useful for anything once the judgment comes.

The baptism by fire in Matthew 3:11 is to be understood in a similar way. It does not refer to the coming of the Holy Spirit at Pentecost, but the impending destruction on Israel. Since baptism simply means "immersion," when something is immersed in fire, it is consumed by the fire. The fact that Jesus is said to be the one who will bring this immersion in fire does not mean that Jesus is the one who performs or sends the destruction. Instead, that the destruction will come upon Israel *by means of* their rejection of Him as the Messiah (cf. Luke 12:49).

This fire will not come upon all, for John teaches that the Messiah will gather the grain into the barn, while the chaff gets burned with unquenchable fire (Matt 3:12). This reference to unquenchable fire causes some to think that John is referring to hell. But the term "unquenchable" (Gk., *asbestos*) simply means that the fire completes its task. It burns all that it was meant to burn and fully consumes all that is fed into it.[2] Chaff does not burn eternally. Quite to the contrary, it burns quickly and then is gone. So the fact that this fire is described as unquenchable means that it burns hot and fast until there is nothing left to burn. It completes its task of burning so quickly and thoroughly, there is little trace of the flames or its fuel after the fire is gone.

Eusebius, in his *Ecclesiastical History* (Book VI: Chapter 41), writes about a Christian named Julian who was burned to death for being a Christian. Eusebius describes this fire as being an immense fire. The Greek words he uses are *puri asbestō,* exactly the same words used by John in Matthew 3:12. Eusebius goes on to use the exact same term to describe how other Christian martyrs were killed. Clearly, when Eusebius used this phrase, he was certainly not saying that these Christian martyrs went to hell. Instead, Eusebius was simply describing the immense inferno which consumed their bodies in the flames. Their bodies were reduced to ash in the fire; not sent to everlasting torment in hell.

This is what happened to the nation of Israel within one generation of John speaking these words. In 69-70 AD, some Jewish people tried to revolt against Rome,

[2] As an interesting side note, the term *asbestos* not only means "unquenchable" but also refers to calcium oxide (or quicklime) that was made in the lime kilns of the ancient world, which, after being slaked with water, was widely used for art and construction. When a human body is completely burned, the ash it leaves behind looks very similar to *asbestos,* or calcium oxide. See Isaiah 33:12.

and in response, Rome sent its military to destroy and burn the city of Jerusalem. Its walls were torn down, the temple was ruined, thousands of people were killed, and the city was burned to the ground. The rest of the nation scattered over the face of the earth. In the minds of many, the nation of Israel ceased to exist, and there was almost no trace of it to be found. It was not until 1948 that Israel was resurrected from the ashes and became a nation once again.

This unquenchable fire was not the first time that such fires came upon Jerusalem. Jeremiah prophesied that if the people of Jerusalem did not turn from their disobedience, then an unquenchable fire would be kindled upon the gates and palaces of Jerusalem (Jer 17:27). This fire came upon Jerusalem in 586 BC when Nebuchadnezzar burned the city, destroyed the temple, and razed Jerusalem to the ground. But even though Jeremiah said the fire was unquenchable, the fire burned itself out. Many years later, the city and temple were once again rebuilt. John follows in the prophetic steps of Jeremiah by saying that if the Jewish people do not turn from their ways, the same thing that happened to Jerusalem in the days of Jeremiah would also happen in their own day.

So John is not warning the people about going to hell where they will be tortured forever in flames. He is warning the people of Israel that a fire is coming upon them, and once it is ignited, it will not be extinguished, but will burn until there is nothing left to burn. This is not a reference to hell or the eventual annihilation of unregenerate dead, but only to the temporal destruction that would come upon the nation of Israel if they did not repent and return to God.

Throughout this text, John uses the images of pruning and burning to invite his listeners to repent and prepare their lives for the coming Messiah. He invites his listeners to burn the rubbish out of their own lives *now* in preparation for the Messiah, or have it burned up *later* when the Messiah comes. This is not a threat from John that the Messiah will send people to everlasting hell, but is instead a call to national repentance as a way of preparing the way for the Messiah. As we now know, however, the nation did not properly prepare themselves, and so the Messianic presence resulted in the fires of purification (cf. Luke 12:49).

MATTHEW 13:40, 42 (MATT 13:50)

"Therefore, the tares are gathered and burned in the fire, so it will be at the end of this age. … and will cast them into the furnace of fire. There will be wailing and gnashing of teeth."

Matthew 13 contains several parables which have consistently challenged interpreters and Bible students. In fact, even the first hearers of these parables were confused by them, as evidenced by the fact that the disciples asked Jesus to explain the parables to them (cf. Matt 13:10, 36). As Jesus explains the parables, He also tells His disciples that one reason He speaks in parables is so that people *do not* understand what He is talking about (cf. Matt 13:15-16). In other words, Jesus *wanted* people to be confused by His parables. Why? So that those who wanted to learn what He was talking about would come to Him for an explanation. Therefore, if you've ever been confused by a parable, be encouraged, for you are on the right track. Then allow this confusion to lead you to the feet of Jesus.

By doing this, you will come to discover three keys to understanding the parables of Jesus. First, if Jesus explains some of the symbolism of the parable, this will greatly help in your understanding. Second, it is critically important to learn the historical, cultural, and theological contexts behind the parables. What matters most in these parables is *not* what you and I want them to say, but what the original audience heard and understood Jesus to be saying. This means that if you want to understand these parables, you must get into the mindset of the original audience by seeking to understand their times and culture, how they read the Hebrew Bible, and what sort of concerns and issues were commonly discussed in *their* day, not ours. Finally, it is important to recognize that Jesus had a sense of humor. Many of His stories were told with a twinkle in His eye and a half-smile on His lips. The stories often contain half-jokes, plays on words, and surprising twists and turns that were intended to amuse, delight, and amaze His hearers. His parables used humor to instruct the hearers about what was most important.

With these three keys in mind, a few cultural, historical, and theological details will help us better understand what Jesus is saying in Matthew 13 (and in *all* of His parables). First, most of Jesus' parables are about the kingdom of God. Many people today, when they think about the kingdom of God, think about heaven. But nobody in the days of Jesus thought this. They had daily, negative experiences with the "kingdom of Rome," and they longed for the promised and prophesied Messiah to come and overthrow Rome so that the kingdom of God could take over. The kingdom of God, therefore, is the rule and reign of God on earth, here and now as a replacement for the kingdoms of men.

Second, the people to whom Jesus spoke were nearly all Jewish, who had been immersed in the themes and ideas of the Hebrew Scriptures since birth. Many modern Christians spend little to no time studying the "Old Testament," and as a result, fail to understand much of what the New Testament teaches. This is especially true with the parables. A deep understanding of Old Testament concepts, imagery, and themes is necessary to understand the parables of Jesus.

Finally, it is critical to recognize that the parables of Jesus were politically and religiously subversive, but not primarily against Rome, as the Jewish people wanted and expected. His parables were subversive to the politics and religion of Judaism. This is one of the reasons Jesus didn't want everyone to understand what He was saying. If people among the Jewish political and religious ruling class understood what Jesus was saying, they would have crucified Him much sooner than they did. If we fail to grasp the subversive and dangerous elements in the parables of Jesus, we have likely misunderstood them.

So with all of this in mind, Matthew 13 contains seven parables about the kingdom of God, which is also called the kingdom of heaven. And despite the popular teaching that is found in some Christian circles today, not a single one of these parables is about how to go to heaven when you die, or how to tell if you are truly a Christian. They are not about the afterlife at all. Instead, all seven are about the nature, character, birth, and growth of the kingdom of God on earth.

For example, the Parable of the Four Soils (Matt 13:1-8) is not about who is a Christian and who isn't, or how to determine who gets to go to heaven and who doesn't. The parable is about how different people respond to the teaching about the kingdom (Matt 13:19). Any believer *or* unbeliever can be *any one* of the four soils. Note as well, by the way, the humor in the Parable of the Four Soils. This sower went out and scattered seed all over the place, willy-nilly, not caring where the seed landed. Seed was valuable, and no sower in that day would have been this careless. But apparently, God is careless with the truths of the kingdom, scattering them all over the place without much concern for where they land. It is not very "efficient," but God has never cared much for efficiency.

All of this helps us grasp the meaning of the Parable of the Wheat and the Tares in Matthew 13:24-30 and the explanation by Jesus in Matthew 13:36-43. By understanding this parable, we will discover a surprising truth about the fire mentioned in 13:42 (and 13:50) and the identity of the ones who are burned in this fire.

Jesus says that the kingdom of heaven is like a man who sows good seed in his field (13:24). The kingdom of heaven, of course, is not heaven, but is the way God brings heaven down to earth as Jesus and His disciples spread the rule and reign of God over the earth. It begins with the sower spreading seed. But an enemy comes and sows bad seeds in the field, so that a bunch of weeds, or tares, spring up among the wheat.

The seed that Jesus refers to should be read in light of the first parable of Matthew 13, the Parable of the Four Soils. There, Jesus teaches that the seed is the Word of God. But here in Matthew 13 we see that there are two types of seeds that can be scattered. There are the seeds of kingdom, and the seeds of the devil. These are two contrasting kingdoms, which result in two contrasting types of people. But initially, when the seeds first begin to sprout, there is great difficulty in deciding between the wheat and weeds.

When the servants discover the weeds, they ask how the weeds came to exist and what the owner wants to do about them (Matt 13:25-27). This is where some humor enters into this parable. As anyone who has ever had a field (or even a flower garden) knows, one does not need an enemy to sow bad seeds for weeds to pop up and grow. So when Jesus describes an enemy sowing bad seeds in the owner's field, His audience would have likely snickered a little bit. No enemy would work so hard to ruin a crop.[3] If an enemy really wanted to ruin someone's crop, there were better and easier ways to do it. But the enemy does sow bad seeds in this story, which not only shows his own foolishness, but also provides a humorous backdrop for the rest of the story.

---

[3] Though some suggest this did indeed occur. See A. J. Kerr, "Matthew 13:25. Sowing Zizania Among Another's Wheat: Realistic or Artificial?," *JTS* 48 (1997): 108. However, this article does not find actual evidence of historical accounts of enemies sowing weeds in someone else's fields. Instead, it reports only hints of possible laws from a later time period that prohibit such actions (hints of this law are found in a document from 533 AD). Of course, the existence of a law prohibiting an action does indicate that the action might have been common. But the hints of the laws could also refer to the natural movement of seeds by wind and animals. In other words, the law could be saying that if your land is full of noxious or dangerous weeds, and the seeds from these weeds spread to your neighbor's wheat field through natural means, you are partly liable for the destruction of their crop. Therefore, such a person should burn the weeds in their field or cut the weeds down before they go to seed. Similar laws are in effect today.

Many commentaries and articles point out that the bad seed in the field is most likely darnel, which looks exactly like wheat until harvest time. It is a mimic weed. This is why the owner of the field tells his servants to just let the two plants grow side by side until harvest (Matt 13:27-30). Prior to harvest, it would be nearly impossible to tell the two apart, and so any attempt to remove the darnel would likely result in the loss of wheat as well. Once harvest arrives, wheat turns golden and the heavy heads of grain droop down toward the ground, but darnel tends to remain greener for longer and will continue to stand upright.

Since wheat and darnel appear so identical, the presence of the tares in the field goes unnoticed until the grain begins to "go to crop," or develop a head. This is why the servants only notice the tares once the wheat begins to mature (Matt 13:26). So they ask the owner if he wants them to pull out the tares, but since wheat and darnel look quite similar to each other prior to full maturity, the owner tells his servants to leave the weeds alone and let them grow along with the wheat. At harvest, the reapers will go through and gather the tares, and then they can harvest the wheat (Matt 13:30). The tares are thrown into the fire to be burned.

One of the reasons it was necessary to first harvest and then burn the tares is because darnel can be deadly to livestock and humans if consumed in large quantities. Smaller quantities will cause dizziness if baked into bread or brewed with beer. In fact, there are historical records of people actually cultivating darnel for this very reason, treating it like an ancient form of cannabis. But if too much is consumed, darnel can cause great sickness and even death.[4]

When Jesus explains this parable to His disciples, He begins by identifying the various characters in the story. He says that the sower is the Son of Man (Matt 13:37), which is one of Jesus's favorite titles for Himself. The field which the sower plants is the world, and so the good seeds that go out into the world are the sons of the kingdom (Matt 13:38). The tares are therefore the opposite of the sons of the kingdom; Jesus calls them the sons of the wicked one. The enemy is the devil, the harvest is the end of the age, and the reapers are the angels (Matt 13:38).

Now each of these characters need to be more carefully explained, but first, it is critical to notice that there is one set of characters Jesus does not identify. This missing identification is the key to the parable. Who is it that Jesus does not identify? It is the servants. Jesus does not explain who the servants represent. I have heard some say that the servants are the reapers, but when the owner is speaking to the servants, he clearly identifies the reapers as a different group (cf. Matt 13:30).

---

4   https://www.atlasobscura.com/articles/wheats-evil-twin-has-been-intoxicating-humans-for-centuries

The solution to this problem is to return to the image of the field as the world. The Son of Man sowed seeds in the field, and the servants went out and worked in the field. Since the field is the world, and Jesus is the one who sowed the seeds in the world, then the servants are the ones who tend, cultivate, and work in the fields. Who are they? They are the followers of Jesus. They are disciples. The servants in the story are the Christians. Christians, or followers of Jesus, are those who work in the world to grow and expand the kingdom of God which Jesus planted and initiated.

But if the servants are Christians, then who are the "sons of the kingdom"? Jesus says the seed is the sons of the kingdom. But if the servants are Christians, then the sons of the kingdom (the seed) cannot also be Christians. To put it another way, since the servants are the followers of Jesus, then this means that the sons of the kingdom must be someone else. And when we understand the identity of the sons of the kingdom, we will also understand the identity of the sons of the evil one (which might be better translated as "sons of wickedness"; Matt 13:38).

To understand the identity of both, it is first necessary to understand how the word "son" is used in Scripture. Typically, a "son" is understood to be a child of someone else. But the word "son" can also be used metaphorically. When the word "son" is used in connection to a concept or idea, instead of to a person or family, it refers to the characteristics or inner attributes of someone, rather than to the person themselves. So "sons of this world" are contrasted with "sons of light" in Luke 16:8 (cf. John 12:36; 1 Thess 5:5). A student or disciple of the Pharisees could be called a "son of the Pharisees" (Matt 12:27; Acts 23:6). Scripture can also speak of "sons of the resurrection" (Luke 20:36), "sons of this age" (Luke 16:8; 20:34), "sons of disobedience" (Eph 2:2; 5:6), "sons of the devil" (Acts 13:10) and numerous other similar terms. Such descriptions are not literal (a son of the devil is not *literally* the biological offspring of the devil), but are instead figurative and symbolic ways of referring to someone's character and behavior.

So who are the sons of the kingdom and the sons of wickedness, and how can we tell? One more contextual key is needed before an answer is discovered. In the context before these seven parables of Matthew 13, the Jewish religious leaders accused Jesus of operating according to the power of Beelzebub (Matt 12:24). Jesus responds with a teaching full of symbolism and imagery (Matt 12:25-37) that shows up again in the parables of Matthew 13. He speaks of kingdoms (12:25, 28), sons of the Pharisees (12:27), gathering and scattering (12:30), this age and the age to come (12:32), and the fruitfulness (or lack thereof) of various trees (12:33-37). All the parables of Matthew 13 must be read in light of this confrontation between Jesus and the Pharisees. While they were accusing Him of doing the devil's work, He responded by saying that it was not Him, but they, who were committing blasphemy and speaking evil from their hearts (Matt 12:35).

But how could the onlookers, the disciples, tell who was right? They had grown up being taught to love, respect, and listen to the religious Pharisees. But now they loved, respected, and listened to Jesus. Yet the Pharisees were saying that the teachings of Jesus were from the devil, and now Jesus was saying the same thing about the teachings of the Pharisees. So what were the disciples to do? How could they know who was right and who was wrong? If you have ever had two Bible teachers, both of whom you greatly respect, disagree with each other, then you understand the dilemma of the disciples. How were they to choose between Jesus and the Pharisees?

The Parable of the Wheat and the Tares is the answer to their question. In this parable, Jesus, the Son of Man, tells His servants, the disciples, that two types of seeds have been sown which result in two types of sons of two types of kingdoms. But which was which and how could they know? Jesus tells His disciples to wait until the harvest "at the end of this age" (Matt 13:40). But this is not helpful for them if the end of the age is thousands of years in the future when the new heavens and new earth are created.

So what if "this age" was the age in which Jesus and His disciples were living, and the age to come was the age that followed (cf. Matt 12:32)? Indeed, Scripture indicates in numerous ways and places that a new age did indeed come into existence with the death and resurrection of Jesus and the birth of the church. The death and resurrection of Jesus gave birth to a new age, the age of the kingdom of God, the church age. There were birth pains and many travails as the old age died and the new age began (as Jesus discusses in Matthew 24–25), but the resurrection of Jesus and the birth of the church was the sign that the new age had begun.

Jesus tells His disciples that while it is difficult for them to decide between the wheat and the tares right now, it will become clear to them at the harvest. Though they had trouble deciding between the way of Jesus and the way of the Pharisees, the end of the age would make it clear when the messengers of God arrived and took away the tares. Here we have the religiously subversive nature of the parable. The disciples of Jesus are faced with a choice: they can either follow the way of Jesus or the way of the Pharisees. Jesus tells them that they don't need to figure it out. In fact, it would be dangerous for them to try to do so, for they will not be able to properly and perfectly tell the difference between the good teaching and bad. Instead, they should just wait for the harvest and let the reaping angels separate the wheat from the chaff.

And this is indeed what happened in 70 AD. The way of the Pharisees was destroyed when Jerusalem and the temple were burned with fire. This does not mean that the Pharisees and all who followed their teachings were unregenerate sinners who will spend eternity burning in hell. Everlasting torture in hell is not anywhere in view with this parable. To the contrary, the "furnace of fire" imagery is drawn from Daniel 3:19-25 where Daniel's friends are thrown into a furnace of fire, but only their bonds are burned as they walk around in the flame with one shining like the Son of God. (As a side note, the "Son of Man" imagery is drawn from Daniel 7:13-14, and the imagery of the righteous shining like the sun in Matthew 13:43 is drawn from Daniel 12:3). It can be assumed that when Jerusalem was destroyed by the Roman army, many Christians were also consumed by the flames. But Christianity survived, as it was not (and is not) dependent upon a city, a temple, or a priesthood. Yet the Jewish Pharisaical religion *was* dependent upon such things, and so it died out when Jerusalem fell.

And so we see that the burning of the chaff in the furnace of fire is not about God sending people to hell where they will burn forever and ever. Instead, it is about the disciples of Jesus allowing God to be the one to judge between right and wrong, good and evil, especially when it comes to deciding between the teachings of Jesus and the teachings of the Pharisees. As a result of the events in Genesis 3 when Adam and Eve tried to gain for themselves what should be left up to God, we humans have always done a poor job of judging between good and evil. So God invites us to leave all such judgment up to Him. And this is what Jesus tells His disciples to do as well.

In fact, this theme is found right within the parable itself. In Matthew 13:41, Jesus speaks about "all things that offend." This is the Greek word *skandala* (cf. Matt 5:29-30; 18:6-9), which is the stumbling block, the thing that leads humans to sin (cf. Matt 16:23). We trip over the stumbling block when we listen to the accuser (Satan) and improperly judge between right and wrong, good and evil. For example, when Peter said it was wrong for Jesus to go to Jerusalem to die, this was an incorrect judgment and so Jesus called Peter "Satan," and said that this wrong judgment would cause Peter to stumble in His God-given tasks. Later, before Jesus is arrested, He warns them that they will stumble and desert Him because they will make a wrong judgment about what was happening (Matt 26:31). He does not want them to make bad judgments and suffer the consequences of these judgments, and so He invites His disciples to leave these judgments up to God.

The same truth applies to us today. Humans make bad judgments, and when we do, we stumble and get burned. But this does not mean we go to hell; it means we face the consequences of our poor decisions. While such consequences are painful, we need not worry too much about them, for they do not say anything about our eternal destinies, and indeed, only serve to purify us so that we shine like the sun in the kingdom of the Father (Matt 13:43).

This parable, therefore, is not about how God sends wicked people to burn forever in the furnace of hell, but is instead about how the disciples of Jesus should allow God alone to make judgments between good teaching and bad teaching, and allow His angels to burn up the bad teaching "at the end of this age." This is what happened with the destruction of Jerusalem and the temple in 70 AD.

Some may object that the description of weeping and gnashing of teeth from Matthew 13:42 indicates that Jesus does indeed have hell in mind. The phrase "weeping and gnashing of teeth" occurs six times in Matthew (8:12; 13:42, 50; 22:13; 24:51; 25:30), once in Luke (13:28), and nowhere else in the New Testament. The phrase is not found in any classical Greek literature or in the LXX, and so we must depend on contextual clues within the New Testament itself to determine the meaning of this phrase. This phrase was discussed earlier in this book, but a summary of what it means is helpful here.

What is most important to recognize is that Matthew's six uses of this phrase are all in reference to those who are "part of the family," that is, those who belong to God. In Matthew 8:12, it refers to those who are sons of the kingdom. In 13:42, it refers to those who were gathered out of God's kingdom, indicating that they were in it to begin with. In 13:50, the image is of two types of people caught in the same net (which is a symbol of the kingdom of God), and one type is pulled out and experiences this weeping and gnashing of teeth. In 22:13, the phrase describes a man who is actually at the wedding banquet. And in both 24:51 and 25:30, it is used in connection to the experience of a servant who did a poor job serving his master.

What this seems to indicate, therefore, is that the weeping and gnashing of teeth does not refer to the tortured experience of unregenerate people in hell, but instead to the experience of some people who belonged to God in some way and should have known what He expects of them and how they are to live. While this can refer to believers who might have a negative experience at the Judgment Seat of Christ or who experience the discipline of God in this life (cf. Matt 8:13),[5] it can also refer to Jewish people who should have known that Jesus was the promised Messiah.

The phrase "weeping and gnashing of teeth," therefore, has nothing whatsoever to do with hell. It is instead a graphic and descriptive middle-eastern way of expressing profound regret and shame, and maybe even fury. The weeping and wailing speaks of "extreme loss,

---

[5] The "sons of the kingdom" are believers, and the "outer darkness" does not refer to hell, but to the darkness outside the party. See Zane Hodges and Robert Wilkin, *What is the Outer Darkness?* (Denton, TX: GES, 2016). For more on this phrase, see the chapter on the eight biblical words for hell.

not so much of actual pain" while the gnashing or grinding of teeth could refer to fury and anger directed at someone else.[6]

So when we read in Matthew 13:42 (and later in 13:50) about the tares being cast into the furnace of fire where there is weeping and gnashing of teeth, we should not read this as an image of God casting people into everlasting flames of hell where they scream and wail for all eternity at the painful suffering inflicted upon them. Instead, Jesus is saying that when judgment comes after the end of the age (which ended at the resurrection of Jesus), the good and bad teachings will be made clear because one set will survive and the other will be burned up. This judgment occurred in 70 AD when the city of Jerusalem, along with the Jewish temple, was destroyed and burned by the Roman military. On that day, there were not only flames and fire, but also much weeping and gnashing of teeth.

The Jewish historian Flavius Josephus, in his history of the destruction of Jerusalem, writes that in the time right before the Roman military attacked and burned the city and the temple, chariots and soldiers were seen to be running around in the clouds around Jerusalem, and voices from heaven were heard calling for the removal of the city. It sounds like fiction, and Josephus admits as much, but he also says that many people wit-

---

[6] Fudge, *The Fire That Consumes*, 171.

nessed these events and told him about them. Here is what he writes:

> Besides these, a few days after that feast, on the one and twentieth day of the month Artemisius, [Jyar,] a certain prodigious and incredible phenomenon appeared: I suppose the account of it would seem to be a fable, were it not related by those that saw it, and were not the events that followed it of so considerable a nature as to deserve such signals; for, before sun-setting, chariots and troops of soldiers in their armor were seen running about among the clouds, and surrounding of cities. Moreover, at that feast which we call Pentecost, as the priests were going by night into the inner [court of the temple,] as their custom was, to perform their sacred ministrations, they said that, in the first place, they felt a quaking, and heard a great noise, and after that they heard a sound as of a great multitude, saying, "Let us remove hence."[7]

Could it be that these were the angels whom Jesus prophesied about in Matthew 13:39-41, who were sent to separate the wheat from the chaff at harvest time?

The parable of the wheat and the tares in Matthew 13:24-30 and 36-43 is not about God sending sinners to hell to burn for all eternity. It is instead a prophecy about the destruction of Jerusalem and the Jewish religion (as practiced in that day), and how the disciples of Jesus should not seek to judge or decide between right and wrong when it came to the teaching of Jesus or their

---

[7] Flavius Josephus, *The Wars of the Jews,* 6.5.3.

own Jewish traditions. They should instead allow God and the angels to make this separation on their own, which is what happened in 70 AD.

MATTHEW 18:8-9

"If your hand or foot causes you to sin, cut it off and cast it from you. It is better for you to enter into life lame or maimed rather than having two hands or two feet, to be cast into the everlasting fire. And if your eye causes you to sin, pluck it out and cast it from you. It is better for you to enter into life with one eye, rather than having two eyes, to be cast into hell fire."

The teachings of Jesus in Matthew 18 are very similar to Matthew 5:22, 29. But we are discussing this text of Matthew 18:8-9 because it contains extra details which help us understand both passages.

Jesus speaks of *hell* and describes it as being a place of everlasting fire. The word for *hell* is *gehenna*, which, as we learned in the chapter about the eight words for hell, was a literal place outside the walls of Jerusalem. It was also known as the Valley of Hinnom and was a horrifying place of worms, fire, decay, and death. It was a garbage heap that had been set on fire to consume its contents and cover the stench of rotting refuse and corpses. The everlasting fire, therefore, refers to the fire of Gehenna that burned day and night, seemingly forever and ever.

The nature of city garbage dumps, however, is that they attract the poor and the sick. In that day (as in our own day), those who were stricken by poverty or sickness would visit the garbage dump in an attempt to find something to eat or sell. For example, in the days of Jesus, scavenging for food and clothing in the garbage dump was often the only way that lepers could survive. It is the lepers that often frequented Gehenna which led Jesus to teach what He does here in Matthew 18:8-9.

While leprosy itself does not cause someone to lose their eyes, ears, nose, or limbs, it was not uncommon for people with advanced cases of leprosy to lose body parts or appendages due to infection, amputation, or accident. If someone has no feeling in their feet, it is possible for them to accidentally put their foot too close to the fire at night while sleeping, thereby causing it to burn. If they are burned bad enough, they might need to amputate their foot.

This is the situation Jesus has in mind. Some people, when they first saw a hint of leprosy on their hand or foot, would rather cut off their hand or foot and go through life maimed, than be officially diagnosed with leprosy and be sent to live in Gehenna, where the fire burned day and night. Similarly, if someone's eye is injured, and it begins to putrefy or rot, it is better to pluck it out than to leave it in and allow the corruption to spread to the rest of the body. If this were to happen, the person would eventually be sent to Gehenna. It is better to lose an eye than to spend your last days there.

When this cultural context is understood, we see that Jesus is not warning people that if they sin in this life, they will end up in a fiery torture chamber in the next. Instead, Jesus is saying that sin leads to damaging and destructive consequences in *this* life. If we want to avoid those consequences, some drastic steps are sometimes needed. A person who finds themselves infected with the rot of addiction or the decay of bad influences should cut those places or people out of their life so that the disease does not spread and cause greater damage to themselves or to others whom they love.

So Matthew 18:8-9 is not a warning about the afterlife, but an instruction about preserving your life here and now. The surrounding context gives several applications of exactly how to do this. Jesus teaches that His disciples should cut pride out of their life if they want to experience the kingdom of God (Matt 18:1-5). He provides instructions for how to rescue a lost sheep (Matt 18:10-14) by going to them with one or two others. But if they do not heed or listen, then they should be cut out of your life as well (Matt 18:15-20). Jesus also speaks about the importance of forgiving others as we have been forgiven (Matt 18:21-35) so that we give up our need to be repaid for wrongs done against us. It is better to go through life without pride, certain friends, and a defense of justice than to maintain such things but to lose yourself, your family, your friends, and your finances in the process. This is what Jesus is teaching.

Matthew 18:8-9 is not a warning about everlasting punishment in hell, but is rather a warning about the experience of a hellish life here and now. Some struggle with this interpretation, however, because of the reference to *everlasting* fire. They argue that since this fire is everlasting, it must go on for eternity, and not just during this life. To help us understand what Jesus means by this phrase, let us consider Matthew 25:41 where it is also mentioned.

MATTHEW 25:41

"Then he will also say to those on the left hand, 'Depart from Me, you cursed, into the everlasting fire prepared for the devil and his angels:'"

This text is one of the more difficult passages to understand about fire. However, when studied in connection with what the Bible teaches about hell, this verse is not as difficult as it first appears. As discussed previously in this book, the Bible teaches that hell is a kingdom which is diametrically opposed to the kingdom of heaven. Everything that is true of the kingdom of heaven is also true of the kingdom of hell, but in opposite form. This will help us understand the parallels in this passage between "the fire prepared for the devil and his angels" and "the kingdom prepared for you" (Matt 25:34).

A proper understanding of this passage is further aided by taking careful note of the context in which it occurs. The entire Olivet Discourse (Matt 24–25) must be understood as Jesus' answer to two questions from the disciples. They had just come from the temple where Jesus had said that the entire structure would be destroyed. By this, He wasn't just referring to the building, but to everything it represented. Jesus was "not impressed with splendid buildings" or the religious establishment they represented.[8] He wanted both to disappear so that people could personally connect with God in freedom and grace. So Jesus told His disciples that it would all be destroyed, not just the temple, but what it represented as well (Matt 24:1-2).

In response, the disciples ask two questions. They want to know when these events will take place, and what will be the signs of His coming and the end of the age (Matt 24:3). At this point, the disciples do not realize that Jesus will die on the cross, rise again, and then ascend into heaven. So when they ask about the signs of His coming, they are not referring to His "second coming" the way we think of it today, but to their expectation of how He will be coming into His throne. They expected the Messiah to overthrow Roman rule and come into His rightful place as the ruler of the entire world. These events would indicate the end of the age and the start of the new, Messianic age. They wanted to

---

[8] Keener, *Matthew*, 559.

know when the war with Rome would begin, and what signs would show its beginnings.

All of the teachings and parables of Matthew 24–25 must be read in light of these two questions. Jesus not only seeks to answer their questions, but also to correct their thinking about His coming. Jesus wants to show them that His coming from heaven to earth has already occurred in His incarnation, and that the works they have already seen Him perform are the only type of works that His kingdom produces. His kingdom will spread over the face of the earth as promised, but not with military might, political power, or religious regulations (cf. Luke 4:1-13). It will spread through peace and grace.

He first provides the signs of His coming at the end of the age (Matt 24:4-51). As indicated everywhere else in Matthew, the "age" in which Jesus and His disciples lived ended with His death and resurrection. The new age began with the birth of the church in Acts 2, but there was a transitional period with the dying throes of the old age and the birth pains of the new. Some of these dying throes of the old age were evident in the destruction of Jerusalem, its temple, and the religion it represented.

Many seek to consign the events of Matthew 24–25 into some future time period, but Jesus states in Matthew 24:34 that all these things will take place within one generation. One must engage in several hermeneutical contortions to get this statement to refer to more than forty years. But if we take it at face value, then we see that the words of Jesus did come true within one generation. Less than forty years after Jesus spoke these words, the Roman military laid siege to Jerusalem, and eventually razed it to the ground, burned the temple, and killed over one million Jewish people. Some of those who heard Jesus say these words saw them come to pass, just as He promised.

At the end of this teaching section, Jesus presents the two possible options for living in this world as one of His followers (Matt 24:45-51). They can either look for His coming which leads them to love and serve others, or they can think that He is not coming and so live selfishly and violently toward others. Again, when Jesus talks about His coming, He is not referring to His future "second coming" but to the coming of His kingdom in power and glory, which will spread over the face of the earth. Jesus wants His followers to choose whether they will join Him and participate in spreading His kingdom over the earth, or if they will think that His coming is delayed (cf. 2 Pet 3:4), and so will live according to the values and principles (the kingdom) of this world.

Based on these two options, Jesus then presents three parables as illustrations. These three parables of Matthew 25 compare and contrast the two kingdoms and how the followers of Jesus will affect and be affected by both. And since Matthew 24:45-51 contrasted "believing and wise" servants with "unbelieving and foolish" servants, the three parables of Matthew 25 make a similar contrast. The followers of Jesus are to live in a constant state of readiness for His return and also work to advance the kingdom while they wait. They live in a state of readiness by believing He will return soon, and they advance the kingdom by loving and serving others in His absence. The three parables of Matthew 25 reveal what this new kingdom will be like (and not like) and how His followers can participate in its coming through their beliefs and behaviors.

These three parables not only show the two ways of living in this world as one of His followers, but they also correct the thinking of the disciples about what the kingdom of heaven will look like.[9] Jesus wants them to know that His rule and reign will not be like the Roman rule and reign. Jesus is not trying to simply replace Caesar. Though this is what most Jewish people wanted and expected, Jesus did not come to inaugurate a kingdom that looked and acted like the kingdom of Caesar. The first and last parables, therefore, describe truths related to the kingdom of God, while the middle parable, the Parable of the Talents, describes truths related to the kingdom of Caesar. The followers of Jesus must decide which kingdom they will serve.

---

[9] Capon, *Kingdom, Grace, Judgment*, 4.

Jesus first describes the kingdom of heaven with the Parable of the Wise and Foolish Bridesmaids (Matt 25:1-13). The point of this parable is to encourage His followers to live in a constant state of readiness for the coming of the kingdom. This passage is not about who is going to heaven and who is not. This story is about participating in the wedding celebration when the bridegroom arrives and the kingdom party begins. People can have eternal life and still miss out on most of the party. Whether we watch or sleep, we will live together with Him (1 Thess 5:10).

The next parable is the Parable of the Talents (Matt 25:14-30). This text was considered previously in this book, but since this parable has been terribly misunderstood, a summary of how it should be properly understood is appropriate here. Most assume that it also is about the kingdom of heaven and how Jesus is the man who traveled to a far country and will return, at which point He blesses those who helped increase His wealth and punishes those who did not. But Jesus does not say that He is describing the kingdom of heaven. While most Bible translations do include the words "the kingdom of heaven" in Matthew 25:14, these words have been added by the translators and do not exist in the Greek.

Instead, having just invited his followers to look eagerly for the coming of the kingdom of heaven, Jesus now goes on to warn them what life would be like for them if they tried to live in the kingdom of this world. Numerous lines of evidence support this view. Chief among them is the fact that the actions of this man who travels to a far country would have been understood as quite evil in the first century Mediterranean world. They not only closely follow the actions and behaviors of King Herod and how he went to Rome to become the king of Israel, but the values of this man also reveal the opposite of what Jesus taught and encouraged.

The first century Mediterranean world was guided by the cultural values of honor and shame. Modern western culture is guided by materialism. Today, we value any activity which gets more money and gains more possessions. In an honor-shame culture, such activities were great sins. They believed that money and possessions were zero-sum commodities, which meant that the only way for one person to gain more money and possessions was by taking it away from someone else.[10] This was very shameful behavior. "Anyone who suddenly acquired something 'more' was automatically judged to be a thief."[11] The first two servants, like their master, were exploiters. "They both use the same exploitive economy to increase the plunder that constitutes the master's wealth."[12] This means that "from the

---

[10] Malina and Rohrbaugh, *Social-Science Commentary on the Synoptic Gospels*, 124, 385-386, 400.

[11] Pilch, *The Cultural World of Jesus, Cycle A*, 164.

[12] Herzog II, *Parables as Subversive Speech*, 161.

peasant point of view … it was the third slave who acted honorably, especially since he refused to participate in the rapacious schemes of the greedy, rich man."[13]

So Jesus is saying that if one of his disciples does not look with anticipation for the coming of the kingdom of heaven, their only other option is to participate with the kingdom of this world, by imitating it in its greedy ways. If a person does not follow the way of Jesus, they will either behave very shamefully in stealing from their brethren, or will receive harsh judgment and punishment from the rulers of this world for not participating in their greedy game. The rulers of this world expect and demand their subjects to follow their twisted, thieving ways to enrich themselves at the expense of others. Those who refuse to follow these marching orders will be punished by the rulers, and will be banished to "the dark world of poverty, misery, and certain death."[14] But when followers of Jesus experience such treatment at the hands of the rulers of this world, they should not despair, for the punishment of worldly rulers is not the end of the matter.

Jesus now goes on in the final parable of Matthew 25 to show His disciples that even though they might be rejected by the kingdoms of men, they will not be rejected or despised by the kingdom of God. Since the

---

[13] Malina and Rohrbaugh, *Social-Science Commentary on the Synoptic Gospels*, 125.

[14] Herzog II, *Parables as Subversive Speech*, 166.

values and behaviors of the two kingdoms are diametrically opposed to one another, the consequences for actions are different as well. While a lack of greed brought punishment from the kingdoms of the world, this same behavior brings praise and honor in the kingdom of heaven. With the Parable of the Sheep and the Goats (Matt 25:31-46), Jesus shows the distinctive characteristics that separate the two kingdoms, and calls His disciples to choose which kingdom they will serve.

In this final parable, Jesus reveals that He, as the Son of Man Shepherd King, will be the one who decides which of His servants worked for the kingdom of heaven and which worked for the kingdom of earth. And while the Parable of the Talents showed that the kingdom of earth praises those who steal from the poor and give it to the rich, the Parable of the Sheep and the Goats reveals that the kingdom of heaven works the opposite way. Jesus, the Lord of the kingdom of heaven, values the poor and needy, and gives praise and honor to those who tend to their needs.

So this final parable of Jesus ties the preceding two parables together. Jesus told two parables showing two different ways of living in this world. One can either live in in the light of the kingdom of God or live with the values of the kingdom of this world. This final parable shows the consequences of living in the two opposing kingdoms.

Most studies on this parable go to great lengths trying to discern who Jesus has in view when He speaks of "the nations" (Matt 25:32) and the "the least of these, My brethren" (Matt 25:40). The "nations" can be identified with Gentile nations, unbelieving Jews, or unbelievers from all nations. The "least of these, My brethren" can be identified religiously as the group of people who follow Jesus and do His will (Matt 12:50; Mark 3:35; Luke 8:21), ethnically, so that Jesus' brethren are the Jewish people, and therefore, all nations (Matt 25:32) that help Israel will be blessed (Gen 12:3), or eschatologically, so that the brethren of Jesus are believers who live during the future Tribulation period.

All such proposals, however, allow readers to ignore the overall lesson of the parable: A defining characteristic of the kingdom of God is that it will take care of the poor and needy of this world, wherever they are found, whatever religion or nationality they are of. Those who use this parable as justification to limit their care of the poor and needy to those of only one particular group of people or for people during one particular time period (e.g., the future Tribulation), self-identify themselves as a goat. Those servants of Jesus who believe that Jesus is returning soon, and live wisely as members of the kingdom of God, will work to feed, clothe, and serve all the poor and needy, regardless of religion or race. The kingdom of God breaks down all such barriers, so that those who work for the kingdom see all people as their brothers and sisters.

This finally brings us to the description of the everlasting fire near the end of the story. Jesus says that those who do not take care of the poor and needy will go away into "everlasting fire prepared for the devil and his angels" (Matt 25:41). He later describes this as "everlasting punishment" (Matt 25:46). Since this later term helps guide and define the earlier image of fire, it is important to begin there.

The Greek word used for punishment is *kolasis*. The word "punishment" is likely not the best translation. Moulton-Milligan argue that "cut short" is the original sense of the word, with the idea of pruning in the background (cf. John 15:1-6).[15] The word itself is only used one other time in the New Testament, in 1 John 4:18, where it speaks of fear involving torment. The point of John is that as we come to understand the love of God, fear is cast out, because fear has to do with punishment. In other words, fear, and the related concepts of torment and punishment, are the opposite of what we see through the love of God in Jesus Christ.

William Barclay wrote this about *kolasis*:

> One of the key passages is Matthew 25:46 where it is said that the rejected go away to eternal punishment, and the righteous to eternal life. The Greek word for punishment is *kolasis*, which was not originally an ethical word at all.

---

[15] Fudge, *The Fire That Consumes*, 197.

It originally meant the pruning of trees to make them grow better. I think it is true to say that in all Greek secular literature *kolasis* is never used of anything but 'remedial punishment.' The word for 'eternal' is *aionios*. It means more than everlasting, for Plato—who may have invented the word—plainly says that a thing may be everlasting and still not be *aionios*. The simplest way to put it is that *aionios* cannot be used properly of anyone but God; it is the word uniquely, as Plato saw it, of God. Eternal punishment is then literally that kind of remedial punishment which it befits God to give and which only God can give.[16]

The word *kolasis* is also used several times in the Greek translation of the Hebrew Scriptures (LXX). Ezekiel 14 contains this word three times (14:3, 4, 7) in reference to the idolatrous stumbling blocks that the leaders of Israel had set up in their hearts. God tells Ezekiel, as the son of man (Ezek 14:3), to inform the leaders of Israel that their idolatrous ways would lead to the devastation of Jerusalem and those who lived there (cf. Ezek 18:30; 43:11; 44:12).

Of further interest in the context of Ezekiel is that the people of Israel are equated with the cities of Sodom and Gomorrah (Ezek 16:44-59). And what was the sin of these two cities? According to God, Sodom and Gomorrah were destroyed because although the people of these cities had lots of food and time, they did not help

[16] William Barclay, *William Barclay: A Spiritual Autobiography* (Grand Rapids: Eerdmans, 1975), 66.

the poor and needy (Ezek 16:49). This behavior was a shameful abomination (Ezek 16:50-52) which led to the destruction and desolation of not only Sodom and Gomorrah, but Israel as well (Ezek 14:15-16; 15:8; cf. Jer 7:30-34).

The abomination that leads to desolation, therefore, is the failure of God's people to take care of the poor and needy in their midst, which then leads to the destruction and devastation of the nations in which they live (Jesus defines an abomination this way as well in Luke 15:14-15). This is the repeated theme of the last half of Ezekiel, that all the nations which practice the abominable behavior of not taking care of the poor and needy in their midst (whoever they might be), will come under the judgment of God and become desolate wastelands destroyed by fire, famine, pestilence, and war. In some places, this destruction is even called "everlasting desolation" (cf. Ezek 35:9).

All this is to say that when Jesus tells the Parable of the Sheep and the Goats, where the nations are brought before Him so that He might determine which nations took care of the poor and needy in their midst, and which did not, Jesus has the prophetic message of Ezekiel in mind. The everlasting punishment is not everlasting torture in hell, but is referring to the temporal destruction and desolation that comes upon nations when its people do not take care of the poor and needy in their midst.

Of course, even here, there is redemption for these nations, for God says in numerous places throughout Ezekiel that He will eventually restore the various nations to their former places (cf. Ezek 16:53-63). Their wicked, selfish, and greedy ways will be eternally destroyed, but the nations themselves, as geographic and political entities upon this earth, will be redeemed and restored so that they properly serve within God's kingdom and purpose on earth.

So in light of all this, the word *kolasis* is best understood as a disciplinary pruning by God upon the people within the various nations who refuse to take care of the poor and needy among them. Though God gathers the nations, He separates the people *within* the nations one from the other for judgment.[17] God sends this *kolasis* upon them so that they might turn from their shameful and selfish behavior and start looking after the poor and needy in their midst. Once they learn this lesson, God will restore these nations to their place in this world.

But how does a nation learn to live as God wants? Such behavior is not accomplished through laws or courts. You cannot legislate generosity. Instead, such things are learned only through the active example of

---

[17] In Matthew 25:32, the noun *nations* is neuter, and the pronoun "them" is masculine, which means the pronoun cannot refer to the nations themselves, but rather to the individual people within the nations. See Walter Wink, *Unmasking the Powers: The Invisible Forces that Determine Human Existence* (Philadelphia: Fortress, 1986), 96; Craig Blomberg, *Interpreting the Parables* (Downers Grove: IVP, 2012), 398.

the righteous people within that nation. The sons of righteousness who reside within a nation must lead their nation into righteousness by showing them through word and action how to live in light of the kingdom of heaven. If we fail in this, then it is *we* who have been unbelieving and foolish servants, and *we* who lead our nation into destruction.

All of this helps us understand the everlasting fire in Matthew 25:41. It is a refining fire that comes upon the nations so that they learn to practice the principles of the kingdom of heaven by taking care of the "least of these, my brethren" in their midst. When nations live like Sodom and Gomorrah, or Israel and Samaria, by refusing to tend to the needs of the poor, they will come under the purifying discipline of God, which is described as "everlasting fire." It is everlasting in that it is a purifying fire that comes from God, who is Himself everlasting.

But what are we to make of the fact that this everlasting fire is prepared "for the devil and his angels"? This does not mean that the fire is some sort of place or state of existence in which God punishes spiritual beings for their rebellion. There are two possible ways of understanding this descriptive phrase.

First, we could say that just as this world was created for humans and God intends for us to live in this world according to the rules and values of the kingdom of heaven (Matt 25:34), He also created a realm of fire for the devil and his angels (cf. 2 Pet 2:4-9, Jude 6), in which they live and move. But this doesn't mean that the fire causes suffering for fallen angels. Since angels occasionally appear as beings of light and fire (Ps 104:4; Heb 1:7), it does not seem that an abode of everlasting fire would cause them torment, torture, or pain. Such a realm or "dimension" might instead be quite suitable for them, just as this physical world is a suitable place for humans. Living in fire is not necessarily a bad thing for a spiritual being, as even God descended onto Mount Sinai in fire (Exod 19:18).

There is a second option, however, which has more merit. This second option depends on understanding that the devil is the god of this age, the spirit of the air that is at work in the sons of wickedness (2 Cor 4:4; Eph 2:2; 6:12). Since the word "devil" could also be translated as "accuser" or "slanderer," this means that the world is guided or directed by a spirit of accusation and slander. As seen in Genesis 3, the spirit of this age is a spirit of accusation and judgment in which we humans try to take the place of God in deciding between good and evil. Accusation and blame are the guiding forces of everything in this world. The angels of the accuser, therefore, are the principalities and powers that guide and direct the nations of this world (cf. Dan 10:13; 12:1).

This imagery fits perfectly with what Jesus is describing in Matthew 25:41. God created the nations of the world to function in a particular way. He gave them power and authority in this world, not to dominate and destroy others, but to protect and care for others, especially for the poor and needy. But the accusatory spirit (the devil) that guides the spirits of the nations (his angels) leads these nations into war and violence, which accomplishes the opposite of what God desired or intended. So the fire prepared for the devil and his angels is once again the fire of discipline, so that the spirits of the nations will be guided and taught to live as God wants.

Satan and his angels seek to set the world on fire through accusation and blame (Jas 3:5-6), but God fights fire with fire, by sending forth the kingdom of God through the followers of Jesus to show the world a better way to live. The fire of the kingdom of God is the cleansing fire of grace, humility, patience, mercy, and forgiveness. As we live in such ways, we give instead of take, love instead of hate, bless instead of accuse, and believe instead of condemn. The nations, as they see our good deeds, will glorify our Father in heaven by learning to live in similar ways themselves (Matt 5:15-16).

Since the Parable of the Sheep and the Goats is the last part of the last spoken "sermon" (or teaching) by Jesus before His crucifixion, He goes on to tell His disciples how to show love to Him and carry on the Kingdom in His absence. While Jesus has told His disciples in various ways that He is going away, He also wants them to know how to live while He is away. Jesus reveals to them that the ultimate truth of His absence is that He is not really absent at all. Instead, He is dwelling with and among the "least of these, My brethren." If His disciples want to spend time with Jesus, they can do so by spending time with the poor and needy.[18] If His disciples want to serve and love Jesus, they can do so by serving and loving the poor, the sick, and the imprisoned. In this way, His disciples will not only be loving and serving others as Jesus did (thereby expanding the presence of the kingdom), but will also be loving and serving Jesus Himself.

So the stories of Matthew 25 are not about some future judgment. They are stories about what is occurring through the arrival of the kingdom of heaven. Jesus is saying that the health and survival of a nation can be affected by whether or not the individual people within that nation take care of the poor and needy in their midst. When people serve the "least of these" in this way, they are not only helping the poor, but are loving Jesus and serving their country as well. True service to your country does not look like marching off to war to kill others, but instead looks like feeding the hungry and clothing the poor that are in our midst. And we do this, not by asking our country to tax people more or to redistribute the wealth of the rich, but simply by being

[18] Kazoh Kitamori, *Theology of the Pain of God* (Eugene: Wipf & Stock, 1958), 98.

generous with our own money and possessions. When this happens, we avoid bringing the fires of hellish war upon our country and instead invite the blessings of the kingdom of heaven upon our land and its people.

The Parable of the Sheep and the Goats is the last parable that Jesus ever told. It is, therefore, a summary parable, or a key to understanding all the others. In it, Jesus describes the central truth to living and experiencing the kingdom of God which He inaugurated on earth. Jesus is saying, "If you want to find the kingdom of God and live within it, then you need to follow Me and live where I live. And where is that? It is with the poor and needy. Go serve and minster to them, and you will be serving and ministering to Me, and in this way, will be living within and serving the kingdom of heaven." It is as Robert Farrar Capon wrote in his book on the parables, "In the parable of the Great Judgment [of the Sheep and the Goats] it is precisely in the hungry, the thirsty, the estranged, the naked, the sick, and the imprisoned that we find, or ignore, the Savior Himself."[19]

Many people wonder where God has been hiding for all of history. In this parable, Jesus tells us where. It is the great surprise at the end of the story. It is the final "Here I Am" of the great divine game of Hide and Seek that humans have been playing with God since Adam and Eve first hid from Him in the Garden. And since

[19] Capon, *Kingdom, Grace, Judgment*, 8.

that time, though we are the ones who hid ourselves from God, it is we who think that God has been hiding His face from us. We wonder why He doesn't show up in strength and power to fix the world and right all wrong. We think God is distant and neglectful. We think God is shirking His duties. And when bad things happen (and continue to happen) we cry out to the silent sky, "God! Where are you?" But now Jesus tells us where God has been hiding all along. He has been living and dwelling with "the least of these, My brethren."

The people we neglected and rejected throughout life are the very people among whom God has lived and dwelt. God has lived among the poor, the sick, the weak, and the hungry. And when we love and serve them, we love and serve Him, and paradoxically, He loves and serves them through us, so that they love and serve us in return, revealing the kingdom of God, and indeed, God Himself, to us. Throughout the ministry of Jesus, the disciples have been saying, "Show us the Father. We want to see God. We want to understand God and know what He wants of us." And now, finally, Jesus has given the answer. "You want to see God?" He asks. "Go serve the poor, for that is where He lives."

When we live in this way, we will experience the kingdom of God in this life, which has been prepared for us since the foundation of the world, thereby fulfilling our God-given destiny and purpose. Those who live this way will see righteousness rise like the morning sun and blessing will come upon them like the dew. But when we refuse to follow Jesus in this way, we will live in and experience the kingdom of hell during this life, which is guided only by selfishness, greed, hatred, rebellion, and emptiness. Those who live this way, though they live for themselves, will only see their life burn away into nothingness, losing all purpose and significance. Such people have chosen to dwell in a hell of their own making.

MARK 9:42-50

Their worm does not die, and the fire is not quenched… (Mark 9:48).

Mark 9:42-50 is very similar to Matthew 18:6-9, and can be understood in a nearly identical way. However, there is one primary difference between the two passages which is important to consider. The passage in Mark 9 contains the refrain that "their worm does not die, and the fire is not quenched."[20]

Though many take this passage as a clear reference to eternal suffering and torment in the flames of hell, there are several reasons to doubt such a view. The first reason is that the images of worms and the fire cannot both be taken literally. Indeed, those who see the reference to fire in Mark 9:42-48 as a reference to literal flames in

---

[20] Most Greek manuscripts repeat this refrain three times (Mark 9:44, 46, 48), while a few only include it once in verse 48.

hell do not typically understand the reference to worms in a literal way. Instead, they interpret the worms metaphorically, as a symbol of intense remorse or regret.[21]

Why? Because the word used for worm is *skōlex,* which is the kind of worm that feeds on dead bodies. This worm would not feed on a living body in hell, and especially not if the body was being burned by flames. In the literal Valley of Hinnom, which was a graveyard for the dead and dying, worms and maggots would eat the bodies that were not being consumed by flames.[22] Proper hermeneutics requires that either both terms be either literal or symbolic. But since they cannot be literal, for worms cannot "feed" on living beings in hell that are being burned alive for eternity. Therefore, both terms must be symbolic. But symbolic of what?

In Mark 9:48 (and 9:44, 46 as well), Jesus is quoting from Isaiah 66:24, which is the final verse in the book of Isaiah. These final lines of Isaiah describe the eternal state of the new heavens and new earth, in which all flesh will worship Him forever and ever, "from one New Moon to another, and from one Sabbath to another" (Isa 66:22-23). Part of this everlasting worship of God includes the ability to "go forth, and look upon the corpses of the men" who transgressed against God, "for their worm does not die, and their fire is not quenched" (Isa 66:24). Though some look forward to such an expe-

[21] Cf. Fudge, *The Fire That Consumes,* 111-112, 185.

[22] Cf. Butler, *The Skeletons in God's Closet,* 322.

rience with anticipation,[23] I find it impossible to think that as part of eternal bliss with God, people will want to take regular field trips to gaze upon a mass grave full of rotting, burning, maggot-filled corpses. To the contrary, since we will have glorified bodies, and will be sinless as God is sinless, I doubt that any glorified person in eternity would ever desire such a thing. So why does Isaiah end his book this way? What did Isaiah have in mind?

The key is to recognize that throughout the book of Isaiah, fire and worms are used as imagery for the destruction and corruption that come upon people and nations for rebelling against God (cf. fire: Isa 5:24; 9:18-19; 33:11-12; 47:14; worm: 14:11; 51:8). And quite often, this destruction and corruption is self-inflicted. God set up the world with rules and guidelines for how to best live and function in this world, but when we live outside these boundaries and guidelines, negative consequences are the result. He does not send the consequences of sin, for they are inherent within sin itself. God loves us, and does not want to see us hurt by sin, which is why He warns us against it. But when we ignore His warnings and practice sin anyway, the consequences of sin come upon us. This is why Isaiah speaks of "*their* worm" and "*their* corruption." It is theirs and theirs alone. They brought it upon themselves, and they live with it.

[23] Cf. Balthasar, *Dare We Hope*, 158.

But how does this help us understand Isaiah 66:24? Isaiah is describing the new heavens and the new earth, in which all the peoples of all the nations of the earth dwell (Isa 66:18-20). And when he writes that the people of God will be able to gaze upon the corpses of the dead, he is not imagining that there is literally a field of corpses in eternity that we can stare at with dread fascination or morbid satisfaction.

Instead, Isaiah is answering an age-old question about eternity. He writes that in the new heaven and new earth, all flesh will come and worship God (Isa 66:22-23). But the question that people have always asked is how this eternal existence of worshiping God will differ from that of Adam and Eve who were supposed to worship God for eternity as well. In other words, since they were perfect and sinless but still fell into sin, what will keep us from rebelling against God in the new heaven and new earth?

Isaiah 66:24 is the answer. We will have what Adam and Eve did not, namely, the knowledge of good and evil. This knowledge is not something that God intended to withhold from humanity forever, but was instead something He wanted to teach to humanity over time within the reality of an ongoing relationship with Him. But Adam and Eve "jumped the gun" and tried to take a shortcut before they were ready. In eternity, the thing that will separate us from Adam and Eve, and therefore, allow us to avoid their same mistake, is that we will have knowledge of evil and will understand its devastating and destructive consequences. We will be able to go out and look upon the corpses of men who have transgressed against God, and will be able to see how their words and actions led to nothing but the worms of corruption and the fires of destruction.

And who are these "corpses" we will look upon? There are all the people of human history, including ourselves. We will be able to view human history, and how we have all lived at various times in the kingdom of hell, which is the realm of death and darkness, the world of worm and fire. Human history will serve as an everlasting reminder about where a life of rebellion leads. Human history is the everlasting object lesson that provides the knowledge of good and evil to the redeemed.

While some people think that heaven cannot be a blessed existence if we are able to remember or view the horrors of human history, the truth of the matter is the opposite: Eternity will not be much of a blessed existence if we cannot remember what God redeemed us from. Besides, since all events in our lives are connected, God cannot wipe some of our memories without wiping them all. But as painful as human history will be to watch and remember, it will carry a much different meaning when viewed through the lens of God's redeeming grace.

So the group of "corpses" that we will be able to view is the corpse of human history. The field of the dead in Isaiah 66:24 is the field of human history, including all of our mistakes and failures. It is our observation and remembrance of human tragedy and horror that will help us avoid similar mistakes in eternity. We will have gained the knowledge of good and evil, and by remembering the fires and worms of our past, will be able to judge between right and wrong, good and evil, so that we can worship God in righteousness and holiness forever. This will enable us to worship God in eternity by learning from our past mistakes and seeing how God has redeemed these mistakes to bring glory and honor to Himself for all eternity.

It is this understanding of Isaiah 66:24 that Jesus appears to have in mind. We see this because of His reference to fire and salt in Mark 9:49-50. First, Jesus says that "everyone will be seasoned with fire." If Jesus is thinking of the eternal fires of everlasting torment in hell, then He would be saying that everyone is going to hell. Clearly He is not saying this, and so therefore, some other meaning must be sought. His reference to salt helps clarify the picture. In the ancient world, salt was not only used as seasoning, but also as a preservative for meat. Since there was no refrigeration, salt kept meat from decaying, and kept worms from eating the meat.

So Jesus is saying that purifying fire can be used to stop the fire of destruction, and preserving salt can be used to stop the worm of decay and corruption. Jesus talks about salt as a seasoning as well, but equates this seasoning to having "peace with another" (Mark 9:50). Since, as we have seen time and time again, the fires of destruction often come upon humans as destructive wars (that often involve fire), then being seasoned with salt for the sake of peace is one of the primary ways to avert human violence and the wars that come from it.

This imagery of fire and salt is also mentioned in the context of sacrifice. This brings to mind not only the sacrifices of the Mosaic Law, but also the invitations in the New Testament for followers of Jesus to offer our-selves as living sacrifices to God (cf. Rom 12:1-2). Jesus has done away with bloody sacrifices, and now calls us to follow Him through a life of self-sacrifice for others (see *Sacrifice*). We put ourselves on the sacrificial altar by purifying our lives through the fire of discipline, and sanctifying our lives through the seasoning and preserv-ing salt of peace. If we do not fire and salt ourselves in this way, our life's work will be burned away forever and will be eaten and destroyed by the corrupting worm.

William Lane presents the truth of Mark 9:43-49 this way:

> The thought of the sacrifice of an offending member of the body (verses 43-47) is here carried a step further: eve-ry disciple is to be a sacrifice for God (cf. Rom 12:1). In the OT the Temple sacrifices had to be accompanied by salt (Lev 2:13; Ezek 43:24; cf. Exod 30:35). The salt-sacrifice metaphor is appropriate to a situation of suffer-ing and trial in which the principle of sacrifice cultivated

with respect to the individual members of the body is now severely tested. The disciples must be seasoned with salt, like the sacrifice. This will take place through fiery trials (cf. 1 Pet 1:7; 4:12).[24]

So the worm and fire of Mark 9:43-49 is not referring to the punishment or torture of the unregenerate dead in the afterlife, but to the self-sacrifice, loving discipline of God, and even fiery trials of persecution that come upon disciples of Jesus during this life as a way of purifying their lives and preparing them for future ministry and effectiveness in this life. As with Matthew 18:8-9, Jesus is encouraging His disciples to take steps of self-sacrifice now, in this life, and to keep their life free from pollution, corruption, and moral decay. This is not so that His disciples can escape hell and go to heaven when they die, but so that they can experience the rule and reign of God in their life here and now, while avoiding the devastation and destruction brought by sin.

LUKE 12:49

I came to send fire on the earth, and how I wish it were already kindled!

The words of Jesus in Luke 12:49 provide further evidence that the judgment He has in mind when He

[24] William L. Lane, *The Gospel According to Mark, NICNT* (Grand Rapids: Eerdmans, 1974), 349.

speaks about fire is not the fire of everlasting torture in the pit of hell, but is instead the fire of judgment that comes upon this earth to reveal truth and purify our lives. In this text, Jesus says that He came to send fire on the earth, and He wishes it were already kindled. Clearly, the fire Jesus is referring to is not a fire of the afterlife that punishes sinners for all eternity, but is a fire brought (or sent) by Jesus upon this earth in our lives.

Jesus goes on to say two things about this fire that He wants to kindle upon the earth. First, Jesus says it will begin with Him. After speaking of the fire that He will bring, Jesus immediately transitions to speaking of a baptism that He will be baptized with (Luke 12:50). This is the baptism of fire which John the Baptist had preached about (Luke 3:16). This baptism was not an event in which people get immersed under water, but is a time that they get immersed in fire, which is the fire of judgment. Before such fires came upon the nation of Israel (or the world), Jesus bore this baptism of fire upon Himself. This occurred when He was judged by the religious and political leaders to be a blasphemer and lawbreaker, and so was sentenced to death by crucifixion. Note that in this case, the judgment that came upon Jesus was not sent by God upon humans, but was sent by humans upon God.

After Jesus took this human judgment and baptism of fire upon Himself, it forced the rest of the world to make a judgment of their own about Him. This is the second point that Jesus reveals regarding this fire He wants to bring upon the earth. Jesus taught about the kingdom of God, and His kingdom was a threat to the religious-political kingdoms of this world. The way of Jesus posed such a threat to the ways of men, that the kingdom of this world crucified Jesus. As a result, everybody is forced to make a decision about which kingdom they will follow. He is the spark that starts the fire on this earth which leads to purification and light for many.

But this judgment (Gk., *krisis*) will also create a crisis. At this point in the ministry of Jesus, the crisis has not yet come, but Jesus wishes that it had. He wants the two available options known. He wants people to see the two roads before them and make a decision about which kingdom they will follow. Sadly, this decision will cause some division between friends and family members. Parents might choose one kingdom, while their children choose another (Luke 12:52-53). This separation and division, even between family members, is part of the fire that Jesus has in mind.

The arrival of the kingdom of God sparks a crisis in the minds of men. They must choose whether to join the party of God's kingdom, or live within the ongoing hell of their own. The choice seems easy, but many prefer to call the shots at their own party than eat the cake and dance to the music at someone else's.

LUKE 16:24

*"Then he cried and said, 'Father Abraham, have
mercy on me, and send Lazarus that he may dip
the tip of his finger in water and cool my tongue;
for I am tormented in this flame.'"*

Every discussion of fire (or hell) in Scripture must include an examination of the story of Lazarus and the
rich man from Luke 16:19-31. With its detailed and
lurid depiction of the suffering of a rich man in the
flames of hell, this account appears to support all the
horrifying ideas of hell as a place of eternal torture for
the unredeemed. It contains the portrayal of a man being tormented in flames, who cries out for just a drop of
water to cool his burning tongue (cf. Luke 16:23-24).
When most people think of hell, this is the sort of image
they have in mind.

Yet not everyone is convinced that Jesus is describing
a literal place with literal flames where literal people suffer and burn for all eternity. Several factors reveal that
Jesus intended some other sort of message with this story.

First, if this is a story about how to escape hell and
go to heaven when you die, then the lesson of the story
is that eternal life and entrance into heaven can be
earned by being poor, or at least by being generous to
the poor. If you don't take care of the poor, then off to
hell with you! But is this what Scripture teaches anywhere else? No. Far from it. Eternal life is the free gift of

God to everyone and anyone who simply and only believes in Jesus for it (John 3:16; 5:24; 6:47). While there are many blessings and benefits connected to taking care of the poor, escaping hell is not one of them.

Second, the presence of Abraham and Lazarus in the same vicinity as the suffering rich man does not fit any other portrayal of hell. In other words, if Jesus is describing the place where the unredeemed dead spend eternity, then what is Abraham doing there, and why does Lazarus get sent there? Is there some sort of annex or suburb of hell where the redeemed can live in relative peace and safety while looking across the chasm at the sufferings of the poor sinners in the torture chamber of hell? Though many scholars try to explain this away by speaking of "Abraham's Bosom" as a temporary holding tank for the redeemed which was then emptied at the resurrection of Jesus, such an idea is tenuous at best and is not taught anywhere else in Scripture.

To the contrary, the image of "Abraham's Bosom" comes from Babylonian intertestamental Jewish literature.[25] The Babylonians believed that there was a single afterlife location for all the dead, and this dwelling place had two regions, one for the righteous and one for the wicked. Some of the Jewish people living in Babylon

[25] See Merrill C. Tenney, ed. *The Zondervan Pictorial Encyclopedia of the Bible* (Grand Rapids: Zondervan), 3:7; Chana Weisberg, *Tending the Garden* (Southfield, MI: Targum), 2:591; Kittel, ed. *TDNT*, 1:147; Jersak, *Her Gates Will Never Be Shut*, 98-99.

picked up on this idea and began telling stories about something similar for Jews. A few of these accounts (which are now found in the Babylonian Talmud) speak of "Abraham's Bosom" as the place that righteous Jews went after they died.

But no passage from Scripture teaches this concept. The fact that Jesus refers to it in this story should not be read as an endorsement of the idea, but as a way of using a common image from that culture to make a theological point. I've mentioned it before, but if I began to tell you about meeting Peter at the Pearly Gates, you would know I was using this common folktale image to tell a fictional (and possibly humorous) story, but you would not imagine that I was speaking of a literal place or that people who die actually appear before Peter at the Pearly Gates.

Third, despite the claims of some, this story of Jesus contains all the markings of a parable. For example, there are numerous and significant elements of this story that are parallel to the other parables in the preceding context. For example, both this story and the Parable of the Unjust Steward begin with the words "There was a certain rich man" (Luke 16:1, 19). These two parables focus the reader's attention on certain rich men of Luke 16:14 and how their treatment of the poor was an abomination to God (Luke 16:15).[26] Some of the other contextual parallels are considered below.

[26] Cf. Ferwerda, *Raising Hell*, 213f.

The only real reason some people think this is *not* a parable is that Jesus specifically names two characters: Abraham and Lazarus. No other recorded parable of Jesus provides a proper name for any of the key human characters. However, "Satan" is mentioned in Mark 4:14, "the son of man" as a title for Jesus in Matthew 13:37, and several personal titles in Luke 10:25-37. Many believe that the story of Job is a parable, in which case, it contains the names of several people. Furthermore, outside of Scripture, many ancient parables often used the names of people in the telling of the stories. So the presence of two names in Luke 16 fails to prove the story is not a parable. Some speculate that maybe Jesus used the name of a popular beggar who was well-known in the streets of Jerusalem. The other possibility (as mentioned previously) is that Jesus was referencing a popular Jewish folktale which His hearers would have immediately recognized as fiction. Again, just because someone mentions Peter's name when speaking of the Pearly Gates, this does not mean they are referring to a literal location or future event.

In fact, the connection between Abraham and Lazarus should not be overlooked. Nothing in the parables is there without reason. The name "Lazarus" means "God is My Help." Though no one else helped Lazarus in this story, God was helping him. More significantly, however, "Lazarus" is the Hellenized (Greek) version of the Hebrew name Eliezer, who was the Gentile slave of

Abraham (Gen 15:2-3).[27] Abraham was a very rich man, and as long as he did not have a son to be his heir, his fortune and property would have legally gone to his servant, Eliezer.

Curiously, this seems to be the same servant that Abraham sends to find a wife for Isaac (cf. Gen 24:2), though in that story, Eliezer is never mentioned by name (Gen 24:1-67). But it is most likely Eliezer, for when Rebecca first sees Isaac, she asks the servant who he is, and Eliezer answers, "It is my master" (Gen 24:65). Soon after this, Abraham died (Gen 25:1-11) and everything he owned went to his son, Isaac (Gen 25:5), which would have included the servant. In light of all this, one wonders if there is any significance to Abraham's words in Luke 16:25 when he speaks to the rich man and says, "Son, remember that in your lifetime, you received your good things …" Is it possible that the rich man in the story represents Isaac? If so, then this is further evidence that Jesus is not saying anything about everlasting torture in the fires of hell, for Jesus elsewhere clearly states that we will sit down with Abraham, Isaac, and Jacob at the wedding feast in the kingdom of heaven (Matt 8:11).

However, Isaac is probably not the rich man Jesus is referring to in this story. Instead, it is better to understand the rich man as all the "sons of Abraham," namely the religious leaders who saw themselves not only as the

[27] Cf. Ibid., 217.

descendants of Abraham but also as the heirs of the Abrahamic faith (cf. Matt 3:9; John 8:39). These religious leaders are, after all, identified as being quite rich in the preceding context (Luke 16:14), men who loved to wear purple and fine linen (Luke 16:19). The rich man is not some pagan sinner or a backslider, but is "an influential and respected leader among God's people."[28] Jesus is teaching that it is not the "sons of Abraham" who will recline at the table (in the bosom of Abraham) with God and all His people among the nations, but rather those who are covered with the sores of sin, who are Gentile dogs, and who are rejected, despised, and neglected by the Jewish religious elite.

There might also be some hint here about the identity of the rich man when we see that he begged Abraham to send Lazarus to warn his five brothers. Some point out that Judah, after whom the nation of Judah and the Jews are named, had five brothers from his mother Leah (Gen 35:23). Furthermore, Annas, who was High Priest at that time, had five sons who were known as "the five brothers" and who shared the responsibility of the high priesthood after Annas and Caiaphas (Annas' son in law, John 18:13) died.[29] Furthermore, the high priestly tunics were made of blue, purple, and scarlet fine linen (Exod 28:5-8, 15, 31, 39), which also describes the rich

[28] Butler, *The Skeletons in God's Closet*, 70.

[29] Anthony W. Bartlett, *Seven Stories: How to Study and Teach the Nonviolent Bible* (Hopetime Press, 2017), 91; Butler, *The Skeletons in God's Closet*, 80.

man's clothing (Luke 16:19). So this again is clear historical evidence that Jesus has the religious leadership in mind.

Fourth, everywhere else Jesus speaks about individual people in "hell," He uses the word *gehenna*, which referred to the Valley of Hinnom outside the walls of Jerusalem. But here Jesus uses the word *hadēs* (Luke 16:23). Elsewhere, Jesus uses this word only as a way of describing the destruction that will come upon certain cities (Matt 11:23; 16:18; Luke 10:15; 16:23). Furthermore, the word *hadēs* was a Greek word for the abode of the dead, and was also the name of the Greek god of the netherworld. Once again, this provides evidence that Jesus is not speaking about hell (the way He understands it), for then He would have used the word *gehenna.*

Instead, Jesus uses a word that He typically uses to refer to the destruction of cities, combines in the Greek idea of the afterlife, mixes in some Babylonian imagery of two compartments in hell, and uses this all in connection with the Jewish history of Abraham and Eliezer. Why? Because this approach makes a memorable story. Jesus is clearly mixing images from numerous sources so that He can tell a parable to His listeners that will connect with them on multiple levels. Jesus is making a point that He doesn't want His audience to miss.

Ironically, due to the Christian preoccupation with sinners burning in the flames of hell, we have mostly missed the point of Jesus. But what was that point? The context makes it quite clear. This context is the fifth and final piece of evidence that helps us know that the story of the Rich Man and Lazarus is a parable rather than a description of a literal place. Jesus has been making one single point in the preceding context, and this story hammers that point home.

The setting for the context is found in Luke 15:1-2. After Jesus welcomes and spends time with the sinners and tax-collectors, the Jewish religious leaders chide Him for eating and befriending such people. They believe it is better to remain separate and distant from such wicked people. So Jesus sets out to correct this entire line of thinking. In doing so, Jesus tells five parables. The first three parables explain why Jesus does what He does, and what will come of His actions. These are the Parables of the Lost Sheep (Luke 15:3-7), the Lost Coin (Luke 15:4-10), and the Lost Son, also called the Parable of the Prodigal Son (Luke 15:11-32).

The third parable is transitionary. It not only shows how the younger son went into a far country to squander his inheritance, but also introduces the elder son, who stayed at home and worked the family farm. Yet as the story closes, it becomes obvious that the Prodigal Son, or the Lost Son, is not the one who went into a far country, but is rather the one who remained. It is the elder son who is actually furthest away from the heart of his father, and wants to keep separate from his sinful, wayward, younger brother. The father invites the older son to the feasting and dancing, but the son refuses, preferring to stay instead in the darkness outside the party. Because he was angry, he would not go in (Luke 15:28).

It is also helpful to recognize that this third parable, the Parable of the Lost Son, not only serves as a transition to the stories that follow, but also serves as a parallel (but opposite) story to that of the Rich Man and Lazarus. In other words, the story of the Rich Man and Lazarus is an inversion of the story of the Prodigal Son.

   -Both the prodigal son and Lazarus find themselves in desperate situations. Both beg for scraps.

   -Both are in the company of unclean animals (dogs, swine)

   -Both stories have father figures: The rich man calls Abraham his "father." Lazarus leans on Abraham like the prodigal son is held by his father.

   -Both contain a theme of distance—there is a great distance between the rich man and Lazarus, and between the father as his wastrel son (in "a far country"). Unlike the father who sees his son from a long way off and runs to meet him, the rich man maintains his structural distance and indifference to the poor, so he sees Lazarus "far away" with Abraham.

-Both the prodigal son and the rich man live sumptuously, but then lose everything. But the prodigal son "comes to his senses" while the rich man does not change his way of thinking. He still treats Lazarus like an inferior wanting him to bring him water with "the tip of his finger," and then to warn his brothers. He is still thinking of his own status and social group, not of the poor.[30]

After these three parables about His own mission and ministry, with the third parable ending with a depiction of the religious rulers as the elder son, Jesus transitions to two other parables, both of which focus on the ministry of the religious rulers. Jesus is seeking to contrast His ministry with theirs by showing where their methods and goals come from and what their methods and goals accomplish.

The first parable that Jesus tells about the ministry of the religious leaders is the Parable of the Unjust Steward (Luke 16:1-13). Though many assume that Jesus is describing how His followers are supposed to function in this world, this is not the point of the parable. If it were, Jesus would be telling His followers to cheat their employers and live unscrupulous lives for the sake of gaining favor with others and wealth for themselves. Does this sound like something Jesus would teach? No. Quite to the contrary, this sounds like the opposite of what Jesus would teach. And indeed, it is.

[30] Bartlett, *Seven Stories*, 90-91.

People get confused, though, because they think that Jesus applies the Parable of the Unjust Steward to His followers in Luke 16:9-12, where He seems to say that we should use riches and wealth for making friends with others. But notice Jesus basically says, "And when your money fails, they will welcome you into their home for ever and ever" (Luke 16:9). We all know that this is *not* true. If Jesus was actually "applying" the parable here, then He is flat-out wrong. Therefore, it is better to see that this so-called "application" in Luke 16:9 is not the application at all, but is a tongue-in-cheek sarcastic reference to how the people of this world will *not* treat you when your wealth is gone. Jesus is saying, "If you use money to gain friends, don't be surprised that when your money runs out, so will your friends. Though they may promise that you will always be welcome in their home, this promise only lasts as long as your money does." This is reality, and this is also exactly what Jesus just taught in Parable of the Lost Son. When the son's money ran out, he had no home to go to, and was sent to live with the swine, and no one gave him anything (Luke 15:14-16).

So the Parable of the Unjust Steward is not about how the disciples of Jesus should act and behave, but is instead about how the world works, and how the religious leaders act and behave to gain friends and influence for themselves. Many of the religious leaders had become very rich by making deals with merchants and political leaders. They were using mammon the way the world used it, to benefit and enrich themselves, and get more money and power for themselves.

Yet it is not just finances that they dealt with; they also trafficked in the forgiveness of sins. Religious leaders have always sold the forgiveness of sins to others for money. Such a practice did not begin with the selling of indulgences by the Catholic Church in the days of Martin Luther. The religious leaders were also engaging in this practice in the days of Jesus. Though the religious leaders were supposed to be stewards of the things of God, they were actually using their position to not only cheat others, but to also cheat their master, God. Jesus, however, gave away forgiveness for free, which is the only way it can be given. But this free forgiveness to the sinners and tax-collectors did not make Him popular among the religious crowd, for it threatened both their teachings and their livelihood.

John the Baptist threatened the religious establishment as well, which is why they had him killed. This is why Jesus mentions John in Luke 16:14-18. John had challenged Herod about his marriage to Herodias (Matt 14:1-12), which eventually led to Herod beheading John. This event in the life of John also explains why Jesus throws in the teaching about marriage and divorce in Luke 16:18. This is not a non-sequitur, but logically follows what Jesus has said about John. John's condemnation of the divorce and remarriage of Herodias led to

John's death. This, Jesus says, is what true followers of God can expect from those who live according to the values and principles of this world.

Now the Pharisees knew that they were being derided by Jesus, and so they sought to deride Him (Luke 16:14). This proves once again, that the Parable of the Unjust Steward is not about how followers of Jesus are to behave in this world, but is instead about how some corrupt religious leaders behave. The Pharisees knew Jesus was talking about them, and they were offended. But Jesus says that their behavior, though highly esteemed among men, is an abomination to God (Luke 16:15). Their use of mammon and religion to garner favor with the rich and the powerful was a great sin before God. It was an abomination that would lead to their desolation.

And indeed, this is exactly what Jesus goes on to describe in Luke 16:19-31, the Parable of the Rich Man and Lazarus. The "Rich Man" obviously represents the rich men who are discussed in the context, which is the Pharisees who were "lovers of money" (Luke 16:14). They were servants of mammon (Luke 16:13). Like the unjust steward, they used their money and position to make friends with the rich and to enrich themselves.

What were they supposed to do with their money and power instead? They were to use it to take care of the poor and needy in their midst. Like who? Like Lazarus, who was covered in sores and laid at the gate, desiring just a few crumbs from the rich man's table (Luke 16:20-21). At what gate did Lazarus lay? In the days of Jesus, there were Gentile converts to Judaism who were called "gate proselytes." Since they were Gentiles, they were kept in the outer "Court of the Gentiles" and could not even pass through the gate into the Court of Women. Many of them wanted to draw nearer to the temple and to God, but were barred from access. So they would hang out at the gate, peering through its opening, and longing to be closer to God. But the religious leaders kept these Gentile proselytes at a distance. They were sinners who could not draw near to God. If Lazarus was a Gentile proselyte, that is, a "gate proselyte," then not only was he overlooked and neglected for his sores and starvation, but also for his desire to serve and honor God.

But now, in this story, the entire situation is reversed. Lazarus is with Abraham, the father of the Jewish faith, while the rich man is far off, thirsty, and separated. And the rich man begs Abraham to send Lazarus to warn his five brothers. But Abraham tells the rich man that his brothers can listen to Moses and the prophets. Apparently, Moses and the prophets contain enough instruction and warning to keep a person from experiencing the fate of the rich man. And what is the central and overriding theme of Moses and the prophets? It was that the people of God are to take care of the poor and needy in their midst. Though there are many sins which Moses and the prophets teach against, the overriding theme of the prophetic message is that God's people must defend the orphans and the widow, provide for the foreigner and the stranger, and take care of the poor and needy. They must do this *themselves*; not by demanding the government make laws which force others to do such things. This generous and loving activity was the clear sign that God was in their midst.

So what then is the story of the Rich Man and Lazarus all about? It is the concluding story of a series of five parables, and it summarizes them all by revealing the danger of living according to the way of this world. This world worships mammon, and uses money to gain friends and power. But greedy living and lusting after money does not satisfy or quench one's thirst for meaning or significance in this world. Money satisfies those who chase after it less than a drop of water on the tongue would satisfy a man who is burning in flames. The quest for money does not quench one's thirst. No matter how much you have, it leaves you desiring more.

The story of the Prodigal Son depicts a man who started out chasing after money, but discovered it was worthless (Luke 15:11-32). The story of the Unjust Steward shows how this world uses and responds to money (Luke 16:1-13). The Pharisees didn't like what Jesus was saying (because they were guilty of such actions), and so in an attempt to justify their own greed, complained about His teaching and derided His message (Luke 16:14). So Jesus provides the example of John, who was a Just and Faithful Steward. John was not greedy and did not use money to make friends with the rich and powerful, but was instead beheaded by them (Luke 16:15-18). And now all of these lessons about greed are wrapped up into the one story of the Rich Man and Lazarus.

Ultimately, the story of the Rich Man and Lazarus is a warning against greed. In Luke 16:15, Jesus identifies the love of money as an abomination to God. The Parable of the Rich Man and Lazarus illustrates that greed does not accomplish the righteousness of God, or help one experience the kingdom of God. Instead, it only invites flames into one's life. Greed brings nothing but desolation and destruction. Greed, and the money which comes with it, does not help one experience the kingdom of God in this life or the next.

The flames in this story, then, are "no more literal than Abraham's bosom. The flames represent the burning agony of his thirsty soul. The rich man is experiencing the agony of thirst and deprivation that Lazarus had known throughout life."[31] We see this by the two different words used to describe the experience of the rich man in this story.

First, Jesus says that the rich man was in "torments" (Gk., *basano*) in *hadēs* (Luke 16:23). The word literally refers to a touchstone, which was used in ancient times

---

[31] Jersak, *Her Gates Will Never Be Shut*, 102.

as a way to test the value and genuineness of the gold and silver found in coins and jewelry.[32] "While the rich man looks fancy on the outside, when placed under the 'touchstone' his veneer comes off. He is being revealed for who he really is … and the revelation is agony."[33]

Second, the word used for "tormented" (Gk., *odunōmai*) in Luke 16:24-25 can also "be translated as 'grief' or 'anguish' and conveys a sense of emotional turmoil rather than physical pain."[34] It is only used two other times in the New Testament, both by Luke. In Luke 2:48, it refers to the "anxiousness" that Mary and Joseph felt as they searched for Jesus in Jerusalem for three days when He was twelve. Then in Acts 20:38, it refers to the "sorrow" that the Ephesian elders experienced when they said goodbye to Paul, knowing that they would never see him again. In neither case does it refer to torture, but to intense emotional grief or anguish.

So the rich man is not being tortured. Instead, he is having the truth revealed to him about himself, about Lazarus, and about what God values in the world. And for a man who has put all his hope in worldly riches and social status, the truth is more than he can bear. The truth is a torment to him. Too late, he discovers that

---

[32] This word is also discussed in our examination of Revelation 20:10.

[33] Butler, *The Skeletons in God's Closet*, 77..

[34] Ibid., 76.

everything he worked for and sought after during his entire life is worthless in this life and the next. And since he cannot accept this truth, he remains in emotional torment and even seeks to continue the life he knew and loved.

We see this in the fact that, even in death, the rich man attempts to command and control Lazarus. He tells Lazarus to bring him a drop of water and to go warn his five brothers about the fate that awaits them. Even in his state of torment, he prefers to stay where he is and order Lazarus around than beg for forgiveness or ask for the opportunity to come over to where Lazarus reclines with Abraham.[35] Furthermore, in his continued haughty arrogance, the rich man never speaks to Lazarus but only to Abraham (Luke 16:24, 27, 30). Even though their roles are reversed, the rich man shows only disdain and derision for Lazarus (cf. 16:14). Notice that in response, however, "Abraham does not call [the rich man] 'fool,' 'disappointment,' or 'idiot,' but 'son.' This is an expression of fatherhood, of filial devotion, of care."[36] Abraham and Lazarus are on the side of love while the rich man continues in his self-centered mindset.

Ultimately, then, the great gulf that separates the rich man from Abraham and Lazarus is a divide of his own making (Luke 16:26). It cannot be crossed, because the rich man will not cross it, for doing so would re-

[35] Cf. Ibid., 74.

[36] Ibid.

quire him to admit that he is no better than Lazarus. This he cannot do, and so his riches, his racism, and his religious arrogance keep him separated from others. Furthermore, though Lazarus and Abraham may *want* to cross the divide to the rich man, they cannot, for the division is not of their making.

> The rich man is the one who creates the divide, so that those on Abraham's side of the chasm who "might want to pass" (i.e., act out of compassion) in fact cannot. The text clearly implies that the rich and privileged, those with status, create the divide, not God. Thus the parable is not a picture of medieval hell but of humanly-created alienation and its suffering.[37]

> The chasm is a spiritual parallel in death to the social chasm fixed in life by the rich man's caste. By making it impossible for the poor or the sinner to cross that great gulf into their pseudo-kingdoms and religious enclaves, the spiritually privileged were unwittingly defining their own distance from God's kingdom.[38]

Luke 16:19-31 is a condemnation of greed. It is a picture of how life looks from God's perspective when the rich create chasms between themselves and the poor and needy. Though the rich could learn much and benefit greatly from the refreshing presence of the poor and needy among them, they separate themselves from those

[37] Bartlett, *Seven Stories*, 91.

[38] Jersak, *Her Gates Will Never Be Shut*, 104.

who are considered "beneath" them. And though the religious elites claim to follow the law and the prophets, their actions and behavior show that they know nothing of what Scripture teaches. Those who rest and live in the way of Abraham, and now those who follow the teachings and example of Jesus, will live in solidarity with the sick, the poor, and the outcast, for it is among them that the kingdom of God most naturally lives and grows. So what are the rich to do? They should use their wealth to serve, honor, protect, and provide for the poor in their midst. They must use their wealth to serve Jesus in the kingdom of God. This meaning and application is supported by James 5:1-3, which will be looked at later in this Appendix (cf. also Luke 6:24-25).

JOHN 15:6

If anyone does not abide in Me, he is cast out as a branch and is withered; and they gather them and throw them into the fire, and they are burned.

Since John 15:6 is similar to Matthew 3:10, it often receives a similar interpretation. Both texts contain the image of a plant being burned in a fire. In Matthew 3:10 it was a tree; here it is a vine. And since the vine and tree are equated with humans, and the fire is thought to refer to hell, these passages are often cited as texts that teach the eternal conscious torment of human beings in the fires of hell. However, it was previously discovered that this is not what Matthew 3:10 teaches. The same thing is true of John 15:1-8, as discovered by considering the broader context of the Upper Room Discourse in John 13–17.

While the tree in Matthew 3:10 referred to the nation of Israel, the vine and the branches in John 15:1-8 refer to Jesus and His church. Jesus is the Vine, and individual believers are the branches. God, as the Vinedresser (John 15:1) wants His vine to produce fruit through the branches. So He walks along the vine looking for branches that are not bearing fruit. When He finds one, He lifts it up so that it might bear fruit (This is the correct translation of John 15:2. He does not cut the branch off.).[39] Branches that have drooped to the ground will not produce fruit and so must be trellised.

But if a branch continues to lack fruit, even after it has been lifted up, Jesus says that it will be cast off (or thrown away), and then gathered up and burned in a fire. Does this mean that those Christians who fail to produce enough good works will find themselves cut off from Christ? Will unfruitful Christians lose their eternal life and spend eternity in hell? The answer is no. The reference to fire in verse 6 is not a reference to divine judgment of any kind, let alone the judgment of eternal burning in hell.

---

[39] Earl D. Radmacher and Gary Derickson, *The Disciplemaker: What Matters Most to Jesus* (Salem, OR: Charis Press, 2001).

We see this by noticing the pronouns that Jesus uses in the text. Neither Jesus, nor God the Father, are the ones who do the burning. In this passage, Jesus refers to Himself with the first person singular pronouns "I" and "Me" (15:1, 2, 4, 5). Whenever Jesus refers to God the Father, the third person singular pronoun "He" is used (15:2). When the branches are in view, Jesus uses the second person "you" (15:3, 4, 5).

But in verse 6 Jesus uses the pronoun "they." He says that when a branch stops abiding and withers as a result, "they" gather them up, and throw them into the fire where the branches are burned. Who does Jesus have in mind? Who are "they"? It cannot be Jesus and God the Father, for then He would say "Us" or "We." Gary Derickson and Earl Radmacher believe that Jesus is talking about the people of this world.[40] Indeed, Jesus referred to the world immediately before His teaching about the Vine and the Vinedresser (John 14:31).

Jesus wants the world to see and know the love that exists within the divine family. He wants the world to see and know the love that the Father and Son share for each other, and that they both share with all of us. It is for this reason that Jesus goes on to invite His disciples to love one another as He has loved them, and as they have been loved by the Father (John 15:9-17). But if a branch does not abide in the vine, then the branch will not show or reveal this love. And therefore, the world

[40] Ibid., 182-184.

will not see any evidence of the love that we claim to have from God or that we claim to share with one another. And if they do not see our love for one another, then they will reject, toss out, discard, and ignore our teachings about love and our invitation for them to join us. In other words, "they" will burn our way of life as just another worthless pile of human philosophy and religious rubbish (cf. similar terminology for "cast out" or "thrown away" in Matt 5:13).

The world is looking for fruit among Christians. They are looking to see if we love one another as we claim, and as Jesus commanded us (John 15:9-17). When the world does not see a difference between us and them, our way of life and our teachings are—in their eyes—good for nothing. If we do not abide in Jesus, and therefore if we do not bear fruit, then our way of life is not any different than the way of the world, and so our testimony among them is useless. If we do not reveal changed lives, the world doesn't care a whit about what we have to say. They just put us in the discard pile for burning. In other words, they disregard and ignore us because they determined that our teachings and our ways are worthless and useless.

So Jesus is not teaching that if Christians fail to abide in Jesus and bear much fruit, He will cut them off and send them to hell where they burn forever. To the contrary, when Christians are not bearing fruit, God's only activity is to tend and care for us as a vinedresser with his vine, lifting us up so that we might only receive nutrients from the vine. But if we still do not bear fruit, we might undergo some pruning and discipline (also known as training), but God does not cut us off from Jesus and send us away to hell. This He will never do. But the world might "burn" our teachings and ideas up as nothing more than worthless garbage.

So while hell is not in view in John 15:6, there are temporal consequences for the believer who does not abide in Jesus Christ and bear fruit. We ruin our witness, we bring shame to the name of Jesus, and we obscure the light of the gospel. These are serious issues, but God does not reject us for doing such things, even though the world might. Nevertheless, this does not mean that there are no eternal consequences for failing to live as Jesus wants. There are. And it is these that Paul writes about in 1 Corinthians 3:13, 15.

1 CORINTHIANS 3:13, 15

> *Each one's work will become clear; for the Day will declare it, because it will be revealed by fire; and the fire will test each one's work, of what sort it is. … If anyone's work is burned, he will suffer loss; but he himself will be saved, yet so as through fire.*

The various texts in this Appendix have repeatedly shown that the image of fire refers to judgment. So far, we have seen that this judgment comes during this life, whether upon individuals or nations. We have not seen one single reference that refers to the fire of judgment coming upon people in the next life. But with 1 Corinthians 3:13, 15, we finally have a text that uses the image of fire in reference to judgment in the next life. But even this text is not about the fires of hell for unbelievers. Instead, Paul writes about a fire that will come upon believers.

In 1 Corinthians 3:13, Paul writes that "everyone's work will become clear; for the Day will declare it." When the New Testament authors write about "the Day," they are referring to the Judgment Seat of Christ, which is the future judgment in which *believers* will give an answer to Jesus for how they lived this life (cf. 1 Cor 1:8; 3:13; 4:3; 5:5; 2 Cor 1:4; Php 1:6, 10; 2:16; 2 Thess 2:2; 2 Tim 1:8, 12; 4:8; 1 John 4:17).[41] No unbelievers will be present at the Judgment Seat of Christ; it is a judgment only for believers.

Paul says that it is on this Day, at the Judgment Seat of Christ, that our works will be "revealed by fire" for "the fire will test each one's work." This is a purifying fire. A refining fire. It burns up those things that have no value for eternity. It incinerates the wood, hay, and straw, while leaving the gold, jewels, and precious stones (1 Cor 3:12). Of course, the fire is metaphorical. For just as our lives do not literally produce wood, hay, and

---

[41] Bob Wilkin, "'The Day' is the Judgment Seat of Christ," *JOTGES 20:39* (Autumn 2007). https://faithalone.org/wp-content/uploads/2016/12/Autumn2007.pdf

straw, but these are only metaphors for the worthless things that we accomplish in life, so also, the fire is metaphorical in that it removes from us the worthless works we have performed. We will not actually be burned with literal fire.

Since the Judgment Seat of Christ is only for believers, we have nothing to fear about this day. Our eternal destinies are not in question. Instead, it is only a time of reflection about our lives, as we learn what sorts of actions and behaviors God values for eternity. Much of this we should have already known from Scripture and following Jesus, but before Jesus creates the new heavens and new earth and sends us to populate and reign over it, He sends us out with only the building materials which we have gained and developed during this life. Much as Adam and Eve were supposed to expand the borders of the Garden of Eden, so also, we will each be given areas of responsibility and oversight in the new heavens and new earth, and our initial "plot of land" which God wants us to expand, and the "building materials" we are given to work this land, will be based on how we have lived for Him and served others during this life.

Paul warns the Corinthian believers that it is entirely possible that some Christians will discover on that Day that they have nothing but wood, hay, and straw. Everything they lived for and everything they worked for in this life will burn, that is, it will all be considered worthless. But even then, Paul says, they themselves will be saved. This does not mean that they will still have eternal life (even though they will!), because in Scripture, the word "saved" doesn't refer to eternal life. Paul is saying that they will still be given some sort of responsibility and oversight in the new heavens and new earth. Not all will be lost. Though some believers will have nothing to show for this life, they will embark on a whole new journey with God which will extend for all eternity. Though they may begin with relatively nothing, they will have eternity to continue to serve and work for God. So they themselves, and who they *really are,* will be saved, even though it will be through fire.

One of the ways we can avoid having our life's work consumed by fire at the Judgment Seat of Christ is to allow the purifying fire of God's discipline in this life to perform its perfect work. God often sends purifying fire in our life now so that we can avoid the purifying fire at the Judgment Seat of Christ. When such fire comes into our lives, we are to allow the fire to burn away the sin, chaff, dross, and impurities that pollute us. We are to let such trials have their perfect work so that we may be complete and ready for whatever task God calls us to perform, both now and in eternity.

So while 1 Corinthians 3:13, 15 are talking about a fire that comes upon people after they die, this is not the fire of everlasting hell. Instead, these verses are referring to the purifying fire of God which comes upon believers at the Judgment Seat of Christ as one final step of preparation before they enter eternity with God.

But what about 2 Thessalonians 1:8-9? Does this text finally contain a reference to everlasting punishment and torture in the flames of hell? Let us turn to it and see.

2 THESSALONIANS 1:8-9

… in flaming fire taking vengeance on those who do not know God, and on those who do not obey the gospel of our Lord Jesus Christ. These shall be punished with everlasting destruction from the presence of the Lord and from the glory of His power …

When considered by itself out of context, 2 Thessalonians 1:8-9 seems to conclusively state that God punishes and destroys people forever with flaming fire. As such, this text may be the strongest passage in Scripture to support the concept of eternal torment in fire for the unregenerate dead. But an entirely different understanding emerges after a careful analysis of the text in its context and the numerous intertextual allusions to other passages in Scripture. And since this Appendix has already considered numerous texts with similar terms and has shown that they do not refer to everlasting torture in the fires of hell but to some sort of temporal destruction, we are well-prepared to see what Paul meant when he wrote this text.

The first thing to consider is the numerous allusions and references in these verses to other passages of Scripture. When Paul wrote these words, he expected his readers to bring to mind the images of fire and destruction that are found in various prophetic texts and the teachings of Jesus. For example, the terminology and imagery used in the preceding verse about Jesus being "revealed from heaven with His mighty angels" (2 Thess 1:7) brings to mind the similar imagery used by Jesus in Matthew 13:36-43 and 25:31-46. As seen previously, both of those passages refer to the destruction of nations and countries that ignore the ways of God and the plight of the needy in their midst. Since Paul is using similar imagery, he must have similar ideas in mind.

Furthermore, when Paul writes about "the presence of the Lord and … the glory of His power," he likely has texts such as Isaiah 2:19-21 (cf. Rev 6:15-16) and 66:15-16, 24 in view. This first text refers to the "terror of the Lord and the glory of His majesty" while the second (which was considered previously) refers to the destruction that comes upon those who sin against God. Yet it is critical to note that while the Isaiah text refers to the "terror" of the Lord, Paul removes the reference to terror and inserts the "presence" of the Lord instead. This change is significant.

The phrase "from the presence of the Lord" is key to understanding Paul's point. Many books and articles focus primarily on the first word of this phrase. It is the preposition "from" (Gk., *apō*), and can refer to location or separation (away from), source or origin (comes from), instrument or cause (caused by), and time (from ages past). But since the preposition introduces a longer phrase, we can know the proper meaning of the preposition by first understanding the phrase it introduces.

So what does the phrase "the presence of the Lord" mean? In English, it appears to refer to that which is in proximity to God, or that which is near God. Therefore, to be in the presence of the Lord is to be near God. But the Greek terminology (and the Hebrew on which it is based) is much more vivid. The phrase Paul uses could literally be translated as "before the face of the Lord" (Gk., *prosōpou tou kuriou*). This was a specific Hebrew idiom which referred to the honor of God.

In biblical times, the greatest cultural value was honor. People sought to gain and keep honor for themselves, their family, their country, and their god(s) while avoiding shame. In honor-shame cultures such as that of the ancient Mediterranean world, honor and shame are often symbolized by certain body parts. The head, face, and right hand were symbols of honor, while the left hand, feet, and buttocks were symbols of dishonor.[42] When Paul (or any biblical author) refers to "the presence of the Lord," or more literally, "before the face of

[42] Bruce J. Malina, *The New Testament World: Insights from Cultural Anthropology* (Louisville: WJK, 2001), 37-39; Jerome H. Neyrey, ed. *The Social World of Luke-Acts: Models for Interpretation* (Peabody, MA: Hendrickson, 1991), 34.

the Lord," they are not referring to God's presence, but to God's honor (cf. Jon 1:3; Acts 3:19).[43] Support for this idea is found in the fact that Paul also writes about the power and glory of God (2 Thess 1:9-12), which are closely connected with honor.

Therefore, when Paul puts the preposition "from" in front of this phrase, he is not writing about something that is located with God or comes from God but is instead referring to God's care for His own honor. Paul is writing about the negative consequences that come "from" neglecting the honor of God. In other words, the preposition "from" is causal, but God is not the cause. We humans are the cause of the destruction, for we despised the Lord's honor and suffered the consequences. It is our responsibility and calling as the people of God to bring honor and glory to God through obedience to Him. If we fail in this, and bring shame upon God instead, we can expect to suffer for it.

But note that the suffering and consequences which come upon humans for neglecting God's honor do not come from God Himself, but "from *the honor* of God." That is, for the sake of His own honor, God has given instructions to humans about how to live and function in this world. These instructions are for our own good and to help us live life in the best way possible. When we ignore these instructions, thereby forsaking the hon-

---

[43] See my commentary on Jonah for a more detailed explanation of Jonah 1:2-3 and the idea that "the presence of the Lord" refers to "the honor of the Lord."

or of God, we suffer the consequences, not because God sends the consequences upon us, but because wrong choices and bad decisions naturally lead to devastation and destruction.

And indeed, according to Paul, destruction is exactly what comes upon those who do not know God and who do not obey the instructions within the gospel about how to live (2 Thess 1:8). Three phrases in the context carry this idea. They are "repay with tribulation" (2 Thess 1:6), "in flaming fire taking vengeance" (2 Thess 1:8), and "punished with everlasting destruction" (2 Thess 1:9). All three of these phrases are in parallel, containing an action and an instrument of that action. So each explains and amplifies the other two. Here they are again in parallel format for comparison:

> Repay with tribulation
> Vengeance with flaming fire
> Punishment with everlasting destruction

Let us consider each phrase. First, in 1:6, Paul says that God will "repay with tribulation those that trouble you." The word for *tribulation* (Gk., *thlipsis*) does not refer to hell, but to temporal calamity. It refers to negative outward circumstances and troubles in this life. Not anywhere in Scripture does it refer to eternal sufferings or torment. So when Paul writes about this, he is saying that when others seek to bring trouble upon us for following Jesus, God will turn these troubles back around upon them. This is not a form of punishment or violence, but simply the principle that "He who lives by the sword, dies by the sword."

Second, Paul writes that this repayment will come "in flaming fire taking vengeance" (2 Thess 1:7). The concept of vengeance is parallel to the idea of repayment from 1:6, and so the idea of flaming fire is parallel to tribulation. And just as the tribulation is in this world, so also is the flaming fire. Paul is not referring to torment in the fires of hell. The image of fire, as seen nearly everywhere else in Scripture, refers to the devastation and destruction that comes upon people in this life as a consequence of disobeying God. This fire destroys their plans and goals for this life, leaving only emptiness behind. Vengeance is something that God reserves for Himself (Rom 12:19; Heb 10:30), but according to 1 Peter 2:14, God often carries out this vengeance through governors and rulers. So once again, this second phrase is about the temporal consequences.

The third and final phrase is parallel to the first two, and can be understood similarly. Paul writes that these people will be "punished with everlasting destruction" (2 Thess 1:9). The word "punishment" is not a good translation of what Paul wrote. A better translation would be "pay the penalty" (Gk., *dikēn tisousin*).[44] God does not punish people for their sin, but sin bears its

---

[44] Dike is the Greek god of Justice. Could Paul be making some allusion to this Greek god?

own punishment with it. And this punishment of sin can come in the form of a penalty that must be paid or exacted. In sports, a player can get sidelined, put in the penalty box, or even ejected from the game if they break the rules. They are not being "punished," but are simply paying the price for their bad behavior in the game. They made a choice, and the penalty is the consequence.

Similarly, the "everlasting destruction" (Gk., *olethron aiōnon*) does not refer to annihilation or everlasting torture in hell. As with the parallel concepts in the preceding verses, this destruction is an event that takes place in this life which brings to ruin all the plans and goals of the people and nations upon whom this destruction comes. In fact, "ruin" is a good translation of *olethron* and better carries Paul's meaning. It carries the idea of plans coming to ruin, or of instruments and tools being of no further use. It does not carry the idea of everlasting torture or a cessation of existence.

When a car is "totally destroyed" in an accident, it still exists; it just exists in pieces and parts. It no longer functions. The same is true of "ruin." If I prepare a meal, and then accidentally drop it on the floor, my meal has been ruined. It is all still there, but it is no longer edible. It cannot be enjoyed for the purpose to which it was prepared. So the term does not require that the object of ruin or destruction be annihilated, or cease to exist. It also has no implication of ongoing destruction or ruination, and especially no implication of torture or infliction of pain.

Now, in the case of 2 Thessalonians 1:9, the word "destruction" or "ruin" is modified with the adjective "eternal" (Gk., *aiōnon*), and so some believe that this is ongoing destruction. And it is, but not in the sense that the *activity* of destruction itself continues. If a car is "totally destroyed" it is beyond repair, and will be eternally destroyed. It cannot be fixed. Similarly, if a meal is dropped on the floor, it is eternally ruined. It cannot be salvaged. I cannot go back in time and catch the meal before it hits the floor. A new meal will have to be made.

So "eternal destruction" means that something has come to ruin, and it cannot be salvaged, restored, fixed, or repaired. In regards to the people about whom Paul is writing, their plans and goals will be ruined and come to nothing. The word *olethros* in the LXX is most often used in reference to foreign nations who seek to destroy and subjugate Israel. God tells them that because they have made plans against Israel, it is actually their plans that will come to nothing, and in fact, they themselves will be destroyed (cf. 1 Kings 13:33-34; 15:28-29; Prov 1:26-27; 21:7; Jer 25:31; 48:3, 8, 32; 51:55; Ezek 6:14; 14:16; Hos 9:6).

This is also similar to what Paul writes later about the man of lawlessness (2 Thess 2:8), and which is discussed in numerous other biblical texts (cf. Psa 18:8, 15;

Isa 30:27-33; Jer 7:31-33), some even by Paul himself (cf. 1 Cor 5:5; 1 Thess 5:3; 1 Tim 6:9). When God opens His mouth and speaks truth to worldly power, the plans of those who disobey God and rebel against Him are ruined. The people themselves might continue to live, and indeed, some of them might even be Christians, but their plans which are contrary to the ways of God and the gospel will have no eternal significance and will even be forgotten in the memories of mankind. Their plans come to ruin, come to nothing for eternity, experience everlasting failure, and have no eternal significance or consequences (cf. John 6:27).

So what is everlasting destruction in the flames of fire? It is the ruination in this life of the plans and goals of the people and nations who array themselves against God and His goals. God has set up this world to bring honor and glory to Himself. When we pursue God's honor, we will also experience the best possible life in this world. But if we live contrary to the honor of the Lord, rejecting His glory and power, then our lives will not bring forth joy, satisfaction, and fulfillment, but only emptiness and failure.

These flames of fire and eternal destruction can come in many forms. It can come temporally in the lives of people, as it did with many of the people in Jerusalem and the Roman Empire after the days of Paul. It can occur in human history, as the lives and work of people, nations, and rulers fade from memory and have no lasting impact on others. It can even come upon believers at the Judgment Seat of Christ when they see everything they have worked for and sought after get burned up as wood, hay, and stubble (1 Cor 3:12-15; cf. "the Day" of 2 Thess 1:10). But one thing that is not in view with Paul's words here is the everlasting torture of people by flames of fire in a place called hell.

Second Thessalonians 1:8-9 is not about a future general judgment where unbelievers are consigned to eternal hell. It is explaining that the ways of this world are not the end of the matter, for a day is coming (and has come) when Jesus will vindicate His afflicted people, so that affliction comes upon the afflicters. But even then, this affliction is not everlasting torture, but is the sad reality of seeing their life's work and actions come to nothing for eternity, have no lasting significance on world history or events, and fade away from memory among people. For those of us who want to be remembered and to make an impact on this world, this is a dire warning indeed.

So even the strongest potential passage in the Bible which is often used to support the idea of everlasting punishment in the fiery flames of hell turns out to be teaching nothing of the sort. Contextual and cultural insights about the text reveal that Paul is saying the same thing that every other passage of Scripture says about fiery judgment coming upon people. Such texts are not referring to everlasting torture in hell, but to a temporal judgment in this life.

But what about the famous warning passage in Hebrews 6:7-8? Does this teach that God will send people to burn in hell? By this point in the study, I suspect you already know the answer, but let us consider the text anyway.

HEBREWS 6:7-8

> For the earth which drinks in the rain that often comes upon it, and bears herbs useful for those by whom it is cultivated, receives blessing from God; but if it bears thorns and briers, it is rejected and near to being cursed, whose end is to be burned.

The book of Hebrews contains five warning passages (Heb 2:1-4; 3:7-19; 5:11–6:12; 10:19-39; 12:14-29). The warning passage in Hebrews 6 is both the most severely worded and also the most widely misunderstood. The author of Hebrews uses the imagery of a plot of land which is cultivated and planted so that a harvest might be gained from it. If the land produces crops, it receives blessing from God, but if it does not produce crops, it will get burned. In the context, the land refers to the lives of Christians (5:11; 6:3-4), and so it is upon Christians that the potential blessings or curses can fall. If, therefore, the cursing and burning refers to the fires of eternal hell, then this passage means that some Christians could end up in hell. But is that what it means? No. A careful consideration of three key terms in this text helps the meaning become clear. These words are "rejected, cursed, and burned." All three terms are parallel, and therefore help explain each other.

The word *rejected* (Gk., *adokimos*) could also be translated as disapproved or disqualified. This word has nothing to do with whether or not a person has eternal life, but instead has to do with whether or not God finds a person useful and honest in their dealings with others. Due to this, the word "useful" is a good synonym for the Greek word *dokimos,* while "useless" would be a good synonym for *adokimos.* Therefore, if a Christian is *adokimos*, they still have eternal life, but God considers their "plot of land" to be useless for planting. Rather than being fit for planting, the field of their life is only full of thorns and briars, which are the cares, riches, and pleasures of this world, so that any seed which is planted would get choked rather than produce a harvest (cf. Luke 8:4-15).

The word *rejected* is also found in Hebrews 12:17 (along with the word *blessing* which was mentioned in 6:7) in reference to Esau. Esau sold the blessing of his earthly birthright for a meal, and even though he sought to regain it afterwards with repentance and tears, he was rejected. So the word *rejected* refers to the loss of earthly and temporal blessings and inheritance that God gives to those who obey and honor Him. Those who disobey

God will not receive the blessings, but will be rejected and turned away from them. This is not about going to hell, or getting turned away from the proverbial "gates of heaven," but is instead about being rejected as a useful part of God's plan here on earth.

The word *cursed* (Gk., *katara*) is similar. The word does not refer to an action, but to a verbal, imprecatory declaration about something or someone. In the context, this word *cursed* is the exact opposite of the blessing which was mentioned in Hebrews 6:7. The word for blessing is *eulogia*, and means "verbal praise," and so the cursing is also verbal. It is a negative declaration that something is useless.

The word *cursed* is also used in Galatians 3:10, 13 to refer to the curse of the law and the curse of being crucified. It is used in James 3:10 to refer to the curses that a person can utter with the mouth. And it is used in 2 Peter 2:14 to describe the behavior and characteristics of false prophets (cf. 2 Pet 2:1). On this last text, it is important to note that in the context, Peter writes about the burning of Sodom and Gomorrah (cf. Jude 7), which is similar to how the author of Hebrews goes on to describe the burning of this worthless field. And just as the burning of Sodom and Gomorrah is not equivalent to burning in the fires of hell, so also, the burning of the field is also not referring to hell.

The third key term is the word *burned* (Gk., *kausis*). The word is not the normal word for fire (Gk., *pur*), but is the noun *kausis,* which is the only time this noun is used in Scripture. The verbal form is found in 2 Peter 3:10 in reference to how, at the end of the age, this world will be burned with fire. This Petrine parallel reveals that the word does not refer to hell, but instead to some sort of temporal discipline and judgment in this life.

Indeed, in real life, the burning of a field is actually a way to prepare it for harvest. Often, when a field is full of thorns and briars, the quickest and easiest way to prepare it for plowing and planting is to burn the field. This does not destroy the soil, but instead prepares the ground for future harvest. The burning of the field is a form of discipline and correction to change a useless field into a useful field, making it ready to be planted.

When the meaning and significance of these three terms are considered together, we learn that Hebrews 6:7-8 is not saying anything about how God will send some people to burn in hell. Quite to the contrary, the author is saying that when a Christian fails to live as God wants and desires, and as a result of this failure becomes useless, God might "curse the ground" and burn over the field of their life, *so that* the field can be properly plowed and planted in the future. This is a passage which explains the disciplinary and restorative work of God in helping unfruitful Christians become fruitful again.

This passage is not talking about Christians who lose their eternal life and end up in hell. Just the opposite. This passage affirms our eternal security because it is a passage about the discipline that God gives to His own children when they fall away and stagnate in their lives due to the riches and pleasures of life (cf. Rev 3:19). The author of Hebrews states elsewhere that the Lord disciplines those He loves (Heb 12:6), and that is what the author writes in Hebrews 6 as well.

One of the other warning passages in Hebrews also contains a reference to fire, so it too is worth considering, especially since it seems to be more strongly worded than the imagery of the burning field in Hebrews 6:8. This other text is Hebrews 10:27.

HEBREWS 10:27

… but a certain fearful expectation of judgment, and fiery indignation which will devour the adversaries.

Hebrews 10:19-39 is one of the five warning passages in the book of Hebrews (Heb 2:1-4; 3:7-19; 5:11–6:12; 10:19-39; 12:14-29). In the middle of this warning passage, the author reminds the readers what will happen to them if they reject the truth revealed in Jesus. The author writes that those who disregard what they had previously learned about Jesus will face the judgment of fiery indignation and punishment (Heb 10:27, 29).

Many see this as a clear reference to torment in the flames of hell, but once again, several key insights from the context reveal an entirely different understanding.

First, note that Hebrews 10:27 does not say that the fiery indignation comes from God. Instead, this indignation appears to be self-inflicted. That is, it comes from within the person to consume and devour them. How do we know this? The word *indignation* (Gk., *zēlos*) could also be translated as "zeal" or "jealousy" (cf. Rom 13:13; 1 Cor 3:3). The word itself usually refers to a sinful attitude (2 Cor 12:20; Gal 5:20; Jas 3:14, 16), though there is a form of godly jealousy (2 Cor 7:11; 11:2). So how can one determine whether or not the zeal or jealousy in question is sinful or godly? The word is often accompanied with a modifying adjective or a descriptive noun which helps determine whether the *zēlos* is sinful jealousy or godly jealousy. Here, the modifier is the word *fire* (Gk., *pur*).

As we have seen over and over from Scripture, fire is often a symbol of judgment, discipline, and destruction. Even when used in a positive way to describe the fires of purification (cf. 1 Cor 3:15), the fire itself is still a destructive fire that burns away all that is undesirable. The context of Hebrews 10 reveals something similar here. Phrases such as "fearful expectation of judgment" (Heb 10:27), "worse punishment" (Heb 10:29), and "draw back to perdition" (Heb 10:39) reveal that the fire is to be understood in this negative, destructive sense. Therefore, since the fire is a negative experience, the *zēlos* can also be understood as the negative, destructive, sinful form of jealousy.

Therefore, if this is the sinful form of indignation or jealousy, then it cannot be God's. Since it is sinful, human jealousy, it cannot be godly jealousy. The jealousy, indignation, or zeal which the author of Hebrews is describing is not from God, but from the sinful heart of human beings.

This insight provides great help in understanding this fourth warning passage. The author is warning the readers to not reject the knowledge of the truth they have received through Jesus Christ (Heb 10:26). For if they reject what Jesus revealed, then there is nothing for them to return to except the old religious system of sacrifices, which never did anything to help them with their sin. Indeed, the sacrifices themselves were sinful.[45] The sacrificial system was based on fear, accusation, blame, and scapegoating, and Jesus came to set us free from all such things. But if one rejects the revelation in Jesus, then the only other option is to return to that broken and sinful system.

And what did Jesus reveal? He showed us that we have nothing to fear from God. It is as John writes, the perfect love we have seen in Jesus casts out all fear, because fear has to do with punishment (1 John 4:18). In

---

[45] See J. D. Myers, *Nothing but the Blood of Jesus* (Dallas, OR: Redeeming Press, 2015).

Jesus we have learned that God does not punish, and therefore, we have nothing to fear. Yet those who have not yet seen or understood this revelation of God in Jesus Christ, still live in fear of God. They do not know what God is like and so are afraid of God and live in fear of His judgment.

This explains the fiery indignation that the author of Hebrews has in mind. Fear makes people feel that they are being unjustly judged. Fear causes a person to feel that the one whom they fear will not judge them correctly or justly. Only when a person knows they are loved by the one doing the judging will they feel that this judge has their best interests at heart and will make sound judgments. So when people fear the judge, they become indignant and resentful of the judgment they receive. They feel that all the facts were not properly considered or that extenuating circumstances were not factored in. And so when people fear God, they become indignant and upset that God will judge them for the actions which they feel they were forced to commit by life's circumstances. They become upset, thinking that God only wants to punish them, regardless of the reasons for their actions. They develop a raging indignation against God, or a fiery zeal based on incorrect ideas about God (cf. Rom 10:2). This inner indignation consumes them. It devours them from the inside out.

The author of Hebrews is warning the readers that if they reject what is revealed in Jesus, then they also reject the love and forgiveness of God that is revealed in Jesus. If they reject this, then there is nothing left but the inner turmoil of fiery jealousy and indignation which consumes people from within. This is not eternal torment in the flames of hell, but the inner, psychological turmoil that comes from having an incorrect view of God.

But what about Hebrews 10:29, 31, and 39? These verses contain references to punishment, perdition, and how fearful it is to fall into the hand of the living God. Do these references prove that some sort of punishment from God is in view? They do not.

In Hebrews 10:29, the Greek word for *punishment* is *timōria*. This is the only time this word is used in the New Testament. In other Greek literature, it most often refers to helping someone who has been wronged by assisting them against those who committed the wrong. It is giving the offender what he deserves by doing to him what he did to others. In other words, it carries the idea of a sin against someone else coming back and falling upon the person who committed it. This idea is nearly identical to the concept of indignation from verse 27. The fiery indignation was not from God, but was from inside a person who misunderstands God, and therefore, the indignation is a sin that consumes and devours the person who commits it. The word for *punishment* here has the same idea. Sin bears its own punishment with it.

Similarly, when Hebrews 10:31 says that "It is a fearful thing to fall into the hands of the living God," the author has in mind the exact same concept that was expressed in Hebrews 10:26-27. When people reject the revelation of God in Jesus Christ, that God is only loving and always forgives, then the only alternative view of God is that God is out to judge and destroy them. And for those who have this view of God, for them, it is a fearful thing to fall into the hands of a God who wants to judge and kill. But for the rest of us, who have seen God in Jesus Christ, we need not fear God in such a way.

Yes, God is a judge (Heb 10:30), but Jesus shows us what kind of judge God is. Yes, vengeance belongs to God and God alone will repay people for what they have done (Heb 10:30), but in Jesus, we see that divine vengeance looks like mercy and that repayment for sin looks like forgiveness. When we have this view of God, then we see that God is love (1 John 4:8), and the knowledge of this love casts out all fear (1 John 4:18).

Finally, we must consider the word *perdition* in Hebrews 10:39. The Greek word is *apōleia,* which means "destruction" (cf. Matt 7:13; Rom 9:22; Php 1:28; 3:19; 2 Pet 2:1, 3; 3:16) or "waste" (Matt 26:8; Mark 14:4). The word itself refers to utter loss or complete ruin. It does not have anything to do with eternal damnation (2 Pet 2:3 in the KJV is poorly translated). It simply means that a person is inviting destruction into their life, and into the lives of those who follow them and their teachings. This is exactly what happened with Judas, and what will happen with the antichrist, both of whom are called "the son of perdition" (John 17:12; 2 Thess 2:3). The phrase "saving of the soul" in Hebrews 10:39 also does not refer to escaping hell and going to heaven, but to delivering your life from premature physical death (cf. Jas 1:21; 5:19-20; 1 Pet 1:9).

So although Hebrews 10:19-39 is indeed a dark and ominous text, it is not teaching that some Christians can end up in eternal hell. It is teaching that those who abandon Jesus after believing in Him and receiving the knowledge of the truth that He reveals will experience many negative and harmful consequences in their life. They will become indignant toward God, feeling that He has unjustly judged them, and this fiery indignation will consume them from the inside out. They will live in fear of God, rather than in the experience of His unconditional love. And ultimately, if they continue on this path, they will bring destruction and utter ruin into their life. It is indeed a serious mistake to reject the revelation of God in Jesus Christ, for He alone brings love, hope, and encouragement into our earthly lives (cf. Heb 10:19-25).

JAMES 3:6

And the tongue is a fire, a world of iniquity. The tongue is so set among our members that it defiles the whole body, and sets on fire the course of nature; and it is set on fire by hell.

Since the book of James is likely one of the earliest New Testament writings, he is heavily reliant upon the Hebrew Scriptures. And since James was a leader in the Jerusalem church and a half-brother to Jesus, he seems to base his letter upon the teachings of Jesus in the Sermon on the Mount. Therefore, what he writes about fire and hell is extremely important for understanding the overall imagery of these terms in the Bible. In other words, the image of fire and hell in James can be used to help us understand how these terms are to be understood in the rest of Scripture.

According to Brad Jersak, the imagery of fire and hell in James 3:6 is a definitive text for understanding both terms and how they were used by Jesus and the early church.[46] Jersak writes that the hell (Gk., *gehenna*) imagery in James 3:6 reveals that hell is not a destination to which people go after death, but rather the source of the flames that set the tongue and this world on fire. And since the tongue itself does not actually burn with flames, nor do words literally set our lives, or

---

[46] Sinner Irenaeus, aka Brad Jersak, "Hell is a Kingdom: The Missing Motif Reconstructed," 4, 10. http://www.clarion-journal.com/files/hell-is-a-kingdom-4.pdf

the lives of others, on fire, this imagery too is symbolic of the devastation and destruction that the tongue can cause in a person's life.[47] What then is hell? It is a kingdom of darkness and destruction that is set against the kingdom of heaven in this life. The two kingdoms are at war with each other, and while one brings light and life, the other brings death and devastation.

So James 3:6 is a key interpretive text for the fire and hell imagery of Scripture, and it reveals that neither are referring to a place of literal flames in the afterlife for the unredeemed dead, but instead refer to the devastation and destruction that can come into our lives when we stray from the values and principles of the kingdom of heaven. This is right in line with everything else we have learned in this Appendix. The "fire" is not a place of burning and torture in the afterlife, but an experience of death and devastation in this life. However, some of this fiery devastation and destruction might come upon believers at the Judgment Seat of Christ, which is what James warns the rich about in James 5:3.

JAMES 5:3

Your gold and silver are corroded, and their corrosion will be a witness against you and will eat your flesh like fire. You have heaped up treasure in the last days.

[47] Ibid., 3.

This passage is frequently cited by those who think of hell as eternal conscious torment, because James portrays a vivid image of the gold and silver eating rich people like fire. And yet as James has pointed out frequently in his letter, the people to whom he writes are Christian brethren (cf. Jas 1:2, 16; 2:1, 5, 14; etc.), and James counts the rich among these Christian brethren (cf. Jas 2:1-7). Indeed, it is *because* the rich are Christians that James is able to exhort them to follow Jesus and obey the law of liberty (Jas 2:12-13). So if James writes near the end of his letter that the rich Christians could end up in hell if they are not generous with their money, then James is teaching that a person can lose their eternal life and that entrance into heaven is based on the good works of generosity and giving. Both of these ideas are contrary to everything else Scripture teaches.

Therefore, it is better to understand James 5:3 in light of James 3:6, along with all the other imagery of fire in Scripture. The fire in James 5:3 is symbolic of devastation and destruction that comes upon a person's life for failing to follow the values and principles of the kingdom of heaven. And while this devastation can come into a person's life *now*, it can also come at the beginning of the next life when a person stands at the Judgment Seat of Christ. Our life in eternity begins with standing before Jesus to give an answer for the things we have done in the body, whether good or evil

(2 Cor 5:10). How we live this life helps determine how we start the next life.

James is warning rich Christians that when they hoard wealth for themselves now, they are also storing up "treasure" for themselves at the Judgment Seat of Christ, which will be the experience of seeing all their earthly work and wealth consumed in the flames as if it were nothing more than wood, hay, and stubble (cf. 1 Cor 3:14-15). The wealth of the rich eats away at their life now, and eats away at their life in the new heavens and new earth as well. Therefore, James encourages his rich readers to use their wealth and power to help those in need and to provide fair, just, and generous pay to their laborers (Jas 2:5; 5:4).

This passage is not about how the rich will go to hell because of their riches, but is about how the rich can use their wealth to help others now and store up true, spiritual riches in eternity. If they keep their wealth for themselves, it will only destroy their life now. It will also start their life in eternity with a negative experience.

JUDE 7

… as Sodom and Gomorrah, and the cities around them in a similar manner to these, having given themselves over to sexual immorality and gone after strange flesh, are set forth as an example, suffering the vengeance of eternal fire.

As frequently seen in this Appendix, the image of fire in Scripture refers to the temporal destruction of cities. This is also what is described in Jude 7, where the author points to the destruction of Sodom and Gomorrah as examples of what happens to those who stray from the will of God. However, some point to the phrase at the end of the verse that the cities are "suffering the vengeance of eternal fire" as evidence that Jude is talking about eternal suffering in the flames of hell. However, several contextual insights reveal that this is not what Jude had in mind.

First, this reference to the destruction of Sodom and Gomorrah is parallel to the preceding two examples. Jude loves to give examples in triplicate, and so prior to writing about Sodom and Gomorrah, he writes about the death of some of the Israelites in the wilderness because they did not believe (Jude 5), and the imprisonment of some angels in everlasting chains while they await judgment (Jude 6).

The first example of the Israelites in the wilderness clearly refers to physical death, rather than to eternal torment in hell. The example of the angels is more difficult, since we are not quite sure what event Jude has in mind. But many believe he is referring to the "sons of God" who had sexual relations with the daughters of men in Genesis 6, and were imprisoned as a result. Yet notice that while these angels are imprisoned in chains and darkness, they are not being tortured with fire. In fact, darkness and fire are mutually exclusive. And since angels are immortal, they cannot be killed. Therefore, they were imprisoned and are awaiting judgment.

This third example of Sodom and Gomorrah is a combination of the first two. Like the angels, the inhabitants of these cities committed sexual immorality and went after strange flesh. This is referring to the fact that the cities were inhospitable and attempted to rape the angels who visited them (Gen 19:4-7; Ezek 16:49-50). The result of this behavior was that the cities of Sodom and Gomorrah were destroyed with fire.

Yet how do we know that Jude is not referring to eternal torment in the flames of hell? We know this because Jude says that Sodom and Gomorrah were "set forth as an example," which means that this example could be seen by humans. If Jude were referring to the eternal fires of hell, then Sodom and Gomorrah could not be set forth as an example to be seen and witnessed by humans. Jude cannot be referring to some sort of *future* punishment in hellfire, because then it would not in any way be set forth as an historical example to mankind.[48]

But we also know that Jude was not referring to the eternal flames of hell because of what he writes in Jude 23. Jude writes that it is possible to pull people out of the fire. This is, of course, exactly what happened with

[48] Cf. Thayer, *The Origin and History of the Doctrine of Endless Punishment*, loc 182.

Lot and his family. They were rescued, pulled, or delivered from the flames that destroyed Sodom and Gomorrah, and Jude indicates that similar deliverance can happen today. If Jude was referring to the flames of hell in this text, then he would be teaching that it is possible to rescue and deliver people from hell after they are already there. But few who believe that hell is a place of everlasting torment in fire are willing to say that it is possible to rescue the people who are there. It is better to recognize from the context that Jude is not thinking about eternal torment in the flames of hell, but rather the everlasting destruction of cities due to temporal flames.

Indeed, this is exactly how to understand the phrase "suffering the vengeance of eternal fire." To begin with, "suffering the vengeance" is probably not the best way of translating the Greek (Gk., *dikēn hupechousai*). As mentioned previously under 2 Thessalonians 1:8-9, the Greek word *dikē* means "penalty" or "justice" (Dikē was the Greek god of justice). The second word, *hupechō*, appears only here in the New Testament, and literally means "to undergo" or "hold under," and carries the idea of experiencing something. So the phrase itself means "to undergo justice" or to "experience justice." And as frequently mentioned elsewhere, this experience of justice, or this penalty, is not sent by God but is brought upon someone through their own actions. Sin carries its own penalty with it. This is exactly what Jude says in verse 10 when he writes that the false teachers "corrupt themselves." The corruption and punishment that come upon people is not sent from God but is brought by a person upon their own heads.

Jude says that this self-inflicted punishment upon Sodom and Gomorrah was "eternal fire." This does not mean that the cities are still burning, for they are not. It means that the fire that fell upon these cities destroyed them completely, and they have not been rebuilt.[49] This is true, for the cities of Sodom and Gomorrah were in the location of what is now the Dead Sea.

According to historical accounts from the New Testament era, the Dead Sea was also known as the Lake of Fire, where there were frequent bouts of flame and smoke, burning sulphur, and where everything that went through it collected a tarnish of oily soot and grime (cf. Gen 19:24-28; Deut 29:23; Isa 34:9; Jer 49:17-18; See the discussion of Rev 20:10 in the chapter on the eight words for hell). In the days of Jesus, the valley was still smoking and smoldering, and they assumed it would go on that way forever. This is what Jude has in mind when he speaks of the cities suffering the vengeance of eternal fire. It is not hell, but is the ongoing, physical destruction and devastation that came upon those cities.

---

[49] The smoke of Babylon burning forever means that Babylon will never be rebuilt (cf. Rev 18:9, 18).

CONCLUSION

The word "fire" is a difficult term to understand in Scripture, not only because of the vivid imagery it portrays, but also because of the long and persistent tradition of hell as a place of burning fire that many have grown up with. It is difficult to retrain our minds to get past the fear and horror of those images and see "fire" for what it truly is in Scripture. Yes, the concept of "fire" includes the idea of destruction, but this destruction most often refers to some sort of temporal, historical calamity that comes upon a city or nation. When it does refer to an experience in the next life, it refers to the judgment that *believers* will face at the Judgment Seat of Christ when their bad works are revealed to be worthless in eternity.

The only instances in which the image of fire is used in reference to unbelievers and their experience in eternity are the texts in Revelation that speak about unbelievers being cast into the Lake of Fire. But since we learned in the chapter about the eight terms for hell that "the Lake of Fire" is itself an image for the Dead Sea, which was in turn a cultural symbol for being separated from God, not even the Lake of Fire describes an eternal, tortured existence in flames for the unregenerate dead. The biblical symbol of fire is a serious and critical subject, but the one thing it does *not* symbolize is the eternal conscious torment of unbelievers in hell.

The image of fire in Scripture calls us to be careful how we live now, so that our lives on this earth are not ruined and destroyed, and so that when we enter into eternity with God, we can begin that life in the best way possible. The biblical teaching about fire encourages us to live like Jesus now so that we can have the best experience possible of our life now and as we begin our life in eternity.

AFTERWORD

Your kingdom come,
Your will be done,
On earth as it is in heaven.
–Jesus of Nazareth

Have you ever heard the old Johnny Cash song entitled "No Earthly Good"? It is a song about people who become so focused on heaven as an afterlife destination that they essentially neglect the present hellish realities that are all around us. One becomes so heavenly minded that they are no earthly good. The lesson we can take from this song is that we can be very spiritual, invest our time in prayer, in church meetings, and in studying the Bible, but end up leaving the world behind with little evidence that we were ever here or made a difference while we were on it.

This is not the kind of Christianity that we see lived out in the pages of Scripture. Jesus and those who followed Him had a bit of a reputation for being trouble-makers. Not because they were mischievous, but because they didn't "toe the line." They saw brokenness in the world, in the systems around them, and in the people who were victims of it all, and they chose to stand up and fight against it.

When Christ taught His disciples to pray "Your kingdom come, your will be done, on earth as it is in heaven," He did not encourage them with the future hope of heaven but rather challenged them to bring a little bit of heaven down to earth. "Your kingdom come" has nothing to do with church real estate; rather it is a declaration of war against the kingdom of darkness. It is heaven invading earth with the knowledge that the gates of hell will not be able to stand up against the church's attacking army. And the church is no ordinary army. Most armies bring with them calamity upon the lands and peoples they invade, resulting in hunger, poverty, and destruction. The soldiers of Christ, however, lay down their own lives sacrificially for others. Instead of capturing, they release. Rather than oppress, they set free. And instead of bringing death, they bring life.

Jesus, reading from Isaiah, once said the following:

> *The Spirit of the Lord is upon Me, because He has anointed Me to preach the gospel to the poor; He has sent Me to heal the broken hearted, to proclaim liberty to the captives and recovery of sight to the blind, to set at liberty those who are oppressed; to proclaim the acceptable year of the Lord (Luke 4:18-19).*

The more you think about it the more you realize that this was not just *His* mission on earth, but is also the calling for all who belong to Him. It is our privilege to continue the work that Jesus started here on earth of serving the poor, participating in the healing process where we find brokenness, setting the captives free, and proclaiming the rule of our Lord to those who are surrounded and entrapped by darkness.

Yes, the implications of trusting in Jesus for eternal life or refusing that gift extend far beyond the few short years that we are given before our bodies will one day be laid to rest. But the good news is that eternal life starts now in the present. The kingdom of God which began like a small mustard seed is growing day by day here on earth, light is overcoming the darkness and as it spreads the kingdom of hell is forced to relinquish ground and retreat. This is a battle that we are winning.

My hope for this book by J. D. Myers is that it will help shed light on many of the myths that people have been led to believe surrounding hell and ultimately about God Himself. By properly contextualizing some key verses and understanding various words oftentimes associated with hell and punishment, we can learn to trust that God is indeed good. And it is because of His love for us that He warns us about the dangers of a life lived apart from His ways and guidance. When we fall off the rails, we don't need to hide from God in the bushes like Adam and Eve tried to do. Instead, we can know that the safest place in the world is to run directly into His waiting arms where we will find love, mercy, and help. This is what I take from Jeremy's book and what I hope that you have found in its pages as well.

This book, though it is about hell, is really about the kingdom of heaven, and how to fulfill the prayer of Jesus: "Your kingdom come, Your will be done, on earth as it is in heaven." So read the book, and then get to work by following Jesus to the gates of hell to set the captives free and introduce them to the rule and reign of God on earth.

–**Wesley Rostoll**
Author of *Seeing the Cross with New Eyes*

A RESPONSE BY BRAD JERSAK

I mentioned in the Foreword that Jeremy and I are not entirely in agreement. To me, Jeremy's boldest contention is that *many will suffer permanent (everlasting) separation from God*. For example, he says:

> … Scripture teaches that many people will indeed spend eternity separated from God.

> God does not (and cannot) force people against their will to love Him or to believe in Jesus for eternal life. I believe that that some people, even if they were given infinite chances in eternity, would still reject God forever.

> The only thing God can do is what He has always done. He can let the objects of His infinite love continue to live forever in whatever way they want. He allows them go off into a far country to squander their inheritance on riotous living.

I applaud Jeremy for expressing these views forthrightly. For too long, traditionalists either used bait-and-switch tactics to avoid confessing their position or they doubled down into cruelty and crassness with their literalized fiery furnaces. Myers is better than that. Still, I'm hopeful that we could be more optimistic than these statements allow. Please consider the following thoughts as sincere questions for further discussion—not a direct rebuttal per se.

I am absolutely with Jeremy on the impossibility of a coerced post-mortem conversion. There is no such thing as forced love. Love that is not free and willing is not love at all. One might even question how many millions of so-called conversions in this epoch were nothing more than coercions notched in the belts of evangelists wielding hellfire ultimatums. No, anyone who turns to Christ in this life or beyond the threshold of death can only enter the Kingdom of Christ through a willing and free turn in love to Love. On this point, I'm at least as convinced as Jeremy.

That said, I'm also convinced of a bit more.

First, I believe in the possibility of post-mortem conversion for all. Because Christ now holds the keys of death and hades (Rev 1), death cannot separate us from the love of God (Rom 8). As my friend W. Paul Young likes to say (I'm paraphrasing),

> In his love, Abba has never taken away our right to say "No" to his love. In dying, Christ secured and maintained our freedom to say our "Yes" or "No" to him. Why then would we think he would ever allow the event

of death to take away that freedom to say "Yes" or "No" to his love?

He wouldn't. Our freedom to say "Yes" or "No" is not negated by death. As the early church Fathers say, "In Christ's death, death has died."

I know well the counterpoints—I used to employ them:

> But Brad, what about the parable of the Rich Man and Lazarus? Doesn't the parable teach that no one can cross the chasm between paradise and hades? And doesn't it say that no one in hades can ever return?

To this, Pope Benedict XVI cautioned us not to forget the *punchline* of the parable (and all of Jesus' judgment parables): namely, Christ's death and resurrection! In his death and resurrection, Christ crossed the uncrossable chasm and returned from the unreturnable depths of hades … with a parade of captives in his wake. We must not create a dogma of inescapable hades from the Lazarus parable without reference to the One who died and went there, shattered its gates, bound its strongman, plundered its goods (us) and returned victorious.

> But Brad, doesn't the Bible say, "It is appointed unto man once to die and after that the judgment?"

Of course! But for many of the Fathers—including Clement and Origen of Alexandria, Gregory of Nyssa and Isaac of Nineveh, the final judgment is restorative and remedial, not retributive. Macrina the Younger argues that the fire of divine love will purge us of our earthly attachments. Any torment we experience is not retributive punishment but will be experienced precisely to the degree that we cling to our bondage and our worldly idols (including religious pride!). Similarly, many centuries later, George MacDonald imagined this judgment as flames of love that consume within us "all that is not love's kind."

Nowhere do we read that the final judgment is voluntary. Rather, some texts describe the coming judgment, not as eternal separation, but as a saving ordeal we undergo—the refiner's fire and launderer's soap (Mal 3). Thus, God not only forgives sin, but heals and purifies us of it completely. How? By burning away the wood, hay and stubble of our false selves (1 Cor 3) in the consuming fire of the divinity presence. Isaac assures us: the flames are none other than the glorious passion of Christ's unquenchable love.

If so, is not the final judgment itself God's ultimate saving act? Isn't "hell" an infinitely amplified version of the "trials by fire" we experience even now, by which the willful ego is humbled, we come to our senses and head home to Abba's house? The key question is whether we could or would forever resist the love of God.

"Love could not bear that," says St. Isaac.

But as Jeremy says, neither can divine Love violate our free rejection of Love.

Are we not, then, at an impasse?

Here, I follow Maximos the Confessor's potential solution. He begins with the nature of the human will. The "natural will" created by God was designed to *always freely desire the Good*—that Good is ultimately the love of God. Our glorification in the coming age will include the restoration of our natural will so that we will *freely* choose never to repeat the tragedy of the fall throughout eternity. That is, our eternal obedience to Christ will always be natural and willing.

The "mystery of iniquity" is that somehow (we don't know exactly) in the deception and willfulness of the fall, our "natural will" became dysfunctional. Maximos refers to this dysfunction as the "gnomic will"—a vacillation of our desires between turning toward the Good and turning away in self-will. The "gnomic will" is not absolutely bound (as you get in Calvin or Luther—both still Augustinians in that sense) but it is also definitely *not truly free*. It is blinded and deceived by the seductions of the world, the flesh and the devil. In other words, turning from the Good is always a delusion rooted in this dysfunction.

Maximos, as I understand him, believes that it would be unjust for God to condemn anyone for a bad decision made with a deceived and dysfunctional will. What was God to do? In Christ, the human will is healed—

especially in Gethsemane when Christ vicariously surrenders his human survival instincts to the greater, saving purposes of the divine will. As we participate in Christ's surrender, our own wills are set free. This happens in part in this life for some. But what of the majority of humanity, ensnared and enslaved to its own self-will?

When we all finally see Christ face-to-face—freed from the deluding influences of the world system, the ego and the evil one—when we see what and who we rejected—will anyone willingly turn away from perfect Love? Would they do so forever? And would infinite Love frown and say, "I'm sorry. You died in your stubbornness. There's nothing I can do"?

Would it be coercion or a violation of our freedom if on that great and glorious day, Christ were to heal our dysfunctional wills and graciously restore our natural will, opening our eyes to the fullness of truth then as he does now for those whom he's freed to see (2 Cor 4) and respond to the gospel?

Doesn't Christ promise that in that day, "Every eye will see him"? Doesn't John claim that "When we see him, we shall be like him, for we shall see him as he is"? And having seen the truth with healed eyes, who would persist in their folly? No one, I hope.

None of this denies that our only entry into eternity is through a free will—or better, *freed will*—response to the Love of Christ. What I'm challenging is whether *infinite Love* could be *eternally ineffectual* in transforming hard hearts, especially once they've been released from all attachments, brokenness and deception. To behold Christ *freely* would be to see him as he is through the eyes of our truest selves. What truly *free will* would say "No" eternally? To me, that would be the greater miracle.

As Hans Urs Von Balthasar says, God's commitment to the principle of human freedom maintains the possibility—*however infinitely unlikely*—that some would resist perfect love forever. "Infinitely unlikely": I love those odds.

I'm not a universalist, but my friend Robin Parry is (and not the sloppy kind)—and I concede that in fair debate, I lose to him every time. The reason for this is his devastating theological and biblical logic. He says,

If God is all-powerful (he is), he is able to save everyone.

If God is all-loving (he is), he wants to save everyone.

If he is able to save everyone and wants to save everyone, he will save everyone.

And then he lays out over NT passages to demonstrate that God will do exactly that—without any violation to human freedom. He cites Philippians 2 as a straightforward prophecy of the outcome: "Every knee will bow and tongue confess [the word for confession of faith], in heaven and on earth and under the earth, that Jesus Christ is Lord to the glory of God the Father." How do we know that for sure, given the reality of human freedom? According to Parry, because Scripture says so (repeatedly).

I find Robin's arguments compelling. He might wonder why I wouldn't teach such clear statements as dogma. Some days I wonder too. One reason is that teachers like Jeremy keep a wise foot on the brake by reminding me of all the other texts that we must not marginalize and which ought to give us pause. So whether you agree or disagree with Jeremy's conclusions, his book is worth reading. It carries forward in a thoughtful and accessible way the ongoing discussion about the nature and character of hell. Take it up and read, so that you might think, learn, and be challenged.

A REJOINDER BY JEREMY

I hope Brad is right. I truly do. I agree with his premise that if an unregenerate person in eternity responds to the infinite love of God and wants to join Him in eternity, God will welcome such a person with open arms. Brad quotes Hans Urs Von Balthasar as saying that it is infinitely unlikely that every person will eternally *reject* such an offer. My view is the opposite. I think it is infinitely unlikely that *every* person will accept such an offer. While I hope, along with Brad, that all who see Jesus with renewed eyes would turn from their folly, the pessimistic realist in me recognizes the infinite ability of sinful humankind to deny the truth, reject love, and persist in self-deception. This human trait, I believe, will only strengthen in eternity.

Other than this, I do wish to state one objection to Brad's summary of my view. In the opening paragraph of his response, he states that my boldest contention in the book is that "*many will suffer permanent (everlasting) separation from God.*" I do not actually believe this, nor is it something I ever stated in the book. Yes, Brad provides a few quotes from places in the book where my words could be read to *imply* such an idea, but I never explicitly argue for the idea Brad attributes to me. I do not believe that many will suffer permanent (everlasting) separation from God.

First, I tried very hard throughout the book to never describe an unregenerate person's experience in eternity as "suffering." To the contrary, I stated repeatedly and frequently that God does not ever wish, desire, cause, or send suffering on human beings, in this life or the next. While sin does indeed cause suffering, God does not send or approve of this suffering, but instead, walks through it with us, seeking to help, heal, and protect us along the way.

This, I believe, is what God also does for unregenerate people in eternity. Which brings up my second disagreement with Brad's summary of my view. He said that I believe people will experience *permanent (everlasting) separation from God.* He even includes a direct quote where I said something very similar to this. But in other places in the book, and in the context of that very quote, I point out that since God is omnipresent, God Himself is *never* separated from anyone, either in this life or the next. God is always with all people.

I argue in the book that unregenerate people will have an experience of separation from God, but this experience is self-inflicted. The experience does not reflect reality. Again, it is much like the experience of some people in this life. Many feel like God has abandoned and forsaken them, even though He has not. Incidentally, it is exactly this experience that Jesus felt when He cried out "My God, My God, Why have You forsaken Me?" Jesus was not forsaken by God; He only *felt* like He was. The cry of Jesus from the cross echoed the similar cry of countless humans throughout history who have felt abandoned and forsaken by God, even though He was with them and near them the entire time.

It will be the same for unregenerate people in eternity. They will not be separated from God in reality. But because they choose to go their own way, they will think, feel, or imagine that they are separated from Him. This is exactly what they want, and though God's presence and love will be with such people for all eternity, they will not know it or experience it because they have shut themselves off from the truth.

This brings me back around to the overall point of this book, and the primary area in which Brad and I disagree. Just as Brad finds Robin's arguments for universalism compelling but cannot go all the way with him, so also, I find Brad's arguments compelling but cannot travel with him all the way. To me, it seems that the longer people reject the truth, the more skilled they become at continuing to reject the truth. Even with healed spiritual eyes and a perfect vision of Jesus, I see no reason why many unregenerate humans will not continue to eternally reject love and deny the truth. People make their choices, and then their choices make them. Furthermore, when confronted with truths that challenge their choices, rather than admit they were wrong, people tend to rationalize their choices against the truth. If this is true now, I see no reason why it would be different in eternity.

But again, I hope I am wrong and Brad is right. There has never been a belief I have held, about which I have so longed to be wrong. Regardless, I place my life and the life of all humans in the loving and gracious hands of God, trusting Him to do what is best and right. And until God makes it clear in eternity the direction He has chosen to go, we will keep our eyes fixed on Jesus, our ears attentive to the whisper of the Holy Spirit, our fingers within the pages of Scripture, and our mouths filled with the beautiful and sure truths of the Gospel. May we always seek to make our life and theology—including our theology of hell—look more like Jesus Christ.

WANT TO LEARN MORE?

Take the online course about hell.

You have questions about hell?
Get them answered in the online course about hell.

Learn more at RedeemingGod.com/Courses/

The course is normally $297, but you can
take it for free by joining the Discipleship Group at
RedeemingGod.com/join/

ABOUT J. D. MYERS

J. D. (Jeremy) Myers is a popular author, blogger, pod-caster, and Bible teacher who lives in Oregon with his wife and three daughters. He primarily writes at Re-deemingGod.com, where he seeks to help liberate people from the shackles of religion. His site also provides an online discipleship group where thousands of like-minded people discuss life and theology and encourage each other to follow Jesus into the world.

If you appreciated the content of this book, would you consider recommending it to your friends and leaving a review online? Thanks!

JOIN JEREMY MYERS AND LEARN MORE

Take Bible and theology courses by joining Jeremy at
RedeemingGod.com/join/
Receive updates about free books, discounted books, and new books by joining Jeremy at
RedeemingGod.com/read-books/

WHAT IS PRAYER? HOW TO PRAY TO GOD THE WAY YOU TALK TO A FRIEND

Stop worrying about how to pray, and just start praying!

This book reveals one simple truth: That you already know how to pray!

Once you discover that you know how to pray as revealed in this book, you will also discover that you already know what to pray for and how to see more answers to your prayers.

Read this book and find the freedom and power in your prayer life you have always longed for.

REVIEWS

I LOVE THIS BOOK! J. D. Myers has done such a great job of putting into clear words all the things about prayer that have been developing in my thoughts for years. If you wonder what praying means, if you wonder what praying should be like, or even if you wonder why on earth people should even pray, READ THIS. This is, so far, my favorite Jeremy Myers book. Not too deep, not too theological, not even too serious—though the subject matter is serious and is dealt with seriously. The tone of the writing is perfect, and the advice is genuine and extremely worthwhile. EXCELLENT BOOK. –B. Shuford

The book appears to be too simple but as you progress Jeremy covers many aspects of prayer in a way that is like a breath of fresh air. The book ends up being a natural encouragement to talking to God as a friend. I definitely recommend this book as the reader will definitely benefit from it. Not just intellectually but practically as well. Prayer will change from a chore or obligation to a pleasurable interaction with God. My heart was so filled with joy while reading this book. Jeremy you've reminded me once more that as you walk with Jesus and spend time in His presence, He talks to you and reveals Himself through the Scriptures. –Pete Nellmapius

When you finish this short book, you will know two things: 1) How easy it is to pray, and 2) How dangerous it is to pray! Prayer changes things, I used to hear. I heard in Jeremy's book, prayer changes me. I especially appreciated a page where Jeremy discusses how often we are the answers to our own prayers. I saw a "vision" of someone I am now praying for, and the Lord looking at him and looking at me, as if to say, "Well, I've put you in his life, haven't I?" A beautiful book. –Carol Roberts

WHAT ARE THE SPIRITUAL GIFTS? DISCOVER YOUR SPIRITUAL GIFTS AND HOW TO USE THEM

Let's cut through all the nonsense about spiritual gifts.

Here is a down-to-earth discussion about what the spiritual gifts are, how to discover your spiritual gifts, and how to use them in the real world.

This book answers such questions as:

-Why did God give spiritual gifts?
-What are the spiritual gifts?
-How can I know my spiritual gifts?
-Are some spiritual gifts better than others?
-What are the dangers of the spiritual gifts?
-Have some spiritual gifts ceased?
-What about the spiritual gift of tongues?
-How can I embrace and use my spiritual gifts?

This book also includes a 125-question Spiritual Gift Inventory test.

REVIEWS

J. D. Myers' title *What are the Spiritual Gifts?* is perfect and delivers in identifying spiritual gifts mentioned in the Bible and how to personally discover your gifts to help others. Those who grew up going to church are very familiar with the topic of spiritual gifts. I would encourage those who didn't grow up in the church to read as well if wishing God's help to make a difference in the lives of others through your talents, interests, skills, and abilities.

Those who grew up going to church want to understand more about gifts such as tongues, prophecy, etc. The book does a great job of discussing whether some gifts no longer exist and how we can understand such gifts. –Mike Edwards

Jeremy Myers pulls out all the distractions that keep us from understanding our spiritual gifts given to us from a loving God. –David DeMille

Why do we think spiritual gifts are a mystery? According to Mr. Myers, we shouldn't. In a simple presentation, he offers his view of the Spiritual Gifts, and some of the characteristics for each of them (with strengths and pitfalls). The book also suggests five simple ways of discerning your gift, including a test in the end. While a test can be useful, much more useful are the other ways, like asking yourself what you think other Christians should do more … –The Pilgrimm

WHAT IS FAITH? HOW TO KNOW THAT YOU BELIEVE

You might know what you believe … but do you know *that* you believe?

While many Christians know that they are supposed to believe, they don't know if they actually do believe.

Stop wondering if you have false faith, spurious faith, temporary faith, intellectual faith, or head faith instead of heart faith. All such terms are unhelpful and unbiblical, and cause many Christians to wonder if they have truly believed.

By reading this book, you will not only discover how faith works, but also how to know that you believe.

This book also answers some of your most pressing questions about faith, such as the relationship between faith and works, whether or not God gives the gift of faith, and how it is possible to be certain about your faith. This book also provides explanations for several key Bible passages about faith.

Once again, Jeremy Myers brings clarity to a topic that many are confused about. Faith is such a difficult subject for some. Do I have enough faith? I have doubts, how does that affect my faith? What is child-like faith? Do I have little faith, small faith or great faith? Many Christians put faith in their faith. Jeremy does a wonderful job of explaining these concepts and more in this book. Having read, and listened to, many of Jeremy's books and podcasts, I can attest to his in-depth knowledge and proficient writing style. Whether you agree with all his points or not, you will come away with more knowledge and understanding after reading this book. This is a book that I would recommend all new Christians read and be used in discipleship classes. –Michael Wilson

I was privileged to receive an advanced copy and am happy to report that the book was enormously helpful. Having a firm foundation of knowing that you are fully loved and accepted by God is essential to spiritual growth, and in our day the greatest impediment to having this firm foundation is wondering, "Have I really believed?" Jeremy helps the reader answer this question. To any Christian who is unsure of your foundation, this book is for you! –K. E. Young

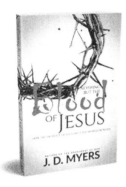

NOTHING BUT THE BLOOD OF JESUS: HOW THE SACRIFICE OF JESUS SAVES THE WORLD FROM SIN

Do you have difficulties reconciling God's behavior in the Old Testament with that of Jesus in the New?

Do you find yourself trying to rationalize God's violent demeanor in the Bible to unbelievers or even to yourself?

Does it seem disconcerting that God tells us not to kill others but He then takes part in some of the bloodiest wars and vindictive genocides in history?

The answer to all such questions is found in Jesus on the cross. By focusing your eyes on Jesus Christ and Him crucified, you come to understand that God was never angry at human sinners, and that no blood sacrifice was ever needed to purchase God's love, forgiveness, grace, and mercy.

In *Nothing but the Blood of Jesus*, J. D. Myers shows how the death of Jesus on the cross reveals the truth about the five concepts of sin, law, sacrifice, scapegoating, and bloodshed. After carefully defining each, this book shows how these definitions provide clarity on numerous biblical texts.

REVIEWS

Building on his previous book, "The Atonement of God," the work of René Girard and a solid grounding in the Scriptures, Jeremy Myers shares fresh and challenging insights with us about sin, law, sacrifice, scapegoating and blood. This book reveals to us how truly precious the blood of Jesus is and the way of escaping the cycle of blame, rivalry, scapegoating, sacrifice and violence that has plagued humanity since the time of Cain and Abel. *Nothing but the Blood of Jesus* is an important and timely literary contribution to a world desperately in need of the non-violent message of Jesus. –Wesley Rostoll

My heart was so filled with joy while reading this book. Jeremy you've reminded me once more that as you walk with Jesus and spend time in His presence, He talks to you and reveals Himself through the Scriptures. –Reader

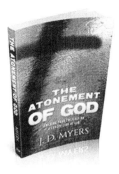

THE ATONEMENT OF GOD: BUILDING YOUR THEOLOGY ON A CRUCIVISION OF GOD

After reading this book, you will never read the Bible the same way again.

By reading this book, you will learn to see God in a whole new light. You will also learn to see yourself in a whole new light, and learn to live life in a whole new way.

The book begins with a short explanation of the various views of the atonement, including an explanation and defense of the "Non-Violent View" of the atonement. This view argues that God did not need or demand the death of Jesus in order to forgive sins. In fact, God has never been angry with us at all, but has always loved and always forgiven.

Following this explanation of the atonement, J. D. Myers takes you on a journey through 10 areas of theology which are radically changed and transformed by the Non-Violent view of the atonement. Read this book, and let your life and theology look more and more like Jesus Christ!

REVIEWS

Outstanding book! Thank you for helping me understand "Crucivision" and the "Non-Violent Atonement." Together, they help it all make sense and fit so well into my personal thinking about God. I am encouraged to be truly free to love and forgive, because God has always loved and forgiven without condition, because Christ exemplified this grace on the Cross, and because the Holy Spirit is in the midst of all life, continuing to show the way through people like you. –Samuel R. Mayer

This book gives another view of the doctrines we have been taught all of our lives. And this actually makes more sense than what we have heard. I myself have had some of these thoughts but couldn't quite make the sense of it all by myself. J.D. Myers helped me answer some questions and settle some confusion for my doctrinal views. This is truly a refreshing read. Jesus really is the demonstration of who God is and God is much easier to understand than being so mean and vindictive in the Old Testament. The tension between the wrath of God and His justice and the love of God are eased when reading this understanding of the atonement. Read with an open mind and enjoy! –Clare N. Bez

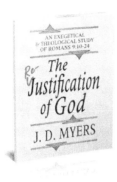

THE RE-JUSTIFICATION OF GOD: A STUDY OF ROMANS 9:10-24

Romans 9 has been a theological battleground for centuries. Scholars from all perspectives have debated whether Paul is teaching corporate or individual election, whether or not God truly hates Esau, and how to understand the hardening of Pharaoh's heart. Both sides have accused the other of misrepresenting God.

In this book, J. D. Myers presents a mediating position. Gleaning from both Calvinistic and Arminian insights into Romans 9, J. D. Myers presents a beautiful portrait of God as described by the pen of the Apostle Paul.

Here is a way to read Romans 9 which allows God to remain sovereign and free, but also allows our theology to avoid the deterministic tendencies which have entrapped certain systems of the past.

Read this book and—maybe for the first time—learn to see God the way Paul saw Him.

REVIEWS

Fantastic read! Jeremy Myers has a gift for seeing things from outside of the box and making it easy to understand for the rest of us. The Re -Justification of God provides a fresh and insightful look into Romans 9:10-24 by interpreting it within the context of chapters 9-11 and then fitting it into the framework of Paul's entire epistle as well. Jeremy manages to provide a solid theological exegesis on a widely misunderstood portion of scripture without it sounding to academic. Most importantly, it provides us with a better view and understanding of who God is. If I had a list of ten books that I thought every Christian should read, this one would be on the list. – Wesley Rostoll

I loved this book! It made me cry and fall in love with God all over again. Romans is one of my favorite books, but now my eyes have been opened to what Paul was really saying. I knew in my heart that God was the good guy, but J. D. Myers provided the analysis to prove the text. ... I can with great confidence read the difficult chapters of Romans, and my furrowed brow is eased. Thank you, J. D. Myers. I love God, even more and am so grateful that his is so longsuffering in his perfect love! Well done. –Treinhart

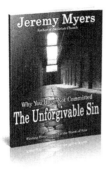

WHY YOU HAVE NOT COMMITTED THE UNFORGIVABLE SIN: FINDING FORGIVENESS FOR THE WORST OF SINS

Are you afraid that you have committed the unforgivable sin?

In this book, you will learn what this sin is and why you have not committed it. After surveying the various views about blasphemy against the Holy Spirit and examining Matthew 12:31-32, you will learn what the sin is and how it is committed.

As a result of reading this book, you will gain freedom from the fear of committing the worst of all sins, and learn how much God loves you!

REVIEWS

This book addressed things I have struggled and felt pandered to for years, and helped to bring wholeness to my heart again. –Natalie Fleming

A great read, on a controversial subject; biblical, historical and contextually treated to give the greatest understanding. May be the best on this subject (and there is very few) ever written. – Tony Vance

You must read this book. Forgiveness is necessary to see your blessings. So if you purchase this book, [you will have] no regrets. –Virtuous Woman

Jeremy Myers covers this most difficult topic thoroughly and with great compassion. –J. Holland

Wonderful explication of the unpardonable sin. God loves you more than you know. May Jesus Christ be with you always. –Robert M Sawin III

Excellent book! Highly recommend for anyone who has anxiety and fear about having committed the unforgivable sin. –William Tom

As someone who is constantly worried that they have disappointed or offended God, this book was, quite literally, a "Godsend." I thought I had committed this sin as I swore against the Holy Spirit in my mind. It only started after reading the verse about it in the Bible. The swear words against Him came into my mind over and over and I couldn't seem to stop no matter how much I prayed. I was convinced I was going to hell and cried constantly. I was extremely worried and depressed. This book has allowed me to breathe again, to have hope again. Thank you, Jeremy. I will read and re-read. I believe this book was definitely God inspired. I only wish I had found it sooner. –Sue

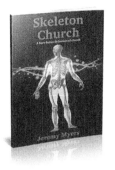

SKELETON CHURCH: A BARE-BONES DEFINITION OF CHURCH (PREFACE TO THE CLOSE YOUR CHURCH FOR GOOD BOOK SERIES)

The church has a skeleton which is identical in all types of churches. Unity and peace can develop in Christianity if we recognize this skeleton as the simple, bare-bones definition of church. But when we focus on the outer trappings—the skin, hair, and eye color, the clothes, the muscle tone, and other outward appearances—division and strife form within the church.

Let us return to the skeleton church and grow in unity once again.

REVIEWS

I worried about buying another book that aimed at re-ducing things to a simple minimum, but the associations of the author along with the price gave me reason to hope and means to see. I really liked this book. First, be-cause it wasn't identical to what other simple church people are saying. He adds unique elements that are worth reading. Second, the size is small enough to read, think, and pray about without getting lost. –Abel Barba

In *Skeleton Church*, Jeremy Myers makes us rethink church. For Myers, the church isn't a style of worship, a row of pews, or even a building. Instead, the church is the people of God, which provides the basic skeletal structure of the church. The muscles, parts, and flesh of the church are how we carry Jesus' mission into our own neighborhoods in our own unique ways. This eBook will make you see the church differently. –Travis Mamone

This book gets back to the basics of the New Testament church—who we are as Christians and what our perspective should be in the world we live in today. Jeremy cuts away all the institutional layers of a church and gets to the heart of our purpose as Christians in the world we live in and how to affect the people around us with God heart and view in mind. Not a physical church in mind. It was a great book and I have read it twice now. –Vaughn Bender

The Skeleton Church ... Oh. My. Word. Why aren't more people reading this!? It was well-written, explained everything beautifully, and it was one of the best explanations of how God intended for church to be. Not to mention an easy read! The author took it all apart, the church, and showed us how it should be. He made it real. If you are searching to find something or someone to show you what God intended for the church, this is the book you need to read. –Ericka

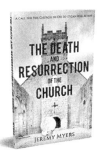

THE DEATH AND RESURRECTION OF THE CHURCH (VOLUME 1 IN THE CLOSE YOUR CHURCH FOR GOOD BOOK SERIES)

In a day when many are looking for ways to revitalize the church, Jeremy Myers argues that the church should die … so that it can rise again.

This is not only because of the universal principle that death precedes resurrection, but also because the church has adopted certain Satanic values and goals and the only way to break free from our enslavement to these values is to die.

But death will not be the end of the church, just as death was not the end of Jesus. If the church follows Jesus into death, and even to the hellish places on earth, it is only then that the church will rise again to new life and vibrancy in the Kingdom of God.

REVIEWS

I have often thought on the church and how its acceptance of corporate methods and assimilation of cultural media mores taints its mission but Jeremy Myers eloquently captures in words the true crux of the matter—

that the church is not a social club for do-gooders but to disseminate the good news to all the nooks and crannies in the world and particularly and primarily those bastions in the reign of evil. That the "gates of Hell" Jesus pronounces indicate that the church is in an offensive, not defensive, posture as gates are defensive structures.

I must confess that in reading I was inclined to be in agreement as many of the same thinkers that Myers riffs upon have influenced me also—Walter Wink, Robert Farrar Capon, Greg Boyd, NT Wright, etc. So as I read, I frequently nodded my head in agreement. –GN Trifanaff

The book is well written, easy to understand, organized and consistent thoughts. It rightfully makes the reader at least think about things as … is "the way we have always done it" necessarily the Biblical or Christ-like way, or is it in fact very sinful?! I would recommend the book for pastors and church officers; those who have the most moving-and-shaking clout to implement changes, or keep things the same. –Joel M. Wilson

Absolutely phenomenal. Unless we let go of everything Adamic in our nature, we cannot embrace anything Christlike. For the church to die, we the individual temples must dig our graves. It is a must read for all who take issues about the body of Christ seriously. –Mordecai Petersburg

PUT SERVICE BACK INTO THE CHURCH SERVICE (VOLUME 2 IN THE CLOSE YOUR CHURCH FOR GOOD BOOK SERIES)

Churches around the world are trying to revitalize their church services. There is almost nothing they will not try. Some embark on multi-million dollar building campaigns while others sell their buildings to plant home churches. Some hire celebrity pastors to attract crowds of people, while others hire no clergy so that there can be open sharing in the service.

Yet despite everything churches have tried, few focus much time, money, or energy on the one thing that churches are supposed to be doing: loving and serving others like Jesus.

Put Service Back into the Church Service challenges readers to follow a few simple principles and put a few ideas into practice which will help churches of all types and sizes make serving others the primary emphasis of a church service.

REVIEWS

Jeremy challenges church addicts, those addicted to an unending parade of church buildings, church services, Bible studies, church programs and more to follow Jesus into our communities, communities filled with lonely, hurting people and BE the church, loving the people in our world with the love of Jesus. Do we need another training program, another seminar, another church building, a remodeled church building, more staff, updated music, or does our world need us, the followers of Jesus, to BE the church in the world? The book is well-written, challenging and a book that really can make a difference not only in our churches, but also and especially in our neighborhoods and communities. –Charles Epworth

I just finished *Put Service Back Into Church Service* by Jeremy Myers, and as with his others books I have read on the church, it was very challenging. For those who love Jesus, but are questioning the function of the traditional brick and mortar church, and their role in it, this is a must read. It may be a bit unsettling to the reader who is still entrenched in traditional "church," but it will make you think, and possibly re-evaluate your role in the church. Get this book, and all others on the church by Jeremy. –Ward Kelly

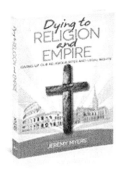

DYING TO RELIGION AND EMPIRE (VOLUME 3 IN THE CLOSE YOUR CHURCH FOR GOOD BOOK SERIES)

Could Christianity exist without religious rites or legal rights? In *Dying to Religion and Empire*, I not only answer this question with an emphatic "Yes!" but argue that if the church is going to thrive in the coming decades, we must give up our religious rites and legal rights.

Regarding religious rites, I call upon the church to abandon the quasi-magical traditions of water baptism and the Lord's Supper and transform or redeem these practices so that they reflect the symbolic meaning and intent which they had in New Testament times.

Furthermore, the church has become far too dependent upon certain legal rights for our continued existence. Ideas such as the right to life, liberty, and the pursuit of happiness are not conducive to living as the people of God who are called to follow Jesus into servanthood and death. Also, reliance upon the freedom of speech, the freedom of assembly, and other such freedoms as established by the Bill of Rights have made the church a servant of the state rather than a servant of God and the gospel. Such freedoms must be forsaken if we are going to live within the rule and reign of God on earth.

This book not only challenges religious and political liberals but conservatives as well. It is a call to leave behind the comfortable religion we know, and follow Jesus into the uncertain and wild ways of radical discipleship. To rise and live in the reality of God's Kingdom, we must first die to religion and empire.

REVIEWS

Jeremy is one of the freshest, freest authors out there— and you need to hear what he has to say. This book is startling and new in thought and conclusion. Are the "sacraments" inviolate? Why? Do you worship at a secular altar? Conservative? Liberal? Be prepared to open your eyes. Mr. Myers will not let you keep sleeping!

Jeremy Myers is one or the most thought provoking authors that I read, this book has really helped me to look outside the box and start thinking how can I make more sense of my relationship with Christ and how can I show others in a way that impacts them the way that Jesus' disciples impacted their world. Great book, great author. – Brett Hotchkiss

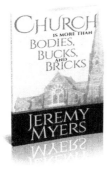

CHURCH IS MORE THAN BODIES, BUCKS, & BRICKS (VOLUME 4 IN THE CLOSE YOUR CHURCH FOR GOOD BOOK SERIES)

Many people define church as a place and time where people gather, a way for ministry money to be given and spent, and a building in which people regularly meet on Sunday mornings.

In this book, author and blogger Jeremy Myers shows that church is more than bodies, bucks, and bricks.

Church is the people of God who follow Jesus into the world, and we can be the church no matter how many people we are with, no matter the size of our church budget, and regardless of whether we have a church building or not.

By abandoning our emphasis on more people, bigger budgets, and newer buildings, we may actually liberate the church to better follow Jesus into the world.

REVIEWS

This book does more than just identify issues that have been bothering me about church as we know it, but it goes into history and explains how we got here. In this way it is similar to Viola's *Pagan Christianity*, but I found it a much more enjoyable read. Jeremy goes into more detail on the three issues he covers as well as giving a lot of practical advice on how to remedy these situations. – Portent

Since I returned from Africa 20 years ago I have struggled with going to church back in the States. This book helped me not feel guilty and has helped me process this struggle. It is challenging and overflows with practical suggestions. He loves the church despite its imperfections and suggests ways to break the bondage we find ourselves in. –Truealian

Jeremy Meyers always writes a challenging book ... It seems the American church (as a whole) is very comfortable with the way things are ... The challenge is to get out of the brick and mortar buildings and stagnant programs and minister to the needy in person with funds in hand to meet their needs especially to the widows and orphans as we are directed in the scriptures. –GGTexas

CRUCIFORM PASTORAL LEADERSHIP (VOLUME 5 IN THE CLOSE YOUR CHURCH FOR GOOD BOOK SERIES)

This book is forthcoming in early 2019.

The final volume in the *Close Your Church for Good* book series look at issues related to pastoral leadership in the church. It discusses topics such as preaching and pastoral pay from the perspective of the cross.

The best way pastors can lead their church is by following Jesus to the cross!

This book will be published in early 2019.

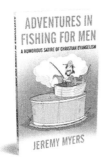

ADVENTURES IN FISHING (FOR MEN)

Adventures in Fishing (for Men) is a satirical look at evangelism and church growth strategies.

Using fictional accounts from his attempts to become a world-famous fisherman, Jeremy Myers shows how many of the evangelism and church growth strategies of today do little to actually reach the world for Jesus Christ.

Adventures in Fishing (for Men) pokes fun at some of the popular evangelistic techniques and strategies endorsed and practiced by many Christians in today's churches. The stories in this book show in humorous detail how little we understand the culture that surrounds us or how to properly reach people with the gospel of Jesus Christ. The story also shows how much time, energy, and money goes into evangelism preparation and training with the end result being that churches rarely accomplish any actual evangelism.

REVIEWS

I found *Adventures in Fishing (For Men)* quite funny! Jeremy Myers does a great job shining the light on some of the more common practices in Evangelism today. His allegory gently points to the foolishness that is found within a system that takes the preaching of the gospel and tries to reduce it to a simplified formula. A formula that takes what should be an organic, Spirit led experience and turns it into a gospel that is nutritionally benign.

If you have ever EE'd someone you may find Myers' book offensive, but if you have come to the place where you realize that Evangelism isn't a matter of a script and checklists, then you might benefit from this light-hearted peek at Evangelism today. –Jennifer L. Davis

Adventures in Fishing (for Men) is good book in understanding evangelism to be more than just being a set of methods or to do list to follow. –Ashok Daniel

CHRISTMAS REDEMPTION: WHY CHRISTIANS SHOULD CELEBRATE A PAGAN HOLIDAY

Christmas Redemption looks at some of the symbolism and traditions of Christmas, including gifts, the Christmas tree, and even Santa Claus and shows how all of these can be celebrated and enjoyed by Christians as a true and accurate reflection of the gospel.

Though Christmas used to be a pagan holiday, it has been redeemed by Jesus.

If you have been told that Christmas is a pagan holiday and is based on the Roman festival of Saturnalia, or if you have been told that putting up a Christmas tree is idolatrous, or if you have been told that Santa Claus is Satanic and teaches children to be greedy, then you must read this book! In it, you will learn that all of these Christmas traditions have been redeemed by Jesus and are good and healthy ways of celebrating the truth of the gospel and the grace of Jesus Christ.

REVIEWS

Too many times we as Christians want to condemn nearly everything around us and in so doing become much like the Pharisees and religious leaders that Jesus encountered. I recommend this book to everyone who has concerns of how and why we celebrate Christmas. I recommend it to those who do not have any qualms in celebrating but may not know the history of Christmas. I recommend this book to everyone, no matter who or where you are, no matter your background or beliefs, no matter whether you are young or old. –David H.

Very informative book dealing with the roots of our modern Christmas traditions. The Biblical teaching on redemption is excellent! Highly recommended. –Tamara

This is a wonderful book full of hope and joy. The book explains where Christmas traditions originated and how they have been changed and been adapted over the years. The hope that the grace that is hidden in the celebrations will turn more hearts to the Lord's call is very evident. Jeremy Myers has given us a lovely gift this Christmas. His insights will lift our hearts and remain with us a long time. –Janet Cardoza

I love how the author uses multiple sources to back up his opinions. He doesn't just use bible verses, he goes back into the history of the topics (pagan rituals, Santa, etc.) as well. Great book! –Jenna G.

JOIN JEREMY MYERS AND LEARN MORE

Take Bible and theology courses by joining Jeremy at
RedeemingGod.com/join/

Receive updates about free books, discounted books,
and new books by joining Jeremy at
RedeemingGod.com/read-books/

Printed in Great Britain
by Amazon